foreword

Ellen Christensen

Children's play is one of the most creative experiences in all of human culture – resulting in new languages, nursery rhymes, imaginary creatures both friend and foe, and entire fantastical universes. The wonder and creativity with which children explore their environment is immeasurable. Influential designers around the world, fueled by recent findings in the fields of psychology, education, and child development, are focusing their ingenuity on shaping the most stimulating and interactive places in which today's children can grow and learn. The projects in Play! Indoor & Outdoor range from nursery schools to outdoor playgrounds to day care centers, and are located everywhere from Japan and Brazil to Portugal and Norway. However, all of the projects share an incredible ability to reinvent space based on the scale, safety, socialization patterns, involvement, and educational and emotional needs of the children whose formative years take place in these buildings. Unprecedented in the extent to which these designers focus on the way a child thinks, the spaces within Play! Indoor & Outdoor surpass all previous designed play spaces through the careful consideration of each element.

A key ingredient of the play spaces showcased is the involvement level of the children for whom each structure is built. These design projects recognize the increased stimulation of children who are actively involved in creating their own play spaces, both in the planning and design process and through day-to-day interaction with spatial elements after construction. For example, design studio Die Baupiloten held creative brainstorming sessions with the young students at Erika-Mann

Elementary School II in Berlin, Germany prior to the building's design. Through these workshops, Die Baupiloten and the school's students together invented a story that inspired the spatial design. The children imagined a fantasy world – the world of the "Snuffle of the Silver Dragon." The designers intentionally carried this inventiveness into design of the space itself so that the children would continue the story through their everyday play. Couches, caverns, lairs, pedestals, and tables are strategically located throughout the space. A "Snuffle Beatle" of 34 reflecting panels was built into the structure as a method of communication, while a "Snuffle Garden" on the school's second story consists of horizontal and sloped surfaces on which children can lie down, sit, slide, and play. The ability of children to recreate their play spaces on a day-to-day basis through their own creativity is fundamental – with moveable furniture, garden spaces within which children can work, interactive amenities, climbing areas, and dynamic rhythmic or changing light and sound possibilities.

Playful use of scale is fundamental. As in Alice's Adventures in Wonderland, different sizes of people and objects can result in heightened curiosity. In Nendo's Baby Café in Tokyo, Japan, the designers emphasized the difference in the way adults and children see and explore by inserting furniture of both extremely large and small sizes in a manner similar to a carnival funhouse's distortion of space. A giant sofa becomes a climbing gym for the infants who are brought to this family café, while a table that is solely functional for adults becomes a secret cavern to the toddlers who play

beneath it. Giant windows are contrasted with tiny windows, big light bulbs are paired with small light bulbs, and interior floorboards vary in size.

Vivid colors, unique materials, and orientation of light in each space are carefully designed to correspond with the activities planned for each room. A giant, rough bark-covered cave functions as a gathering space within SAKO Architects' Kid's Republic in Shanghai, while the library and study spaces feature walls covered with giant round tree trunk sections which also function as a place to put up pictures, instructions, or books – all underneath a ceiling composed of logs with branches interspersed to embellish the forest feel. In multiple projects, windows are designed on two levels – with windows that can be opened and closed at the adult level and permanently closed windows at the children's level for safety. Glass windows in different color shades corresponding to the hues of the rainbow serve as fissures within the long horizontal shape of Alejandro Muñoz Miranda's Educational Center in El Chaparral, Albolote in Granada, Spain – the colorful light is reflected into the space in play and activity areas, while colorless glass reflects muted light into spaces designed to hold lesson plans. Colors are often chosen, either subtly or through painted directional cues such as color-coded arrows, to function as guides for the children to navigate through each space.

Safety and comfort are also essential to these kid-focused spaces. Entrances are carefully oriented, often away from street traffic. Buildings are isolated from noise and vehicle exhaust fumes. Eco-friendly materials and kid-safe materials are prioritized. Unique ground coverings such as interior lawns are introduced to create a cushioned floor for younger children to play on. The social comfort, mobility, and engagement of children are also important design factors for educational facilities. These building's spatial organization takes into account the need for separation versus interaction of different age groups at various times during the day, as well as the importance of children's ability to independently determine their level of privacy or social interaction with others during play times.

Within the spaces featured in Play – Indoor & Outdoor, children have their first experiences with the world of education, recreation, and socialization. They make their first friends, learn to count and recite the alphabet, learn sports - and how to be a good sport, and explore and create their own fantastical worlds within carefully designed spaces. The unifying element of these projects – by highly respected international design and architecture studios – is an understanding of the importance of children's formative everyday life experiences. The featured design professionals are able to completely reinvent architectural notions in order to create the best and most innovative spaces of an unparalleled caliber. These designers' ability to see things from the perspective of the child and transform this understanding into engaging spaces is a skill acquired by years of education and practice – but is fueled by that incredibly important ability to remember and draw from one's own memory of the experience of being a small, curious child in a large, exciting world.

contents

Retail

Dining

Recreation

Art & Leisure

Healthcare

School

Nursery

"wendy, john and michael darling live in a lovely house in london. they have a big, sunny nursery. there are colorful pictures and a big clock on the wall. there are toys here and there..."

–peter pan by j. m. barrie

day care center for benetton

Location/
Treviso, Italy
Design/
Alberto Campo Baeza

Photography/
Hisao Suzuki, Marco Zanta
Area/
1,868 sqm

The architects built a square box composed of nine smaller squares. The central square structure emerges from the building to guide light into the interior. The classrooms are located within the surrounding squares.

This square structure is embedded within a larger, circular enclosure made up of double walls. The four courtyards created by the concentric circles are open to the sky and suggest the four elements: air, earth, fire, and water.

The space between the perimeter walls serves as a "secret" place for the children. The courtyard spaces, located between the curved and the straight walls, are particularly remarkable.

The central space is lit from above and has the highest ceiling. Sunlight is guided into the building by nine perforations in the ceiling and three more peepholes on each of its four façades.

The children have understood and connected with the building's architecture. A book has even been published of their impressions of the space, within which they are happy and feel free.

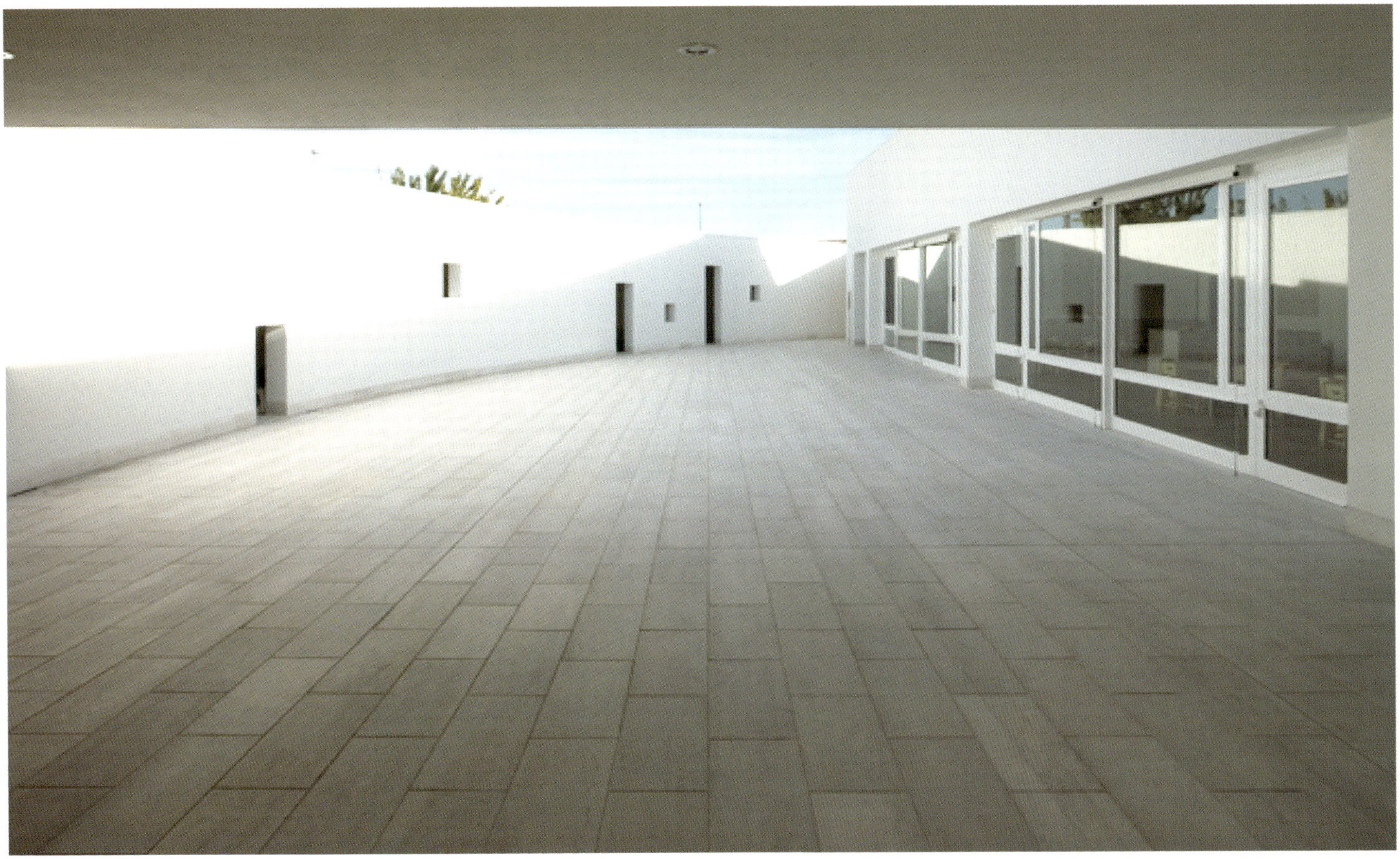

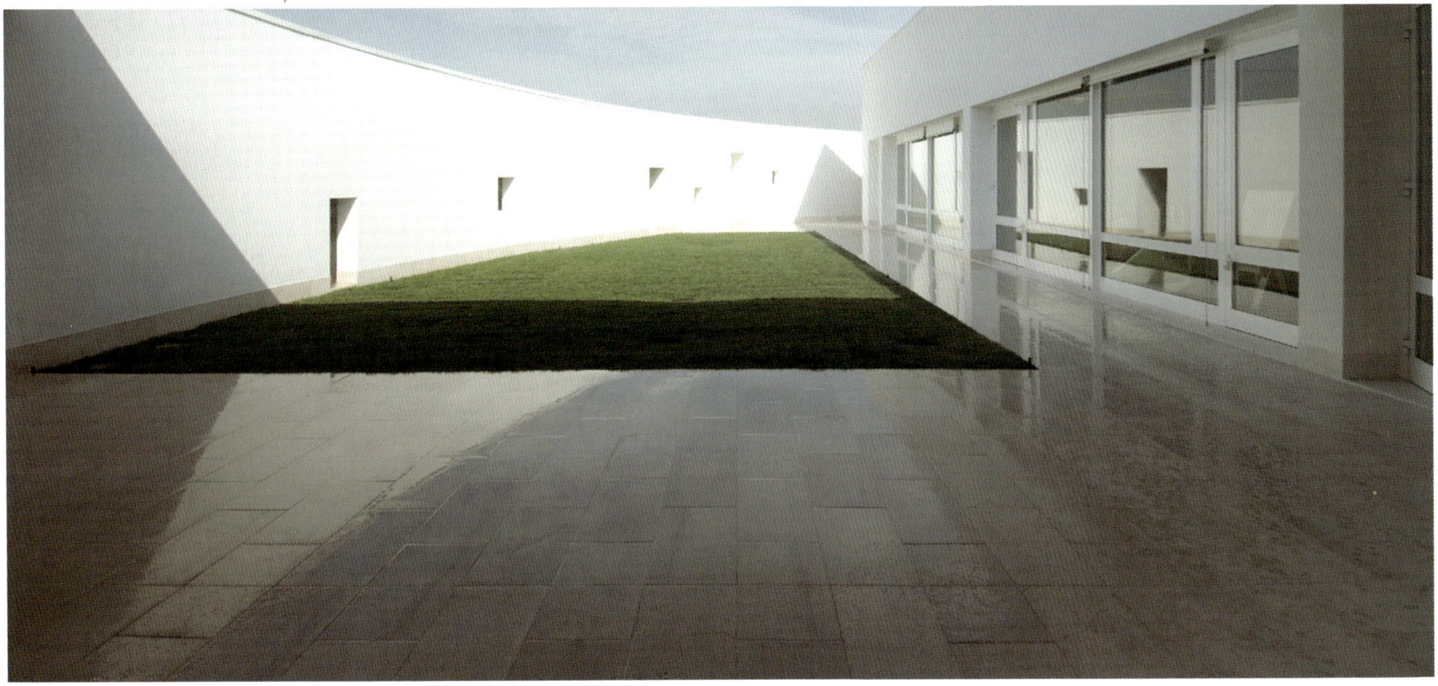

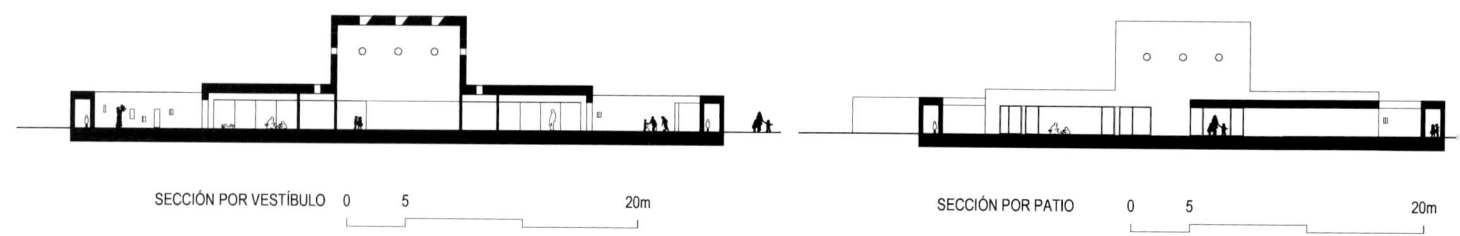

SECCIÓN POR VESTÍBULO   0   5   20m

SECCIÓN POR PATIO   0   5   20m

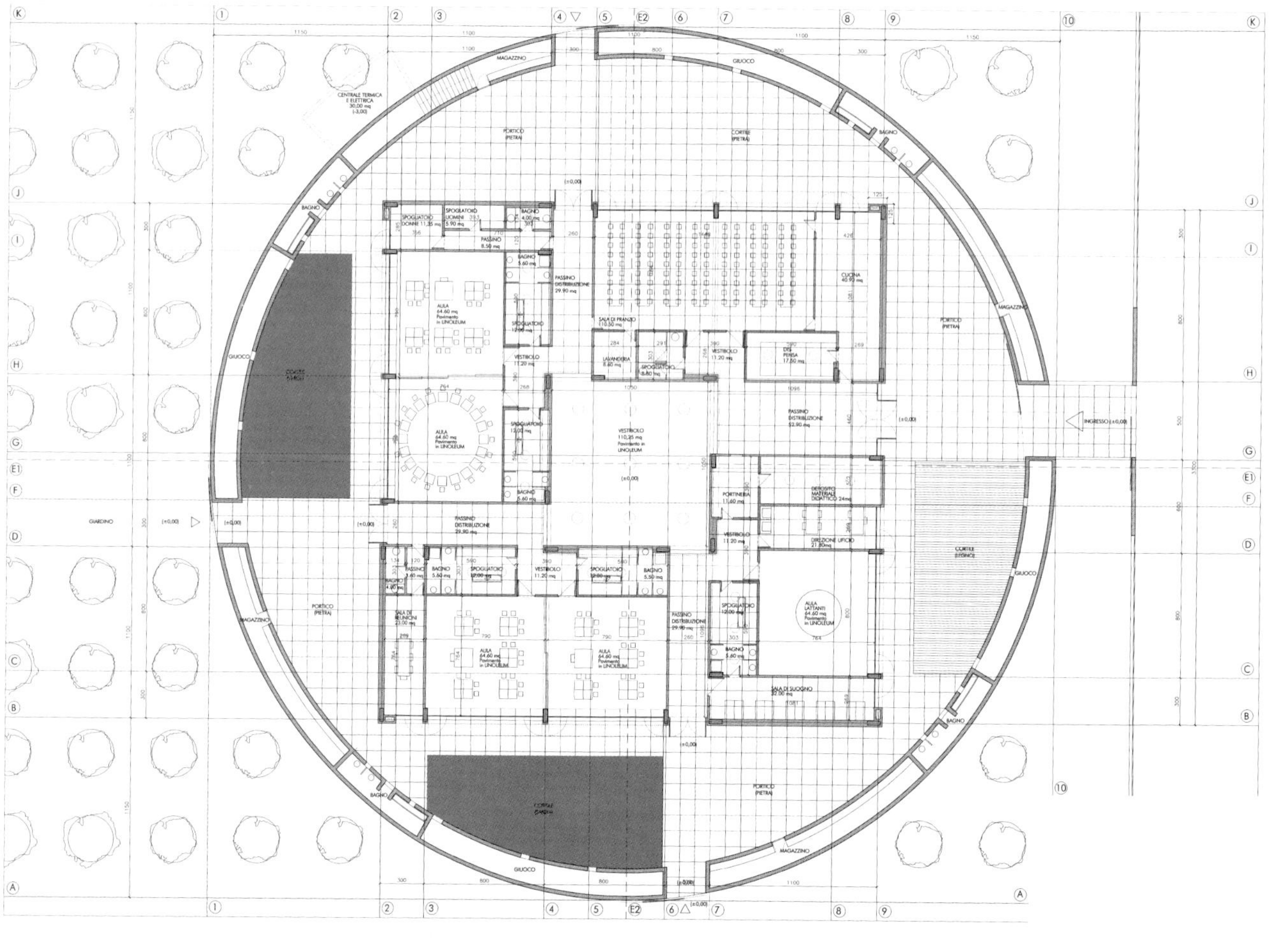

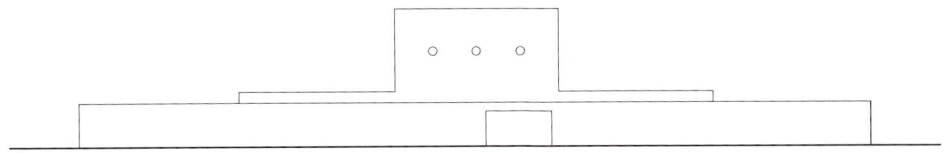

ALZADO POR ACCESO   0   5   20m

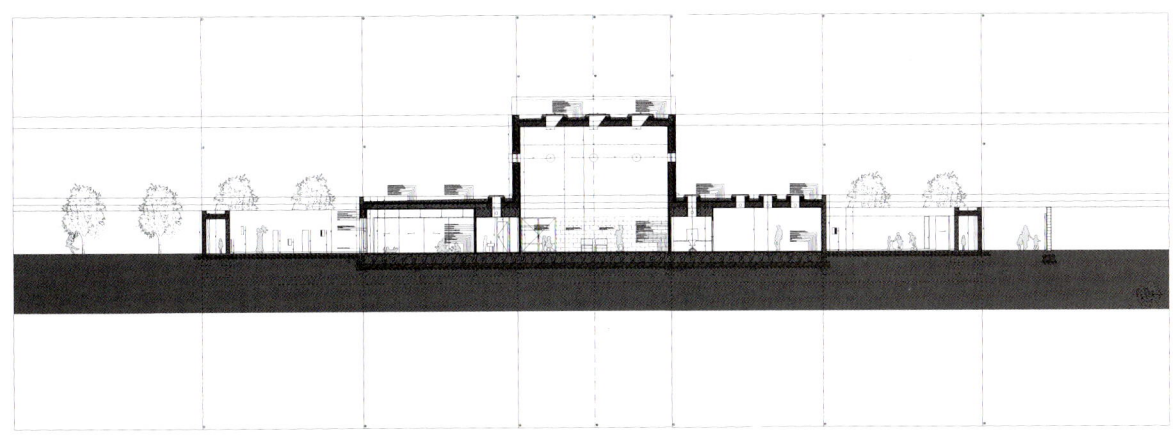

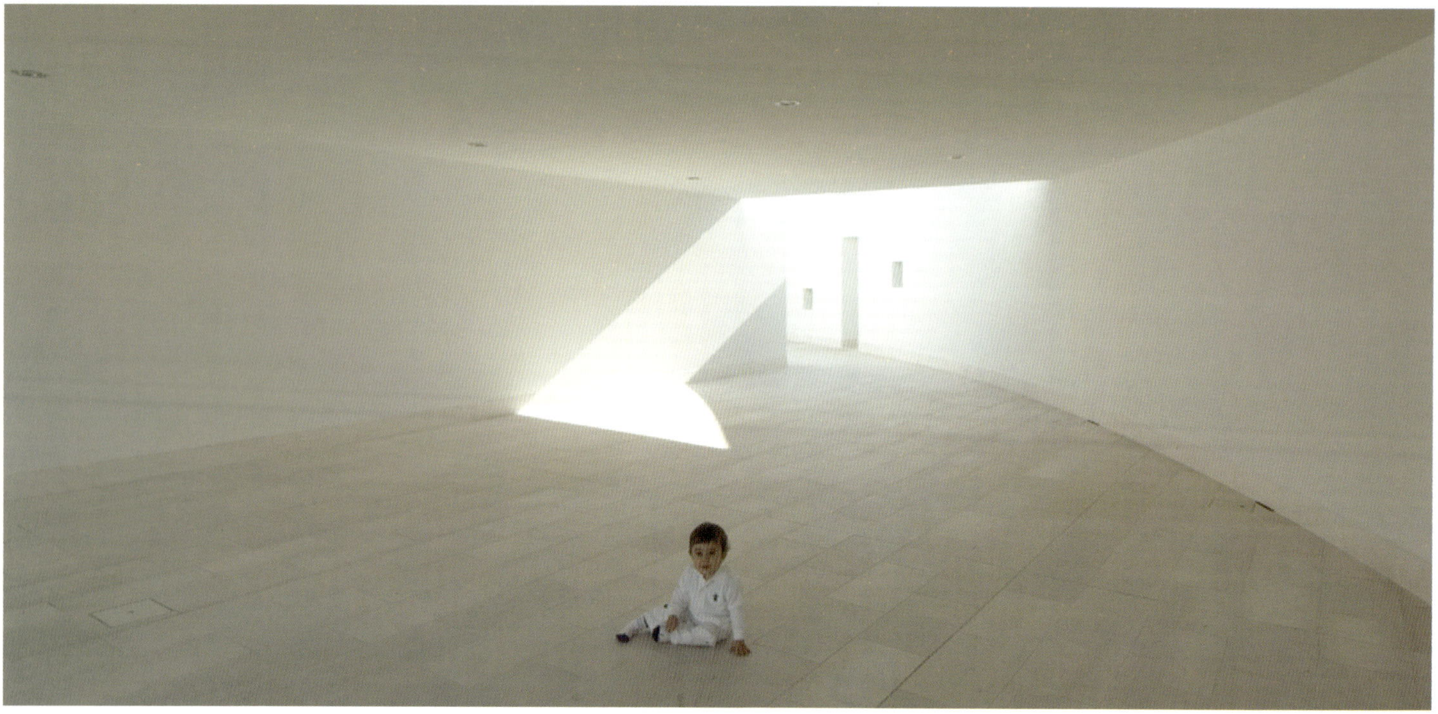

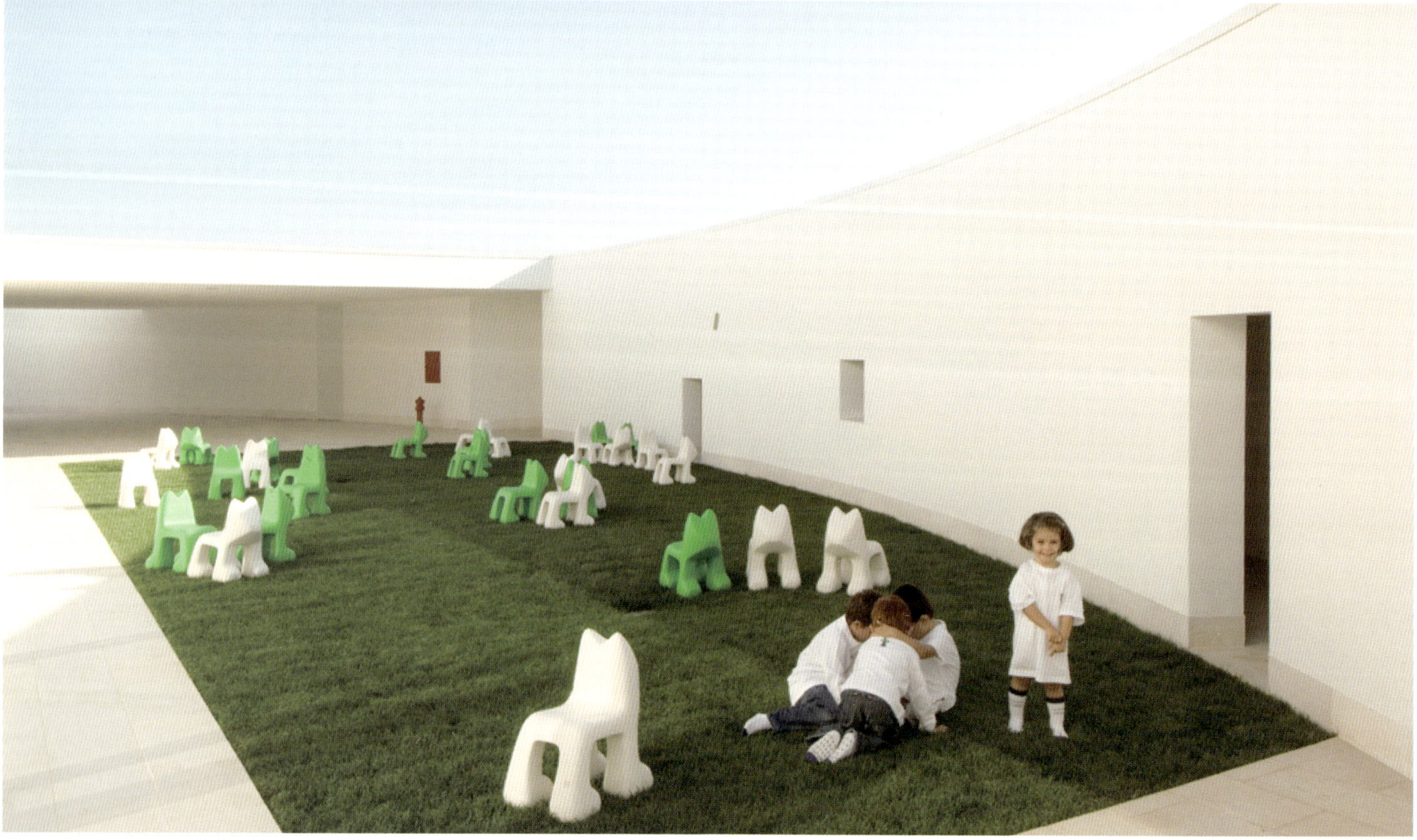

familienservice school berlin

Location/
Lützowstraße 106,
10785 Berlin, Germany
Design/
Die Baupiloten

Photography/
Jan Bitter
(www.janbitter.de)
Area/

The Baupiloten converted the fifth floor of an office building located in the Lützowstraße 106 into a school for the company Familienservice. Anonymous waiting rooms and drab offices were transformed into learning and activity spaces, as well as common areas for pupils.

The ceiling of the activity room opens up to the sky through large glass windows. The expansiveness is reinforced by mirrors on the ceiling, as well as adjustable mirror-walls through which the children can observe, discover, and experiment. The room offers plenty of space in which to play and even boasts a stage for the children to climb around on.

Platforms, counters, and tables jut out from the walls, creating a school lounge in what used to be a sterile waiting room. This is a place to hang out, work with a laptop, or have some alone time. A large counter separates the room from a modestly designed kitchen area.

In contrast to the drab beige and grey tones of the former administrative offices, the new school shines with fresh and cheerful colors. On the school walls, pupils can realize their artistic interests. They can hang artwork on large magnetic surfaces, or learn about geography by inspecting a room-sized world map.

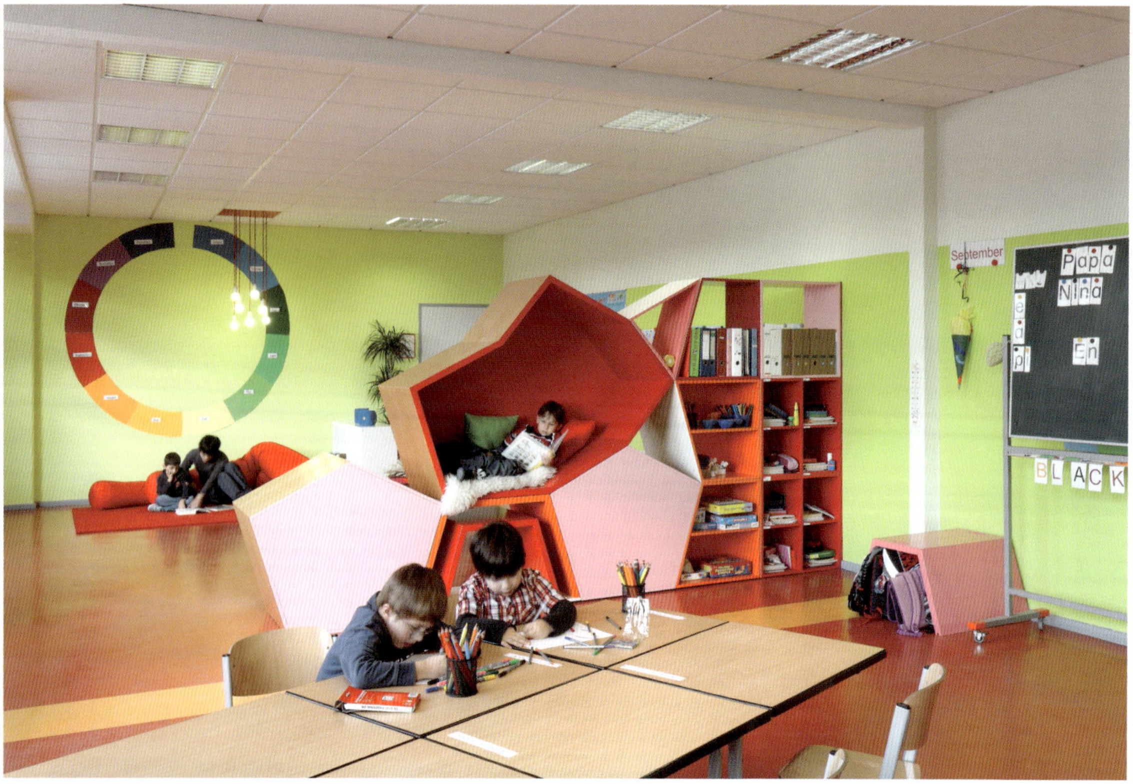
September
Papa
Nina
En
BLACK

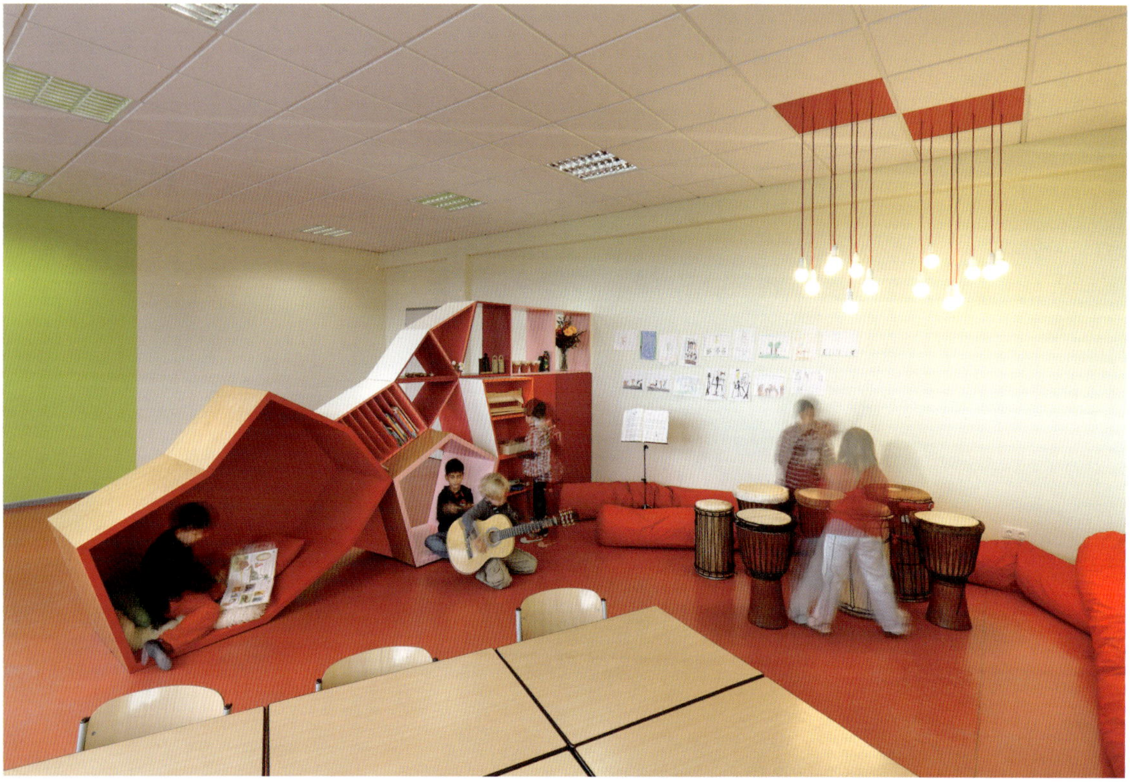

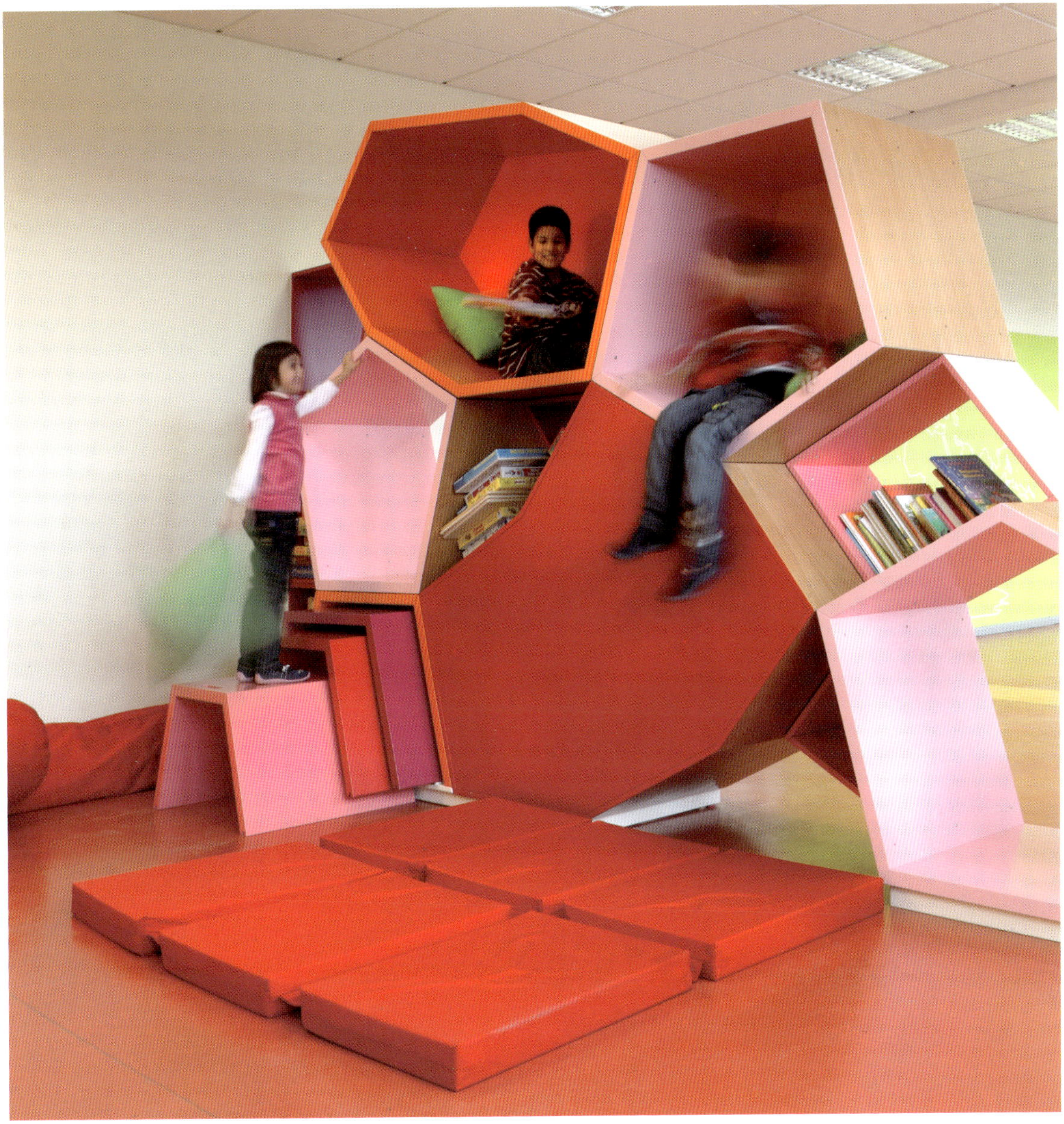

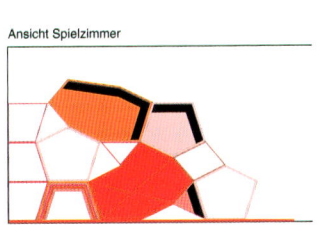

Ansicht Spielzimmer
Ansicht Hort
Ansicht Einzelarbeitsbereich
Klassenzimmer
Ansicht Gruppenbereich
3 x
2 x
1 x
1 x
1 x
3x
1 x
1 x
1 x
1 x
2 x
2x
1 x
1 x
1x
1 x

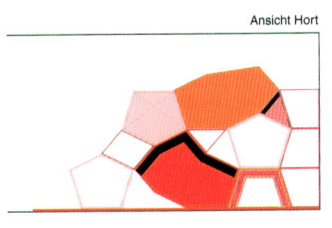

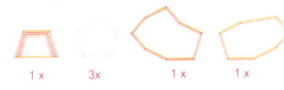

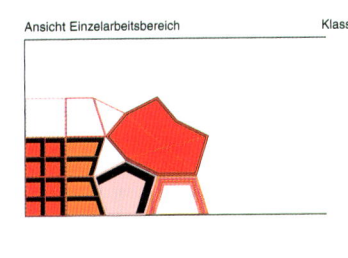

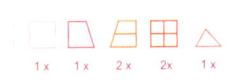

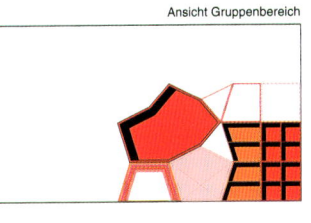

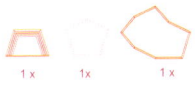

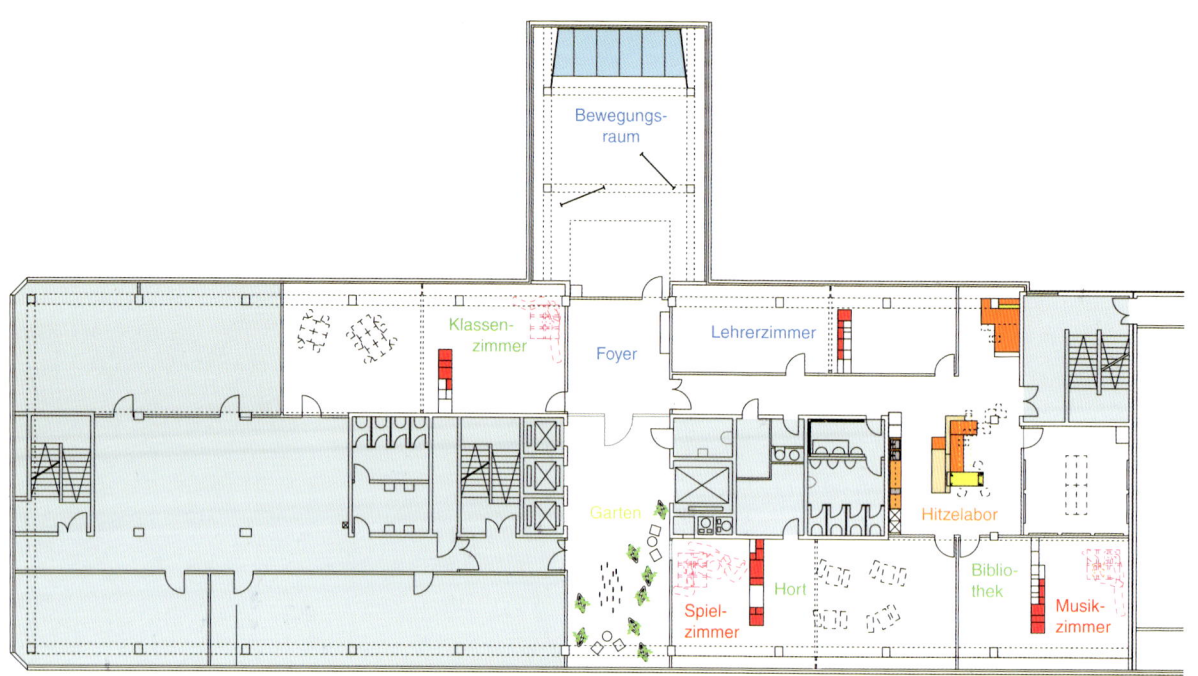

Bewegungs-
raum

Klassen-
zimmer

Foyer

Lehrerzimmer

Garten

Hitzelabor

Spiel-
zimmer

Hort

Biblio-
thek

Musik-
zimmer

erika-mann
elementary school ii

Location/
Utrechter Str. 25/27,
13347 Berlin, Germany

Design/
Die Baupiloten

Photography/
Jan Bitter
(www.janbitter.de)

Area/
727 sqm

Working together with Die Baupiloten in a series of workshops, the students created fantastical and poetic worlds, culminating in the fictional "Snuffle of the Silver Dragon."

The designers believe children should be able to form their own environment through daily interaction with their surroundings, not just in the collaborative design process. An interactive seating landscape was created within each of the school's three uppermost stories. In these areas, children can relax upon soft warm seating. The landscape is composed of five modules: couches, caverns, lairs, pedestals, and tables with fold-out benches. These modules allow the children to explore and find the most comfortable positions in which to learn or play, without conforming to seating norms. The children communicate via the "Snuffle Beatle" which consists of a total of 34 reflectors located around the building.

The "Snuffle Garden" on the school's second story offers a series of horizontal and sloped surfaces on which the children can lie down, sit, or slide. Structures dubbed "the Wings" and "Fireflower" float inside the "Snuffle of the Silver Dragon." These pieces are fold-out chairs and sculptures which children can sit on or disappear into. Warm rays of light shine into the building from the ceiling, covering the seats in a golden glow.

114
ISA KLASSE
113a
MUSIKRAUM
113
ISA KLASSE
112
ISA KLASSE
111
MATHE-WERKSTATT
110
ISA KLASSE
RELIGION
HOLZWERKSTATT
HAUCHSANFTSEIN
HAUCHSANFTSEIN
Leuchtkäfer
Sitzlandschaft

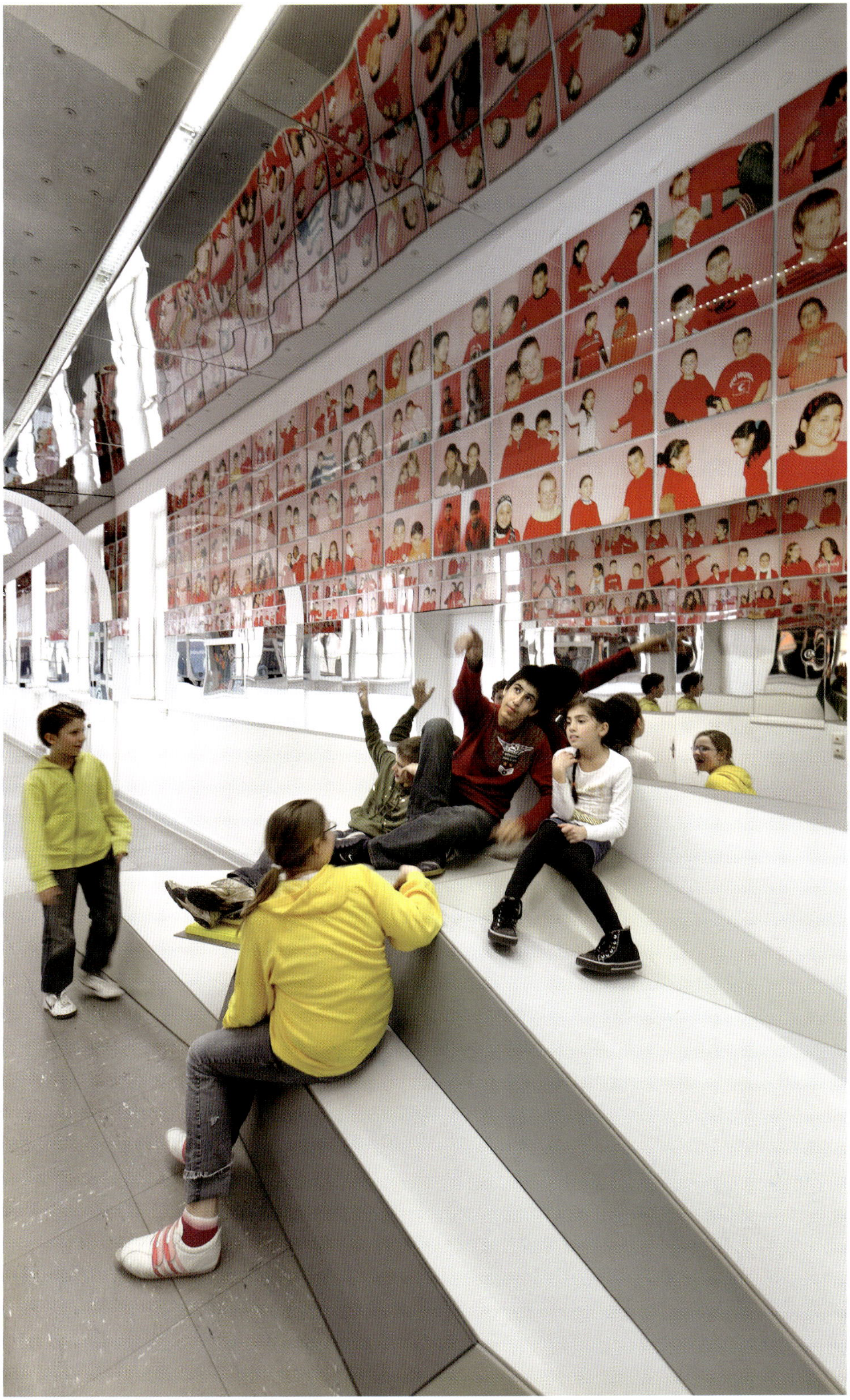

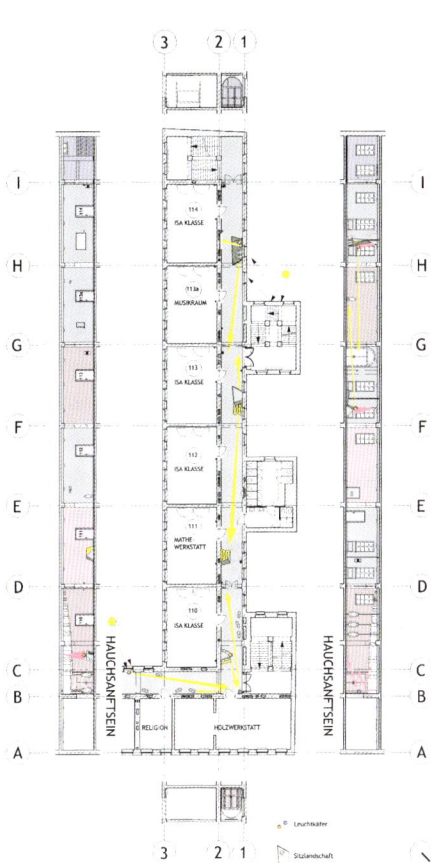

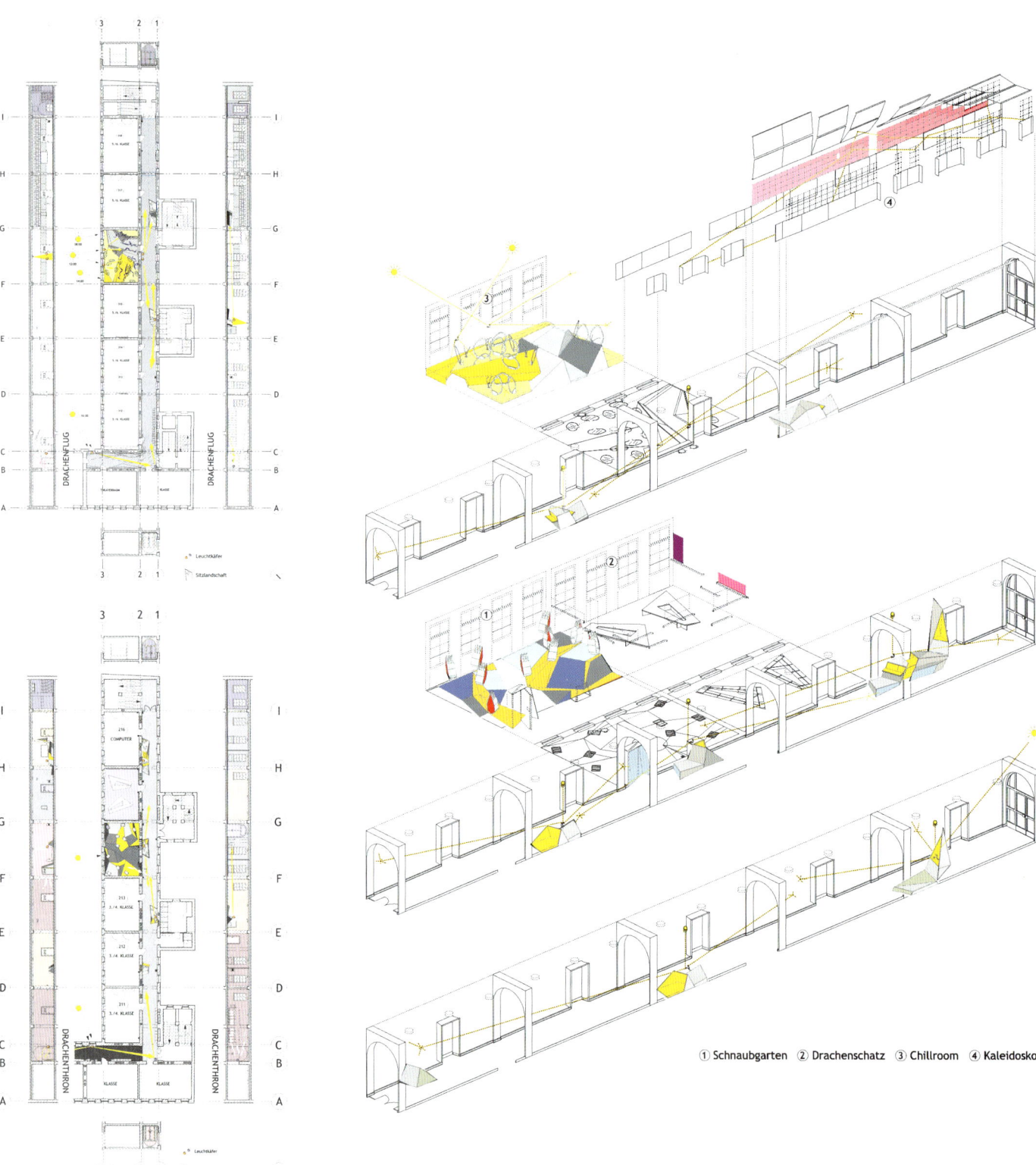

① Schnaubgarten ② Drachenschatz ③ Chillroom ④ Kaleidoskop

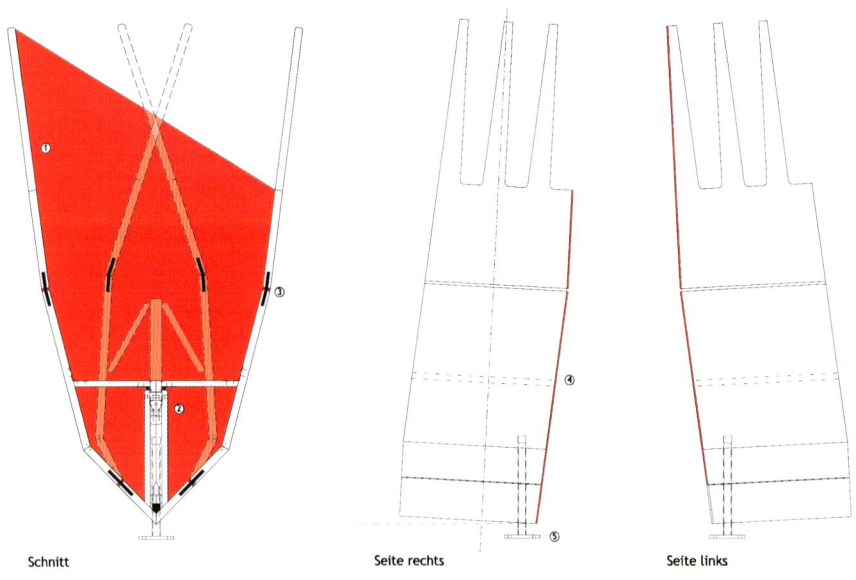

Schnitt   Seite rechts   Seite links

1. DJ-Pult
2. Lautsprecher und LED-Leuchten
3. Bluteninsel
4. Wanderndes Wasser
5. Leuchtkafer

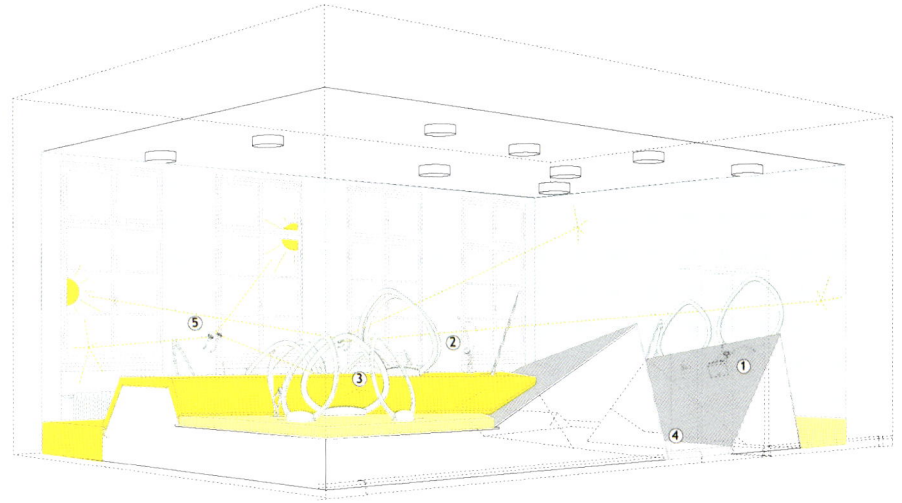

kindergartens in tromsø

Location/
Tromsø, Norway
Design/
70°N arkitektur
Photography/
Ivan Brodey

Area/
622 sqm / kindergarten
(Fjellvegen, Sommereng)
820 sqm / kindergarten
(Elvestrand, Gyllenvang, Solneset,
Kjosen)

The first two kindergartens, Fjellvegen and Sommereng, were built in 2006, followed in 2008 by four more schools: Elvestrand, Gyllenvang, Solneset and Kjosen. All of the schools have the same basic concept, but the kindergartens built in 2008 feature larger common areas and various play wall solutions.

The kindergarten is organized in a number of longitudinal zones including an exterior playground, roofed outdoor terraces that regulate the micro-climate of the building, and an "indoor street" with water play areas and a winter garden. These zones contribute to a soft transition from exterior to interior spaces. The broad exposed exterior landscape leads into quieter and more intimate zones.

In the first two kindergartens each base is furnished with two adjustable play walls that are hinged in the centre, and that can provide multiple combinations of small and large rooms. The walls contain play structures, shelves, drawers, pull-out furniture, whiteboard walls, climbing walls, puppet shows, etc. In the four kindergartens built more recently, the wall is even more experimental, with varied spatiality integrated in a fixed wall. Each kindergarten is a conceptual exploration of children's scale and imagination. Fairy tale elements of transition, conversion, and surprise were the inspiration for the design of each room and play wall.

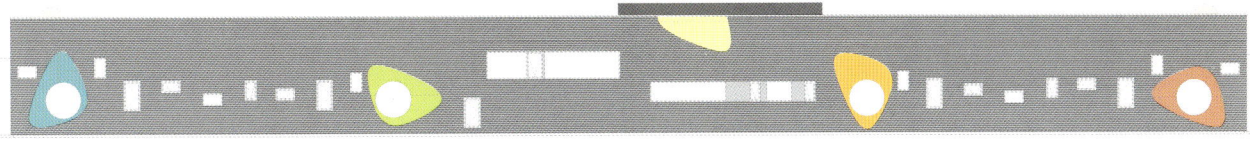

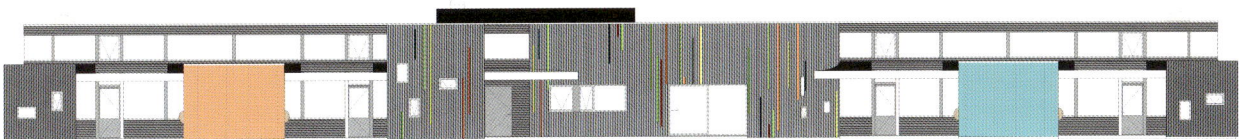

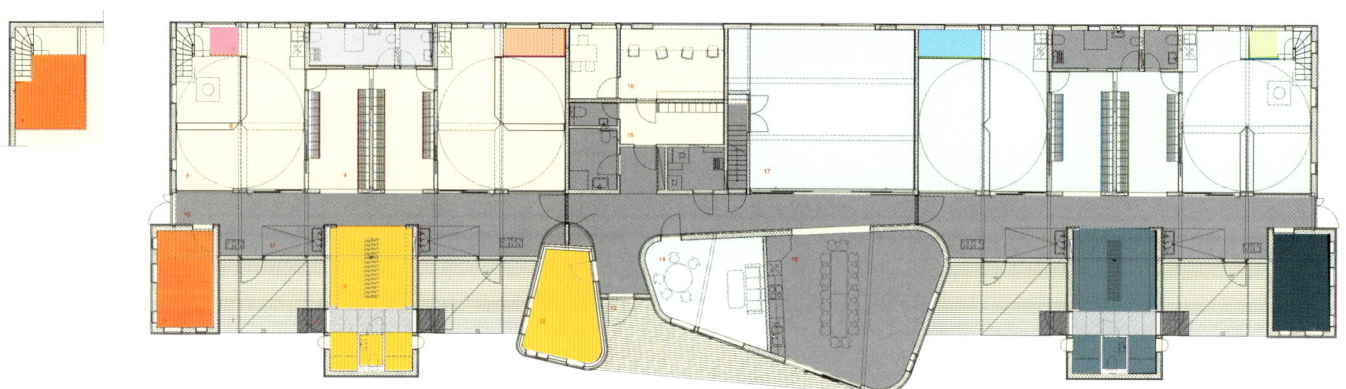

1 terrace under transparent roof 2 entrance for base 3 'rough' cloakroom 4 wardrobe / cloakroom 5 base 6 adjustable playing walls 7 reading corner / shelves 8 mezzanine
9 common play room 10 playing corridor / 'indoor street' 11 water play 12 common play room 13 main entrance 14 staff room 15 staff wardrobe 16 office / meeting room
17 common activity room 18 kitchen / dining room / activity room

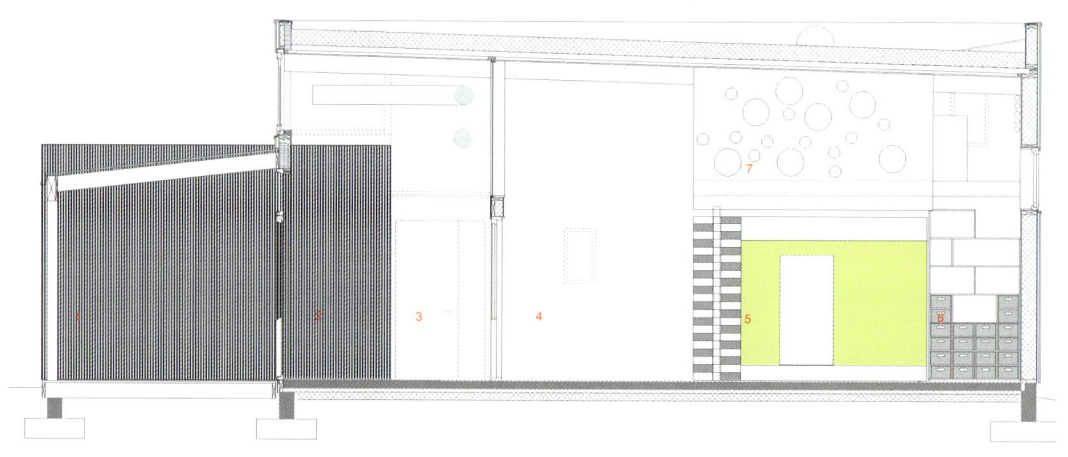

1 terrace under transparent roof 2 water play space 3 play corridor / indoor street 4 base 5 adjustable play walls 6 shelves / reading corner 7 mezzanine

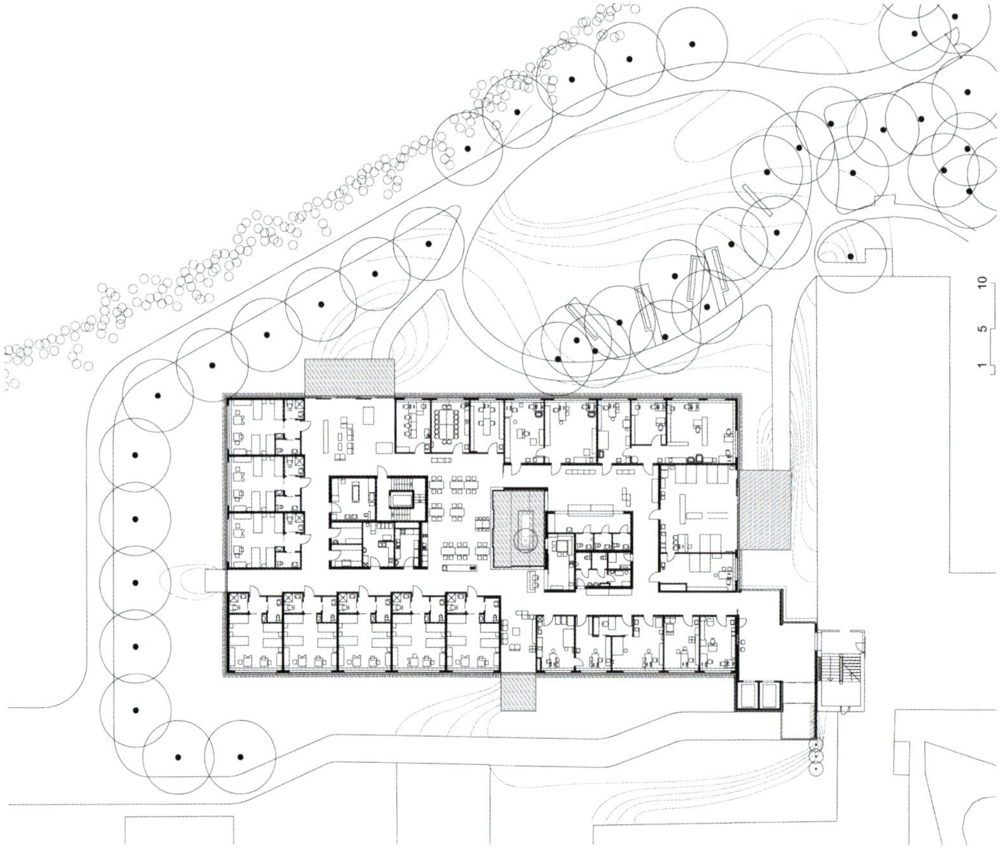

children's department and work therapy

Location/
Ljubljana, Slovenia
Design/
dans arhitekti

Photography/
Miran Kambic, dans arhitekti
Area/
4,570 sqm

The building itself has a rectangular floor plan with an internal atrium. The simple architectural idea of a box in the middle of a park with a wooden atrium is based on the rational and functional plan within which fresh architectural ideas surpass the basic form's rigid functionality.

The atrium with a warm and velvety soft wooden finish enables light to penetrate into the interior. Along the sides of the atrium and the corridors, there are living spaces that open towards the exterior space with wooden terraces. Large windows overlook the old park with old trees that have been retained despite reductions in park size. The corridors and halls are well-lit and graphically exciting. The walls feature playful graphics by Slovenian artist Natasa Skusek. Bold colors and soft flooring in the hallways create a system of orientation through and around the building. Grey concrete walls in the core of the structure contrast with the softness of the wood in the atrium. The hygienic whiteness of the bathrooms is contrasted with bright, colorful ceilings.

The basic white facade, made of fibre cement panels, is articulated with large horizontal windows while vertical yellow accents give it rhythm. The volume of the building is a white canvas on which graphics are projected. In the future, the building may be covered with a layer of greenery, which would integrate the building into its environment and emphasize the poetics of the design.

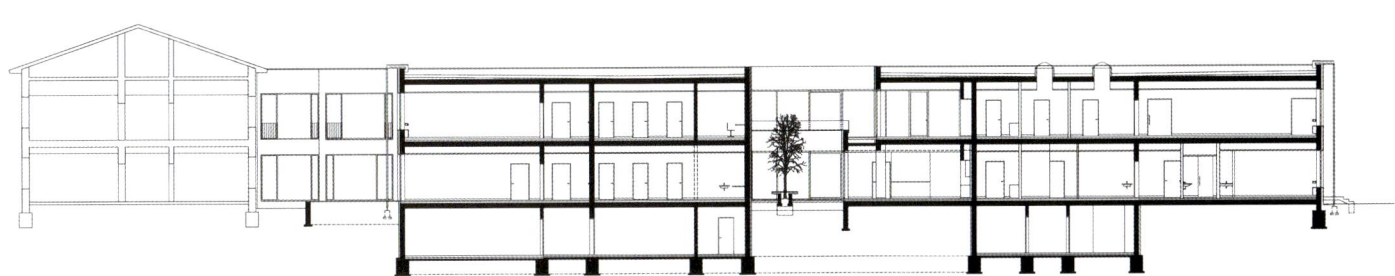

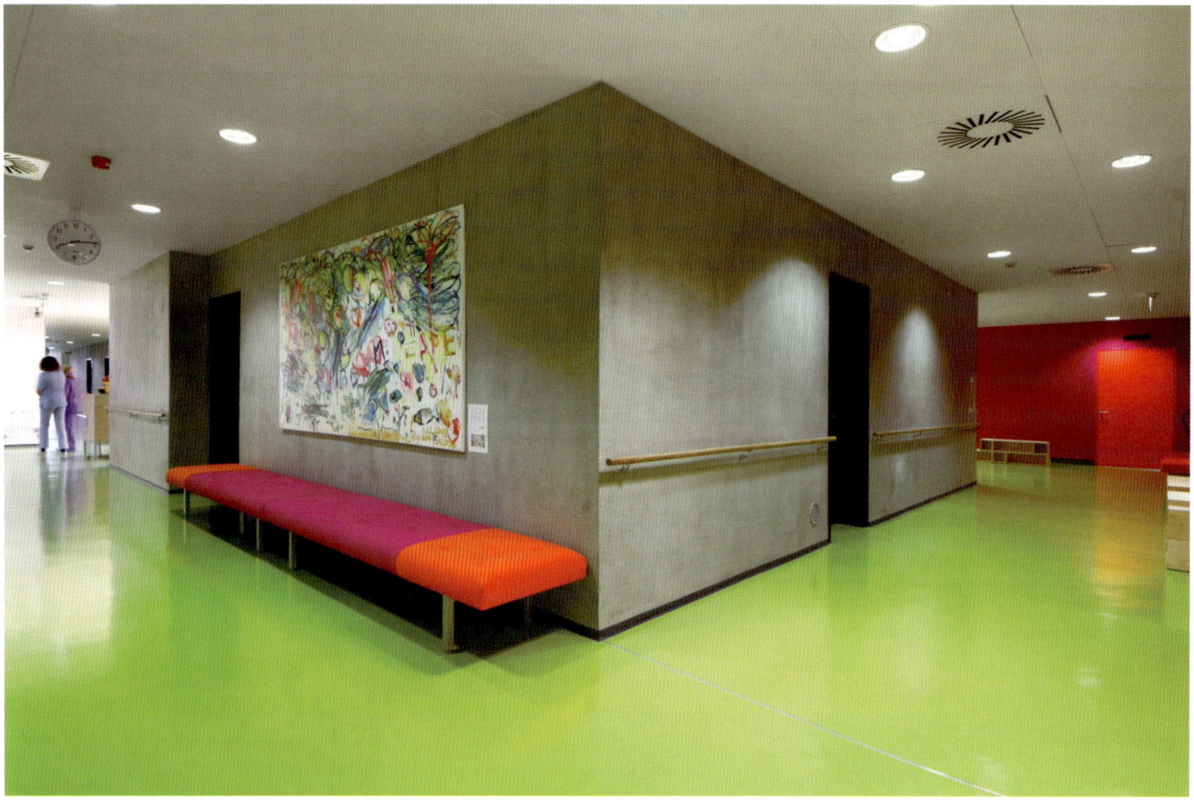

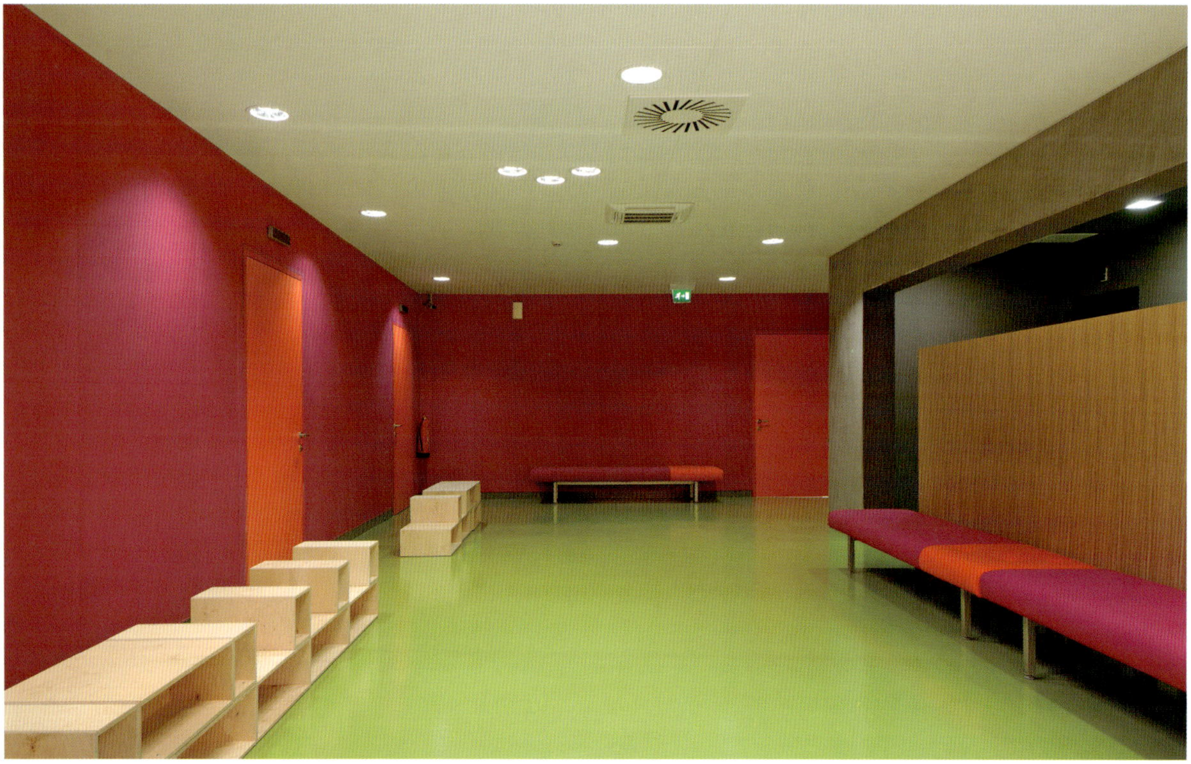

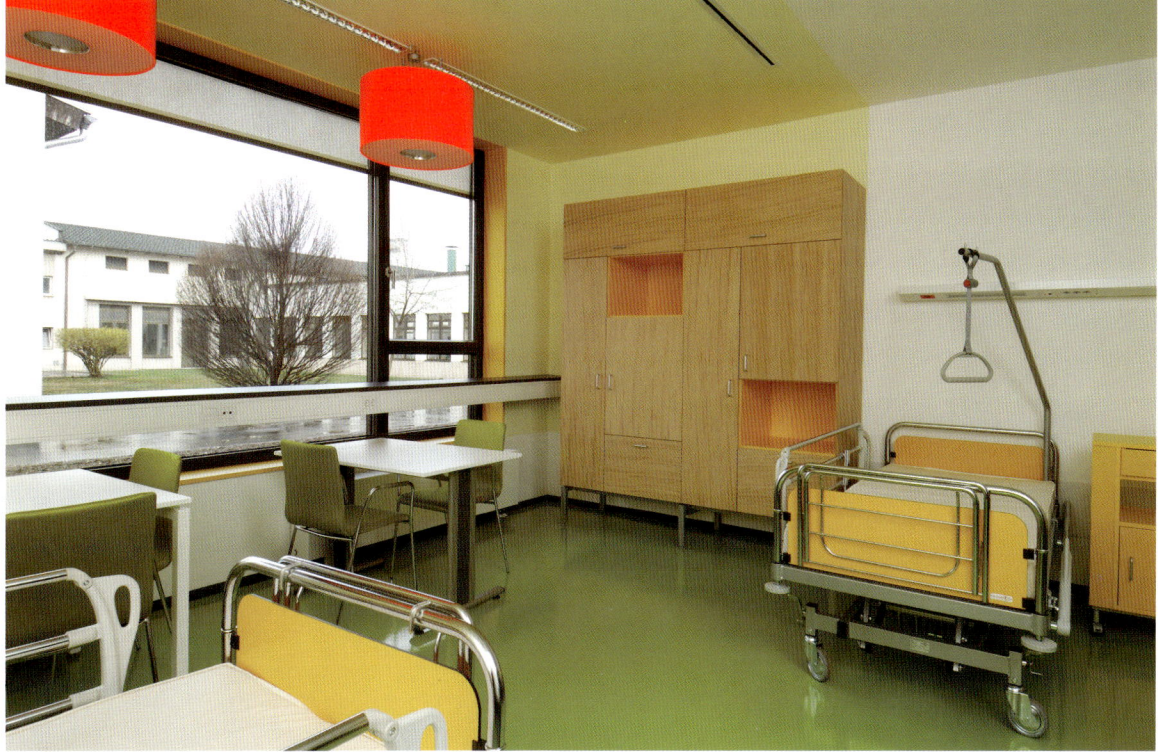

kindergarten 'dandelion clock'

Location/
Buchen, Germany
Design/
Ecker Architekten

Photography/
Constantin Meyer
Architekturphotographie
Area/
630 sqm

The kindergarten "Dandelion Clock" educates children with physical or developmental handicaps. Four similar modules form the building, three of which contain two classrooms and a therapy room. Deep overhangs shade the classrooms and permit outdoor play in poor weather.

The units are radially distributed about an atrium, which serves as a traffic zone, an indoor playing field, and a dining hall. This center is naturally illuminated and ventilated by four prominent roof monitors – the so-called "jester's cap." Vents in the classroom façade and windows at the top of each monitor draw air through the building, providing cooling during warm days or when the atrium is intensively used. Clad in gold-anodized standing-seam aluminum, the roof monitors form a strong visual identity for the school despite sprawling, commercial surroundings.

Repetitive framing enabled factory production of large modular panels. Connection reveals in the timbers, designed to accept aluminum curtain wall profiles, were milled with a CNC wood router in the carpenter's shop to ensure precision on the building site. Construction took eight months to complete. Wood products play a dominant role in exterior and interior finishes. The color concept supports the radial form of the school and defines territories for its young users.

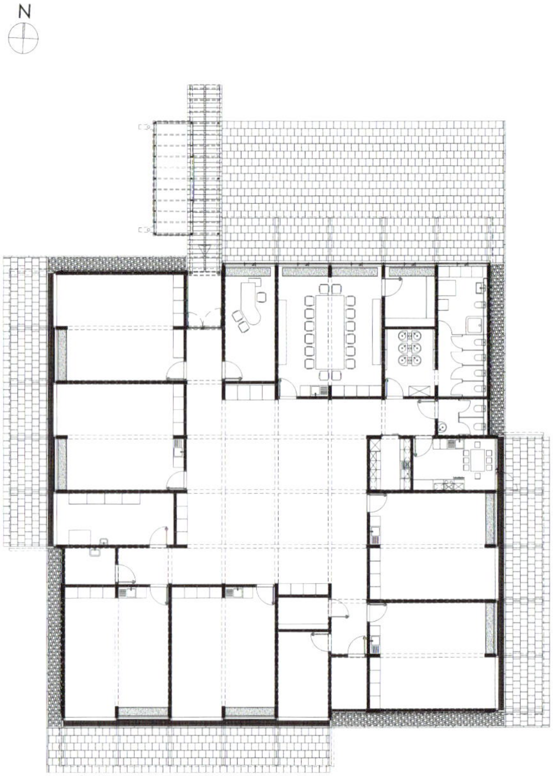

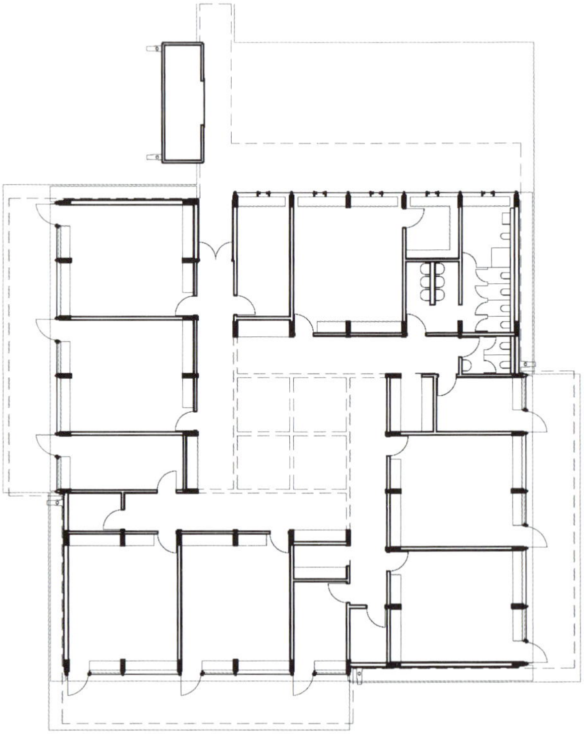

sansaburu kindergarten

Location/
Eibar, Gipuzkoa, Spain
Design/
vaumm arquitectura &
urbanismo

Photography/
Aitor Ortiz
(www.aitor-ortiz.com)
Area/
1,227 sqm

Recessed into a hill on its north and west sides, the building opens towards the south and southeast. The design of the building places the playground at the back of the building in the shade. The building is organized into two wings which cradle an interior courtyard.

The classrooms are lit by morning light, which is appropriate to the children's schedule in the building. The inside of the building is designed according to the scale of a child. The natural light of the corridors and classrooms enters through the ground level windows which allow the children to admire the outside world. The internal cladding colors are warm and lively, giving the school a playful feel that pervades from the interior spaces out onto the balcony overlooking Sansaburu Street.

The random arrangement of lamps in the front entrance above the tramex-made closure provides an inviting entrance into the building.

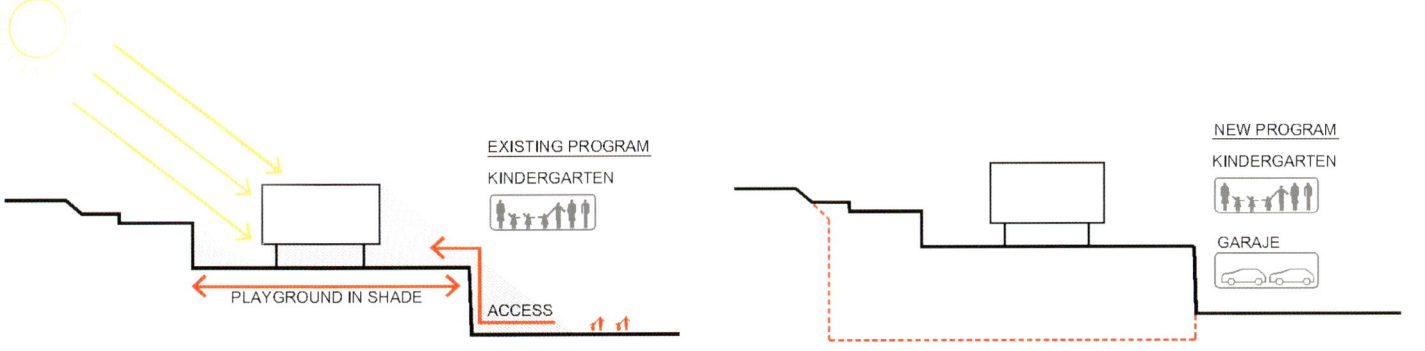

EXISTING PROGRAM

KINDERGARTEN

PLAYGROUND IN SHADE

ACCESS

NEW PROGRAM

KINDERGARTEN

GARAJE

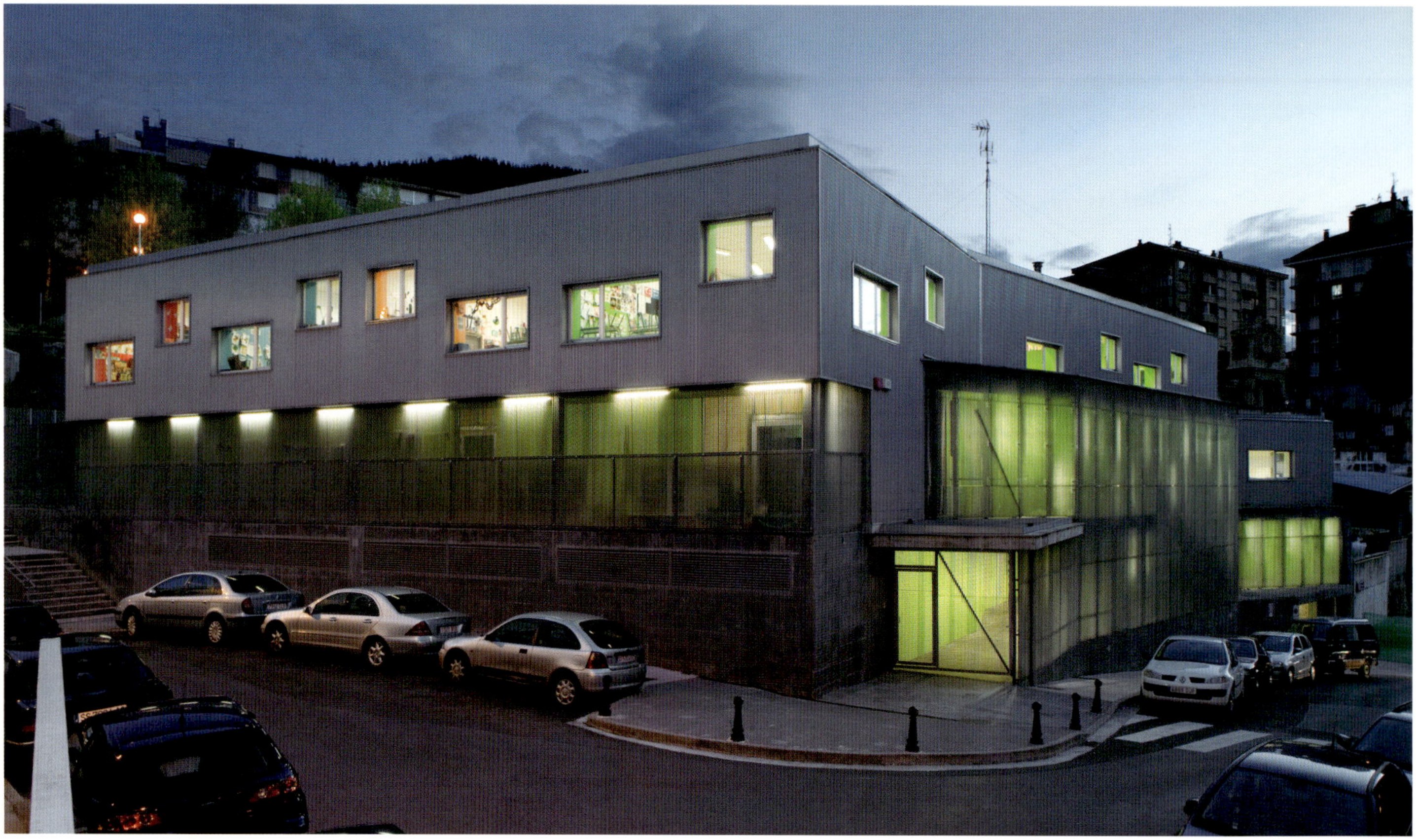

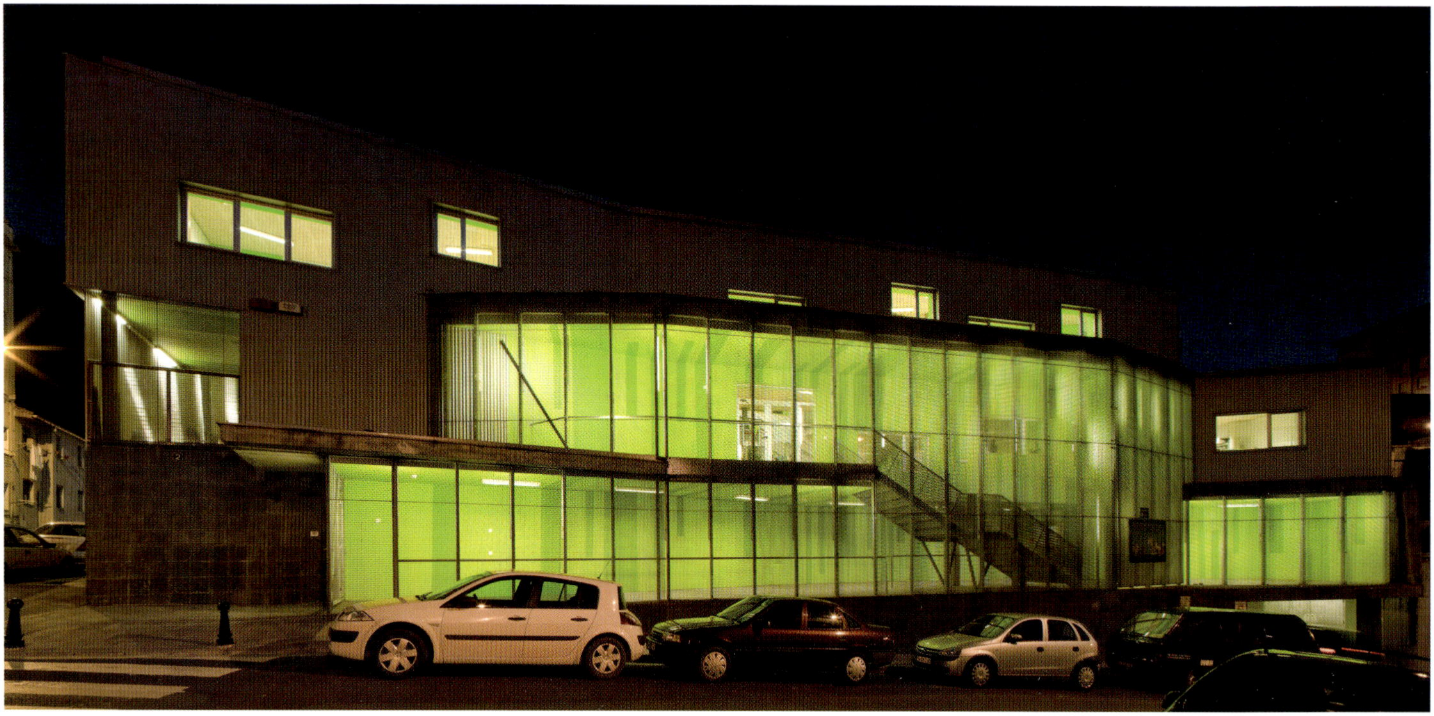

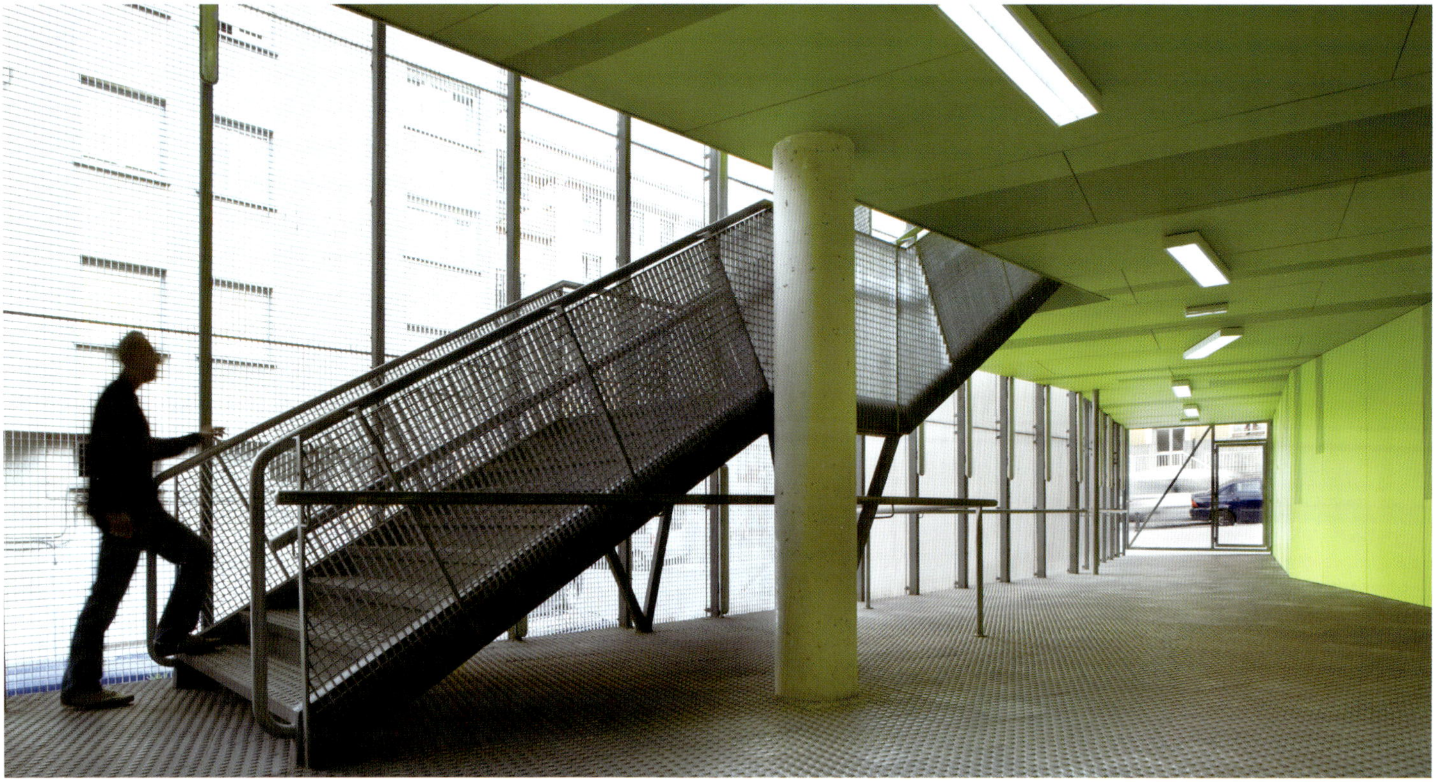

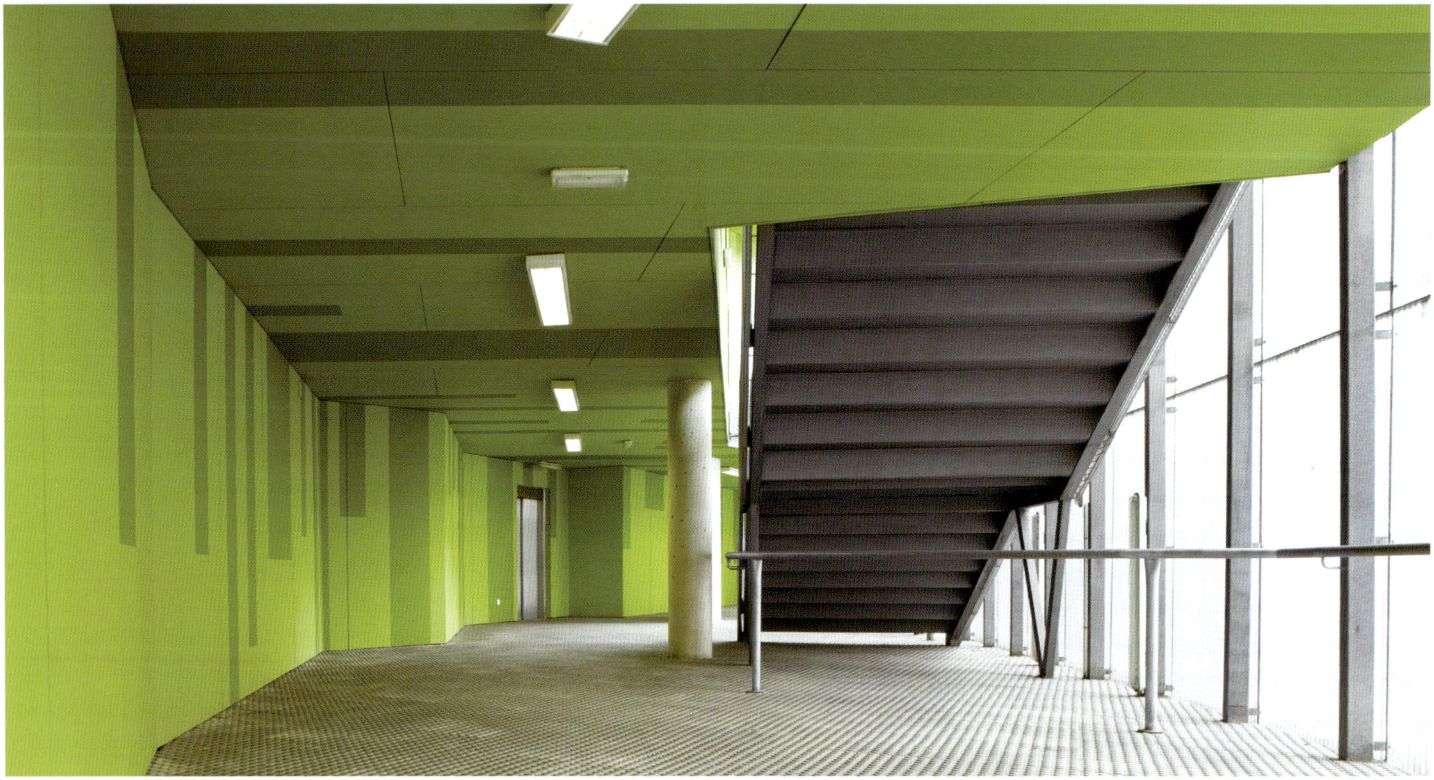

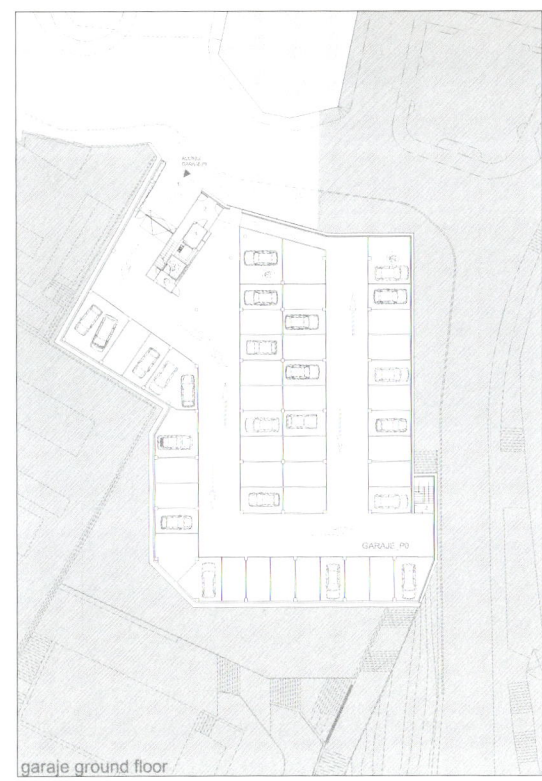

garaje ground floor

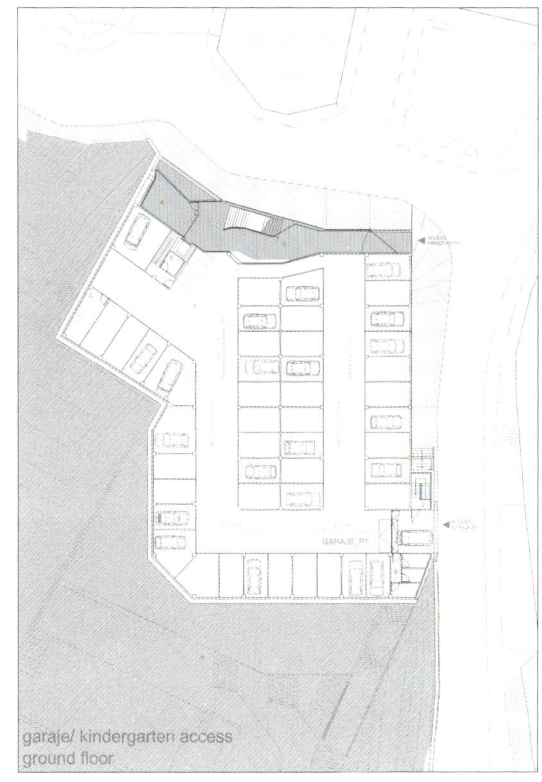

garaje/ kindergarten access
ground floor

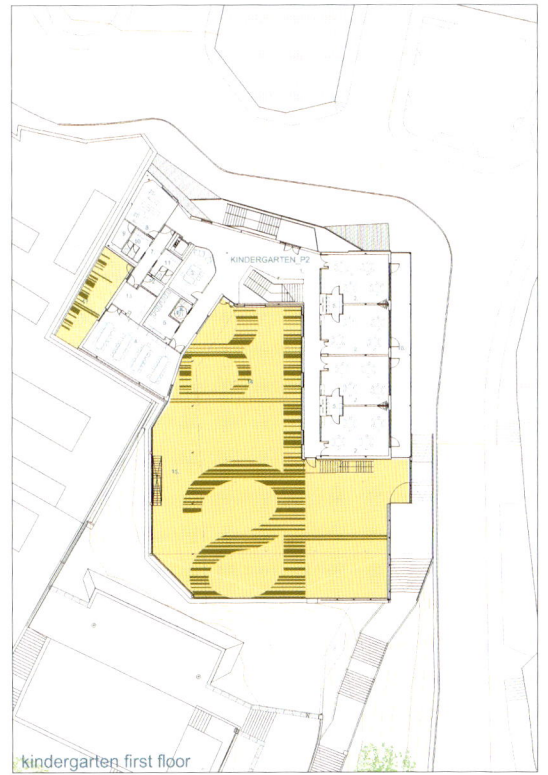

kindergarten first floor

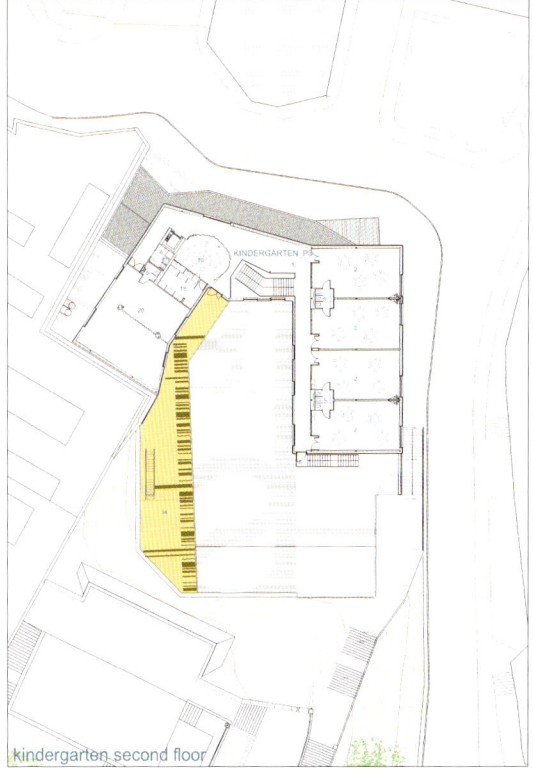

kindergarten second floor

bakkegaard school

Location/
Skolebakken, Gentofte,
Denmark
Design/
CEBRA

Photography/
Adam Mørk, Kragh &
Berglund
Area/
6,200 sqm + 1,800 sqm

The project is a combination of development, rebuilding and extension and it forms part of a school development project – including all schools in the municipality of Gentofte. The project involves rebuilding of the existing school with three-form entry as well as the building of an extension of approximately 1,800 sqm containing a gym, auditorium, and cafeteria.

The new building functions as part of a landscape connecting the school on several levels, with new common spaces created for school and leisure. The new sports center, the auditorium, an educational service center in the old gym, and the café and workshops in the pavilion are integrated together and can act as one coherent room for common activities. The roof of the building is an elevated schoolyard, which opens up new possibilities for play and exploration of outdoor areas. A connecting pathway leads from the roof to the main access roads, the pavilion with workshops, and the playground, as well as up to the pupils' lodging areas and project rooms.

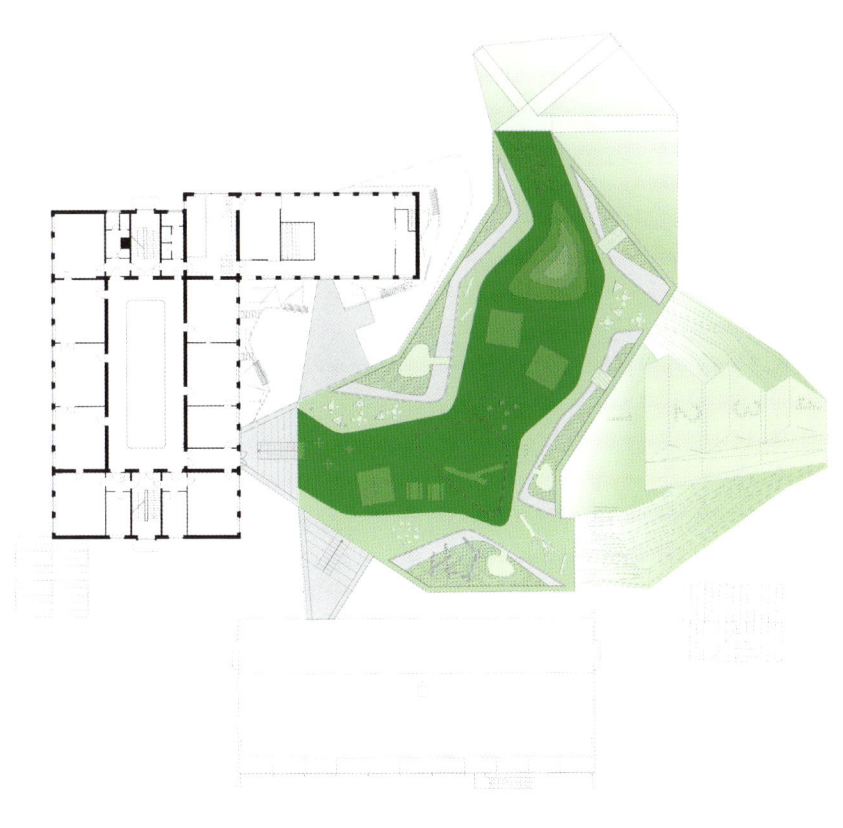

arreletes day care center

Location/
Els Alamus, Spain
Design/
XVSTUDIO

Photography/
Jordi Anguera
Area/
254.36 sqm

The project creates two volumes. The bottom level consists of the classrooms and courtyard, follows the direction of the agricultural fields, and is supported by the existing agricultural wall. The upper level holds the teachers' offices which face houses of the neighboring village and overlook the children's courtyard. The two volumes offer dual access to the school and are connected by a staircase inset into the natural slope of the hill.

The personal experience centers around the designers' memories of childhood amid countless fruit trees, shade-filtered spaces, and trees perfectly planned out in a geometrically pleasing garden.

The spaces are versatile, continuous, and have controlled lighting. The lobby and the first classroom can be transformed into a dining hall and the classrooms can be connected by the changing room which leads into the courtyard. The building is oriented toward the east; the design features a horizontal window resting on the foundation slope which gives the interior corridor screened light from the west.

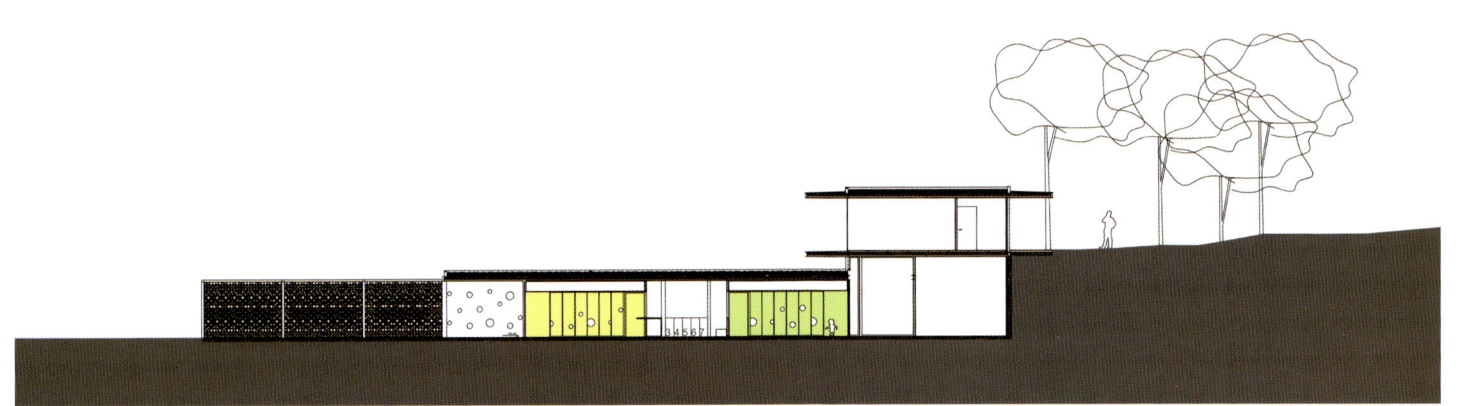

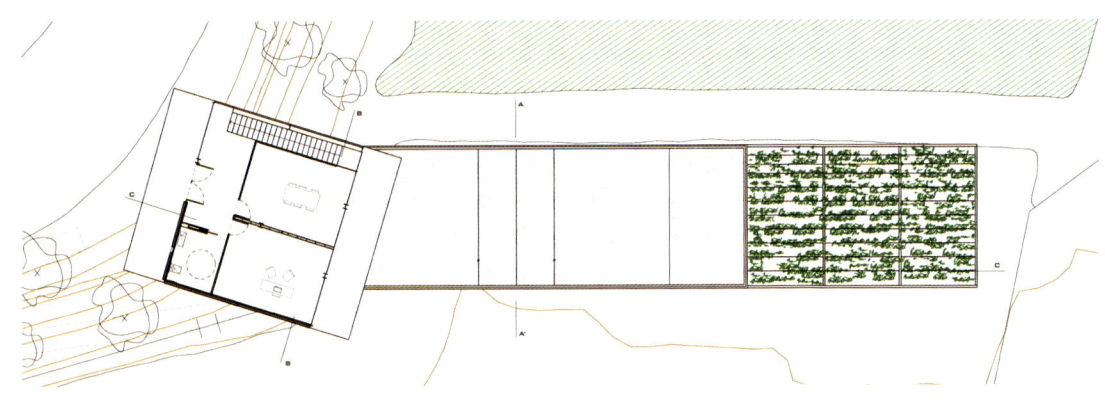

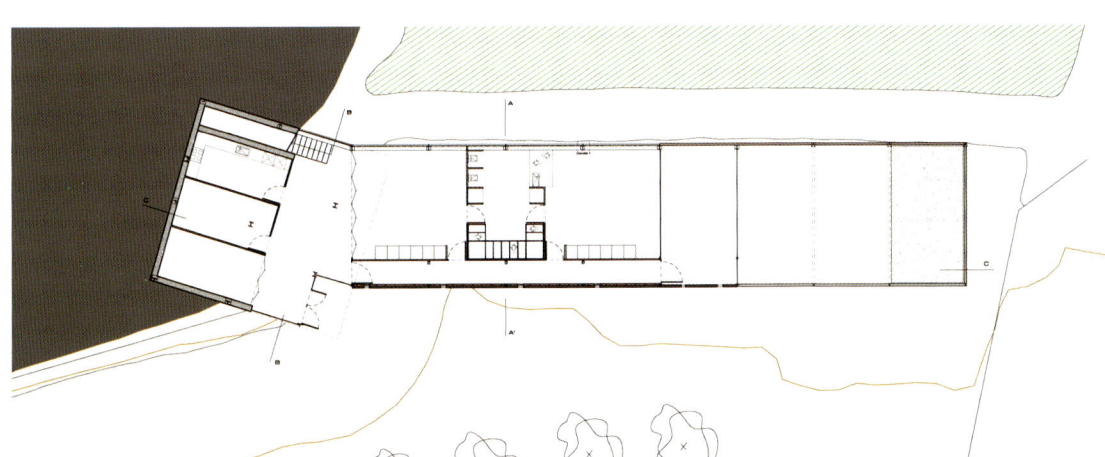

l'atelier des enfants at the centre pompidou

Location/
Paris, France
Design/
Mathieu Lehanneur

Photography/
Hervé Véronèse
Area/
300 sqm

L'Atelier des enfants at the Centre Pompidou is newly up and running in a new area designed by Mathieu Lehanneur. It now offers a more spacious setting, which is better adapted to activities for children ages 2 to 12 years. The rounded corners of the room are a direct allusion to skate parks as recreational scenery. The walls act as a playful element with which children can interact.

L'Atelier des enfants is comprised of three areas: a workshop for the youngest children from 2 to 5 years old; an artist's area for children ages 6 to 12 years old, and last, a multipurpose area. Designed and equipped to accommodate any type of activity (practical work on the floor, walls, or in the central space, visual and sound installations, choreographic sessions, etc.), the area includes a secure entrance, a rest area, a continuous wall seat, alcoves, and a wall of "senses." All that is needed is available for the children who are guided by teachers in activities designed to stimulate their creativity.

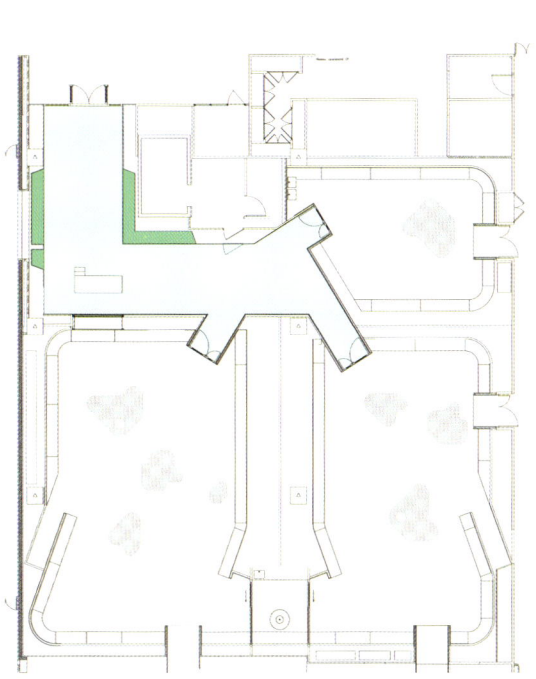

anansi playground building

Location/
Peltlaan 130, 3527
EC Utrecht, the
Netherlands
Design/
Mulders vandenBerk
Architecten

Photography/
Wim Hanenberg, Roel
Backaert, Wouter van
der Sar
Area/
150 sqm

Mulders vandenBerk Architecten of Amsterdam
has completed a playground building in a park
in Utrecht, the Netherlands, with a Corian façade
engraved with images of fairytales from around
the world. The idea of the building is to excite and
stimulate curiosity and creativity of the children.

The pavilion splits the playground in two. One
side is used by teenagers, and the other by young
children. The interior is divided into three separate
playrooms featuring bright colors, simple furniture,
and interactive elements. Each room is related
to an individual façade and offers a specific
orientation to its context. This, combined with
unique "wallpaper," gives a particular identity to
each room. The design invites children to play, to
discover and invent games.

The exterior of the building is the opposite of
the "active" playground with its many climbing
frames and slides. The building is a calm oasis
in the playground. The façade is a large white
Corian surface with milled jagged lines. At first
sight there are only lines. A second view reveals
decorative characters from fairy tales all around
the world. Graphic design studio Design Arbeid
worked together with the neighborhood children to
select the fairy tales which would be featured. The
graphic design is cnc-milled out of the façade to
stimulate the senses and the imagination.

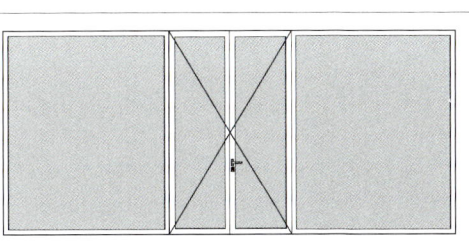

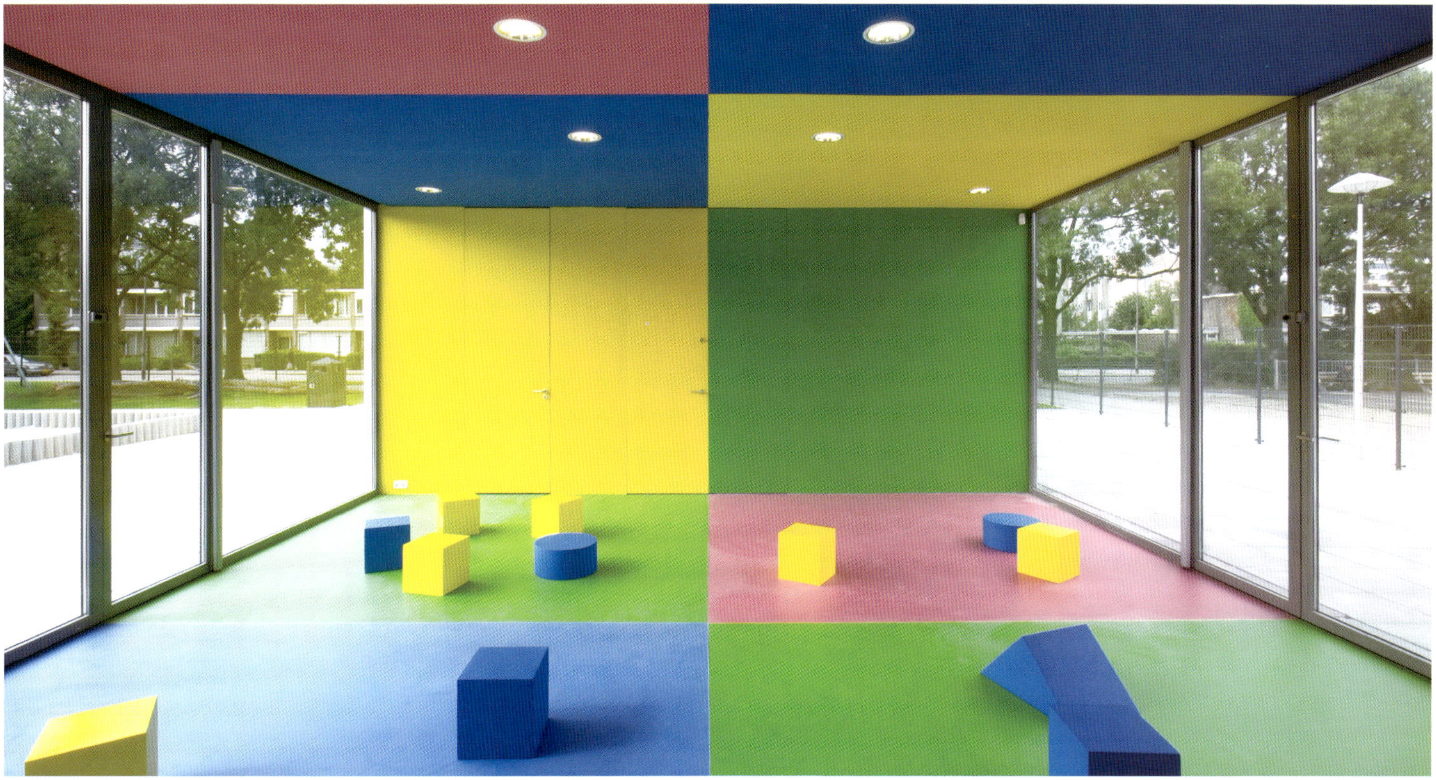

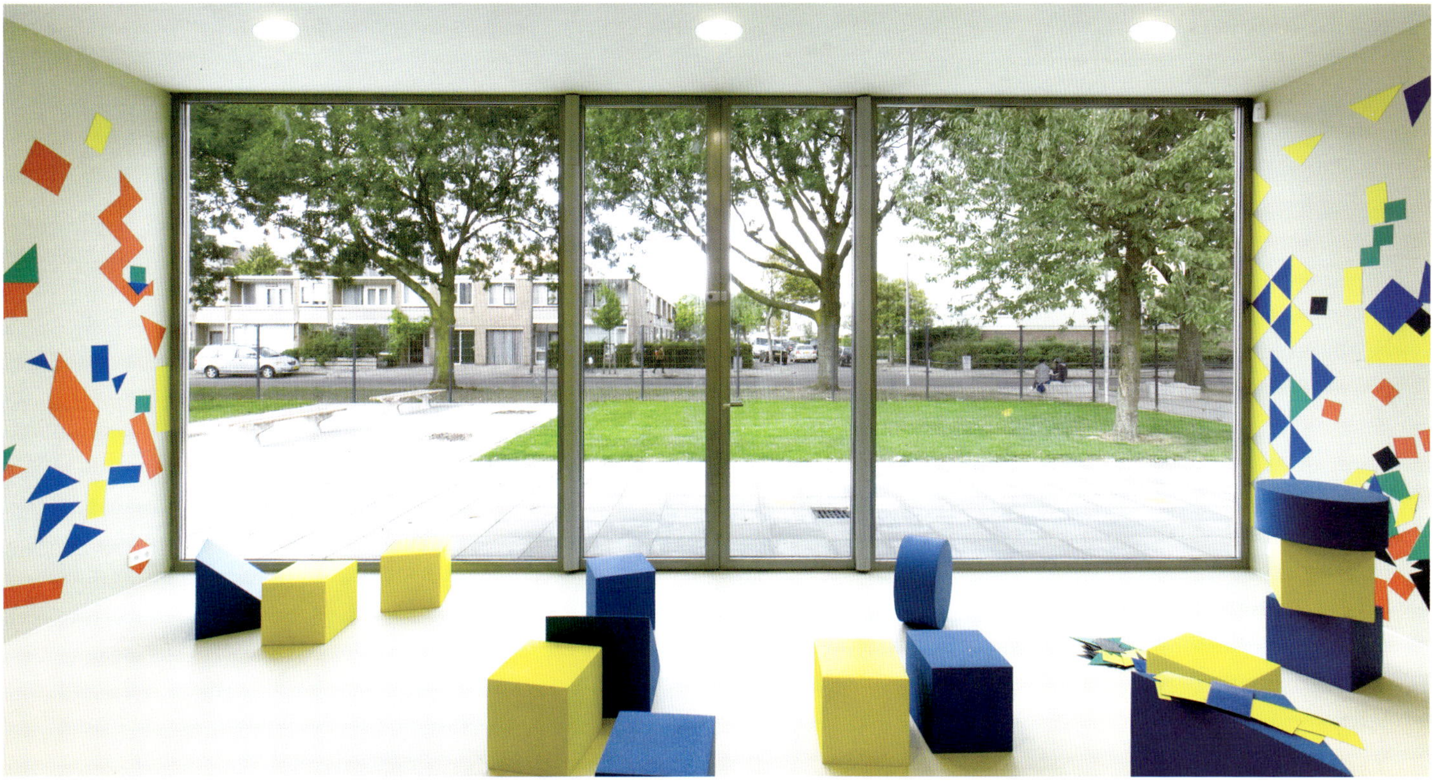

ku65 - kids club

Location/
Berlin, Germany
Design/
GRAFT

Photography/
GRAFT
Area/
505 sqm

The client came to GRAFT with a brief to extend his existing adult-focused dental spa to incorporate a wing for dental care for children as well as orthodontics for both adults and children.

The concept for the existing spa was a sand dune topography, with the treatment rooms located within the dunes to make a disconcerting visit to the dentist feel more like a day by the seaside.

This topography extends into the new wing, and is suffused with a vertical garden at the end where a living green wall is framed by sand dunes. A secret garden space is created to surround the area where the children are treated.

Topographical elements drip from the ceiling, inverting the dune typology to become elements used as either hills or caverns for play or privacy.

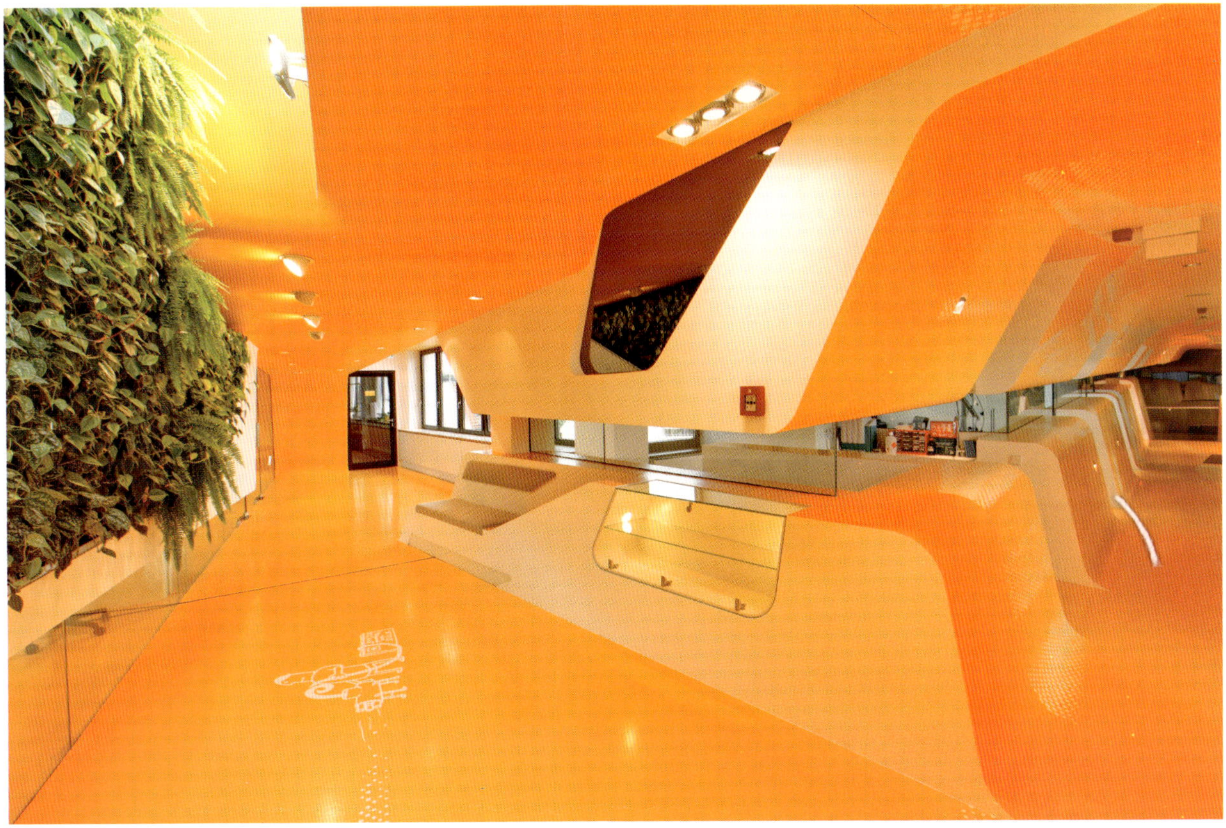

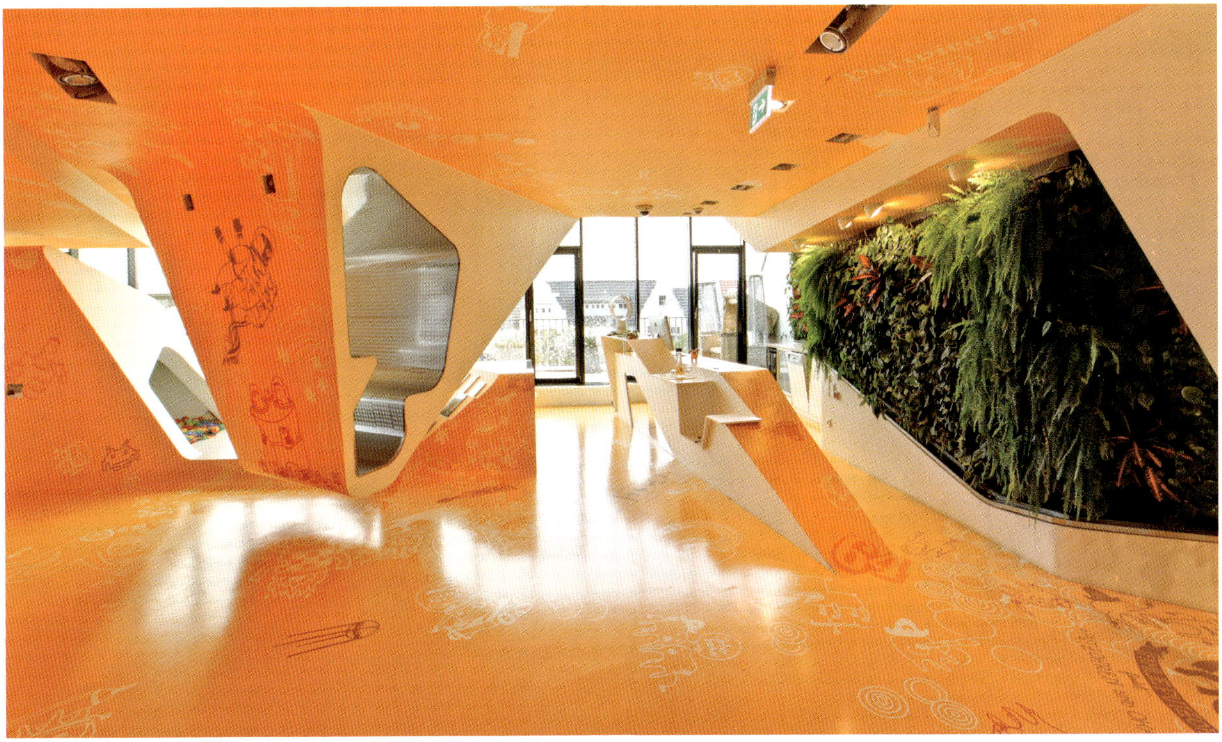

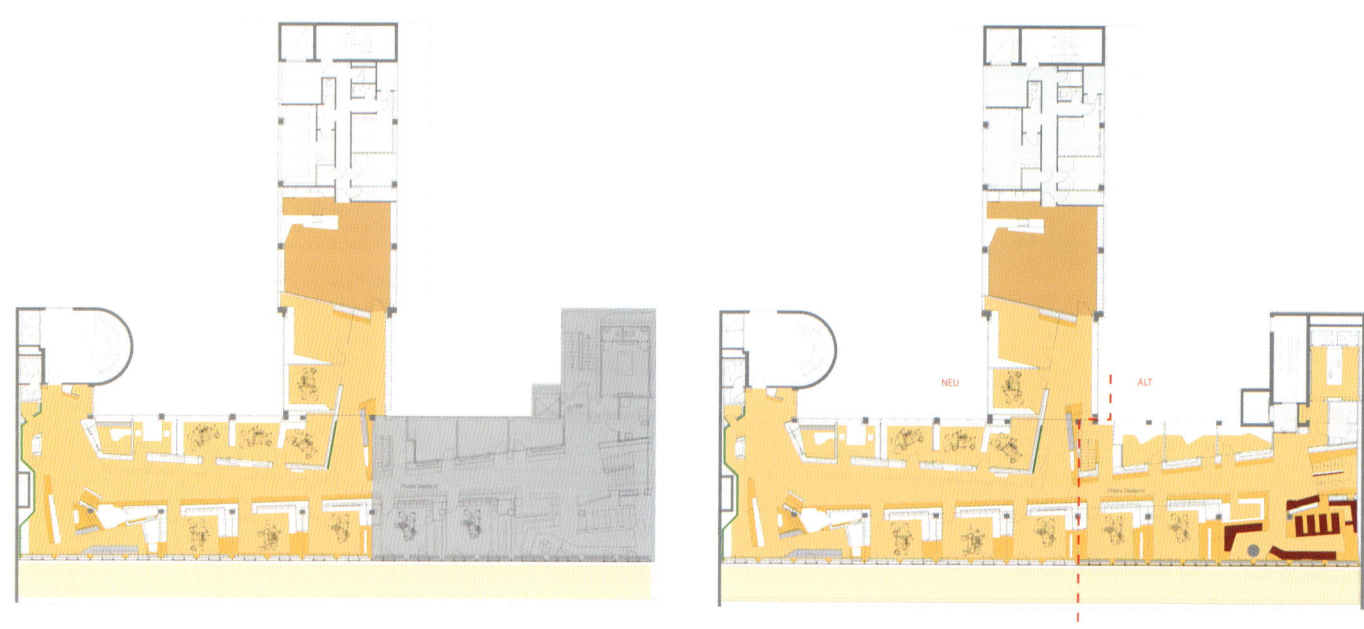

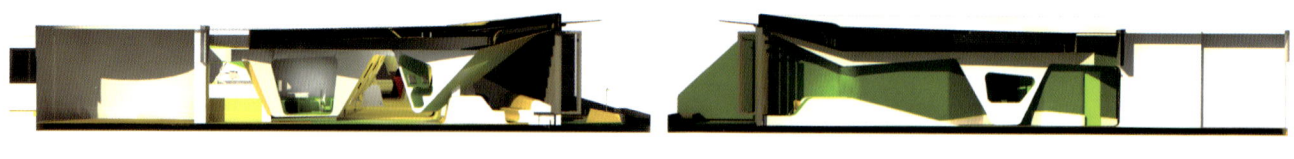

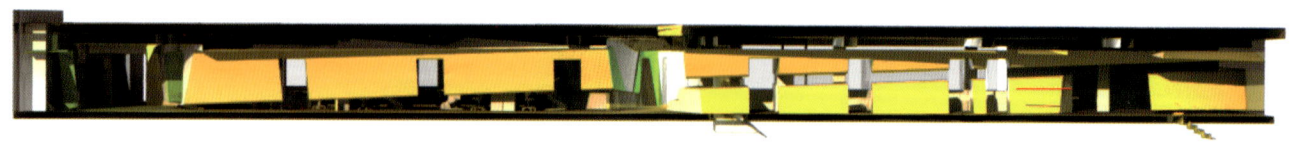

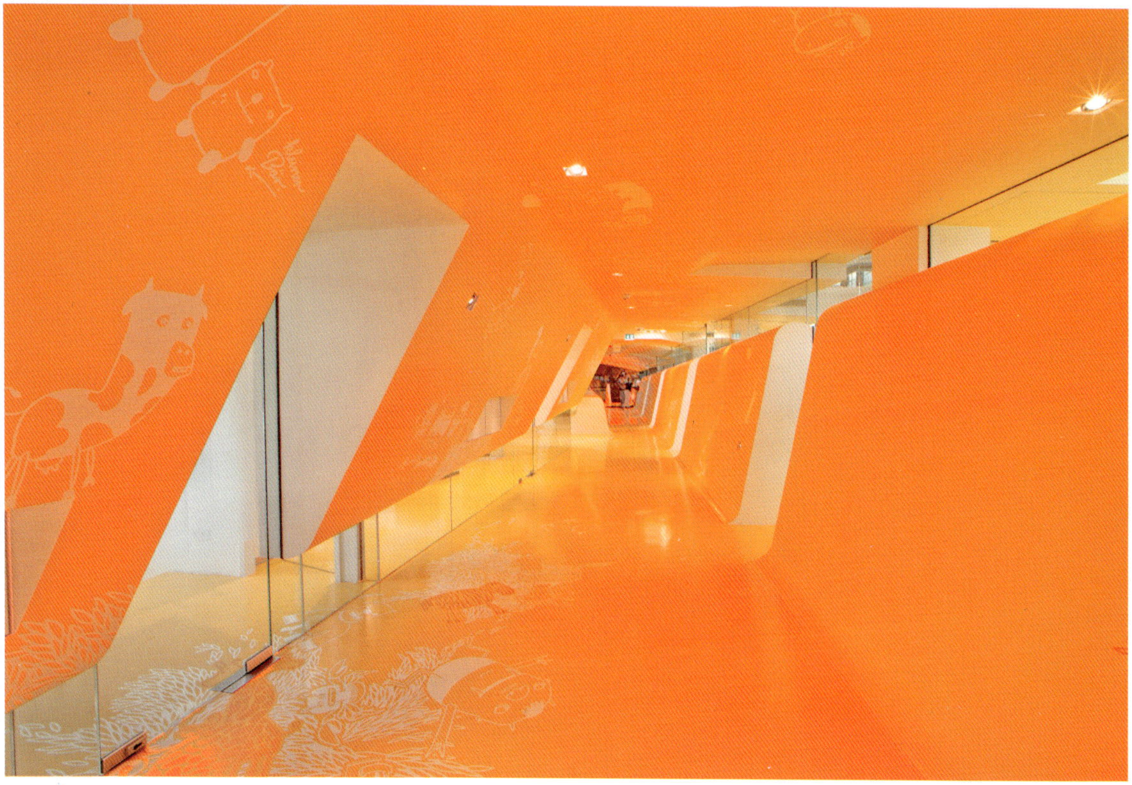

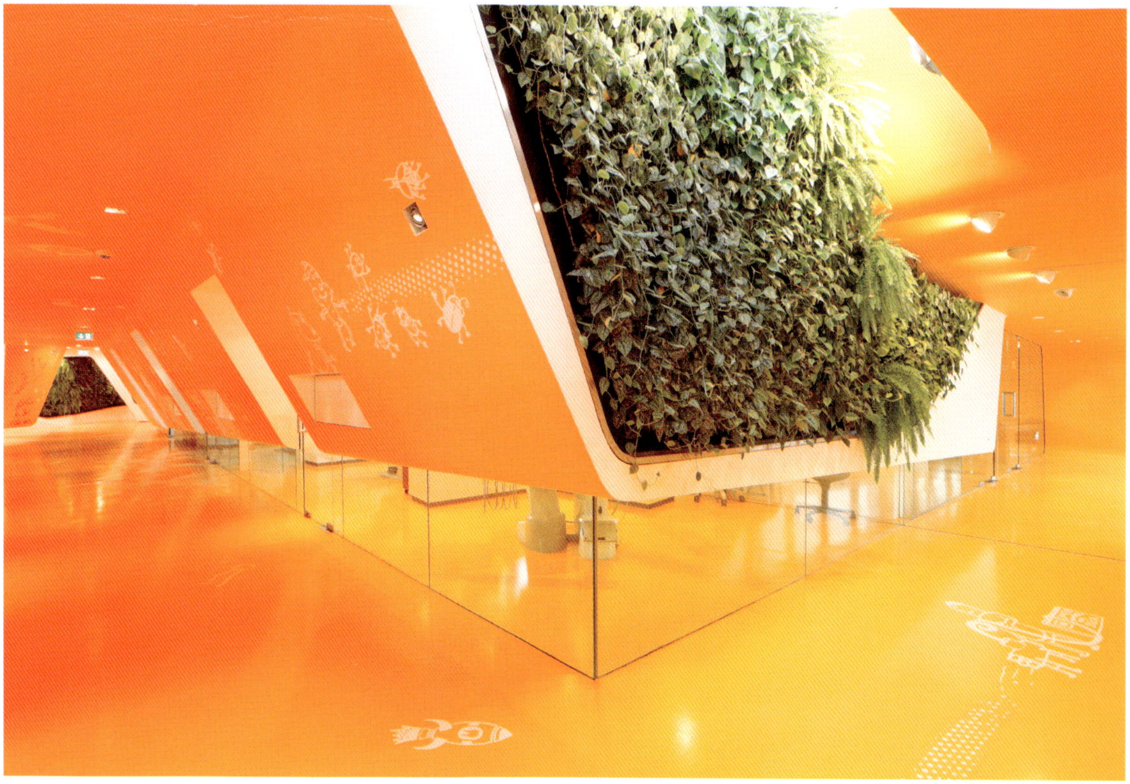

ajurinmäki daycare center

Location/
Espoo, Finland
Design/
AFKS architects

Photography/
Jussi Tiainen
Area/
1,060 sqm

The Ajurinmäki daycare center is situated in the district of Leppävaara in Espoo. The building is comprised of three separate "home areas" for different groups within the children's daycare center, as well as an open door daycare center. The rear of the plot rises up from a steep rock out-crop, where there are also fortification works (which are now protected) dating from the Second World War. Construction was confined to the south side of the plot, where there are favorable climatic and construction conditions. The plot contains a community garden with a variety of garden plants and fruit trees. This area has now been preserved as part of the daycare center and as a local playground, with a fence marking as large an area as possible. The building has the shape of an organic, living entity that feeds the imagination. The interiors vary in height and utilize the attic space below the shallow roof planes. An essential part of the architecture is the seemingly arbitrary placement of the windows and the artificial landscape of slopes formed by the roof, where the 'light lanterns' stand as miniature buildings and enliven the interior.

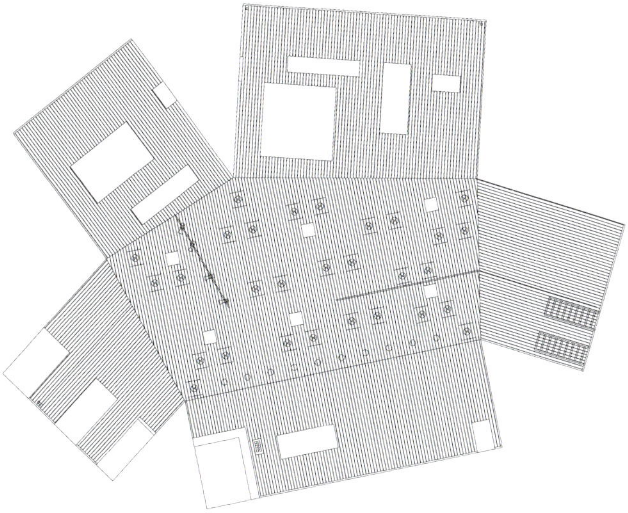

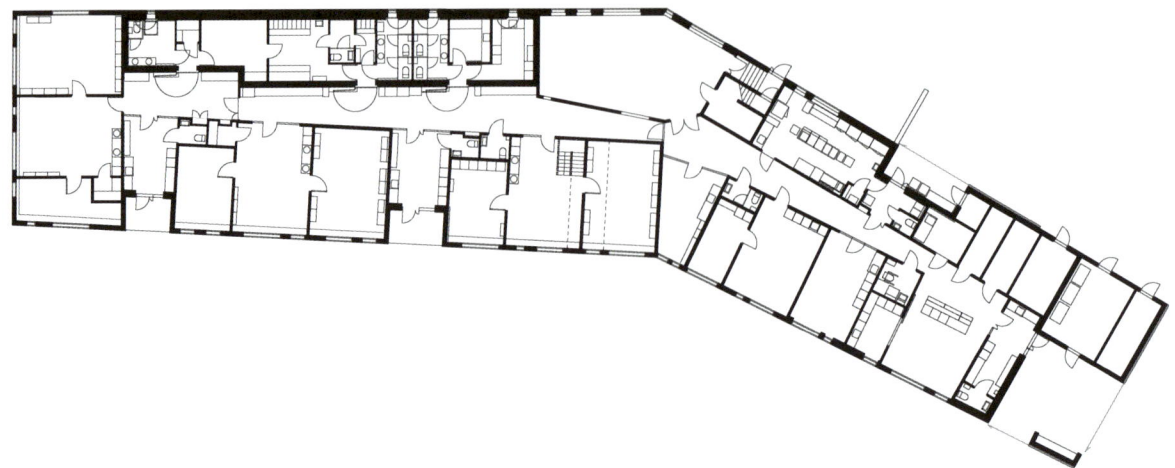

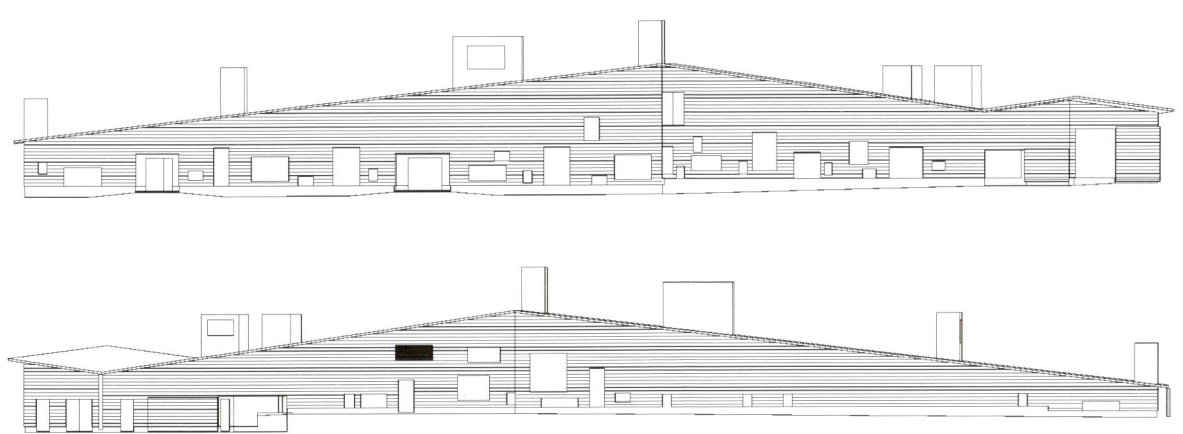

tellus nursery school

Location/
Telefonplan,
Stockholm, Sweden
Design/
Tham & Videgård
Arkitekter

Photography/
Åke E:son Lindman
Area/
1,242 sqm

On the border between a former urban/industrial development and a small forest where new housing is being developed, this nursery school mediates between different contexts and scales. A semi-enclosed entrance courtyard constitutes a primary exterior space for parents and children meeting and leaving. The organic layout encourages movement as space becomes continuous and creates both exterior and interior rooms of challenging shapes. Windows are freely placed at different heights and allow for light and views to be adapted to the scale of children, which adds to the relation between the interior and the exterior playground and the wooded hill.

The clients were inspired by the Reggio Emilia school and a new way to organize the interior of the building was developed. The result is an unorthodox plan which includes a large interior plaza which is used as a common area for the six different groups of children at the school, within which they can engage in different activities together, play, and learn from interactive projects. This main space is complemented by separate workshop spaces for water projects and art, as well as small secluded group rooms for rest and quiet activities.

The facade is made of sawn wood that filters direct sunlight into the nursery space and creates hidden windows that underscore the curved interior and exterior spaces. The building complies with the highest standards for environmentally friendly and long term sound construction.

083

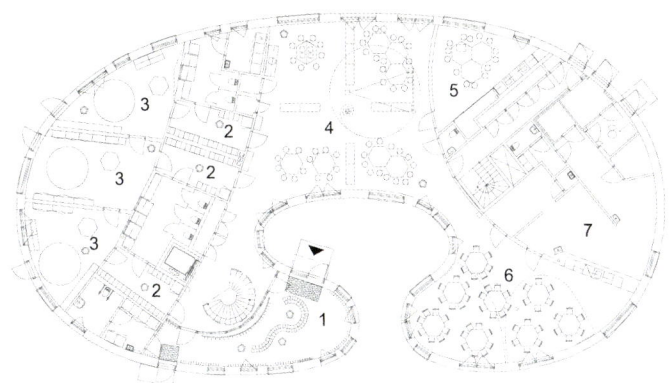

LEVEL 1 - ENTRANCE

1 ENTRANCE 2 CLOAK ROOM 3 GROUP ROOM
4 COMMON SPACE 5 ATELIER 6 CANTEEN / ATELIER
7 KITCHEN 8 LOADING

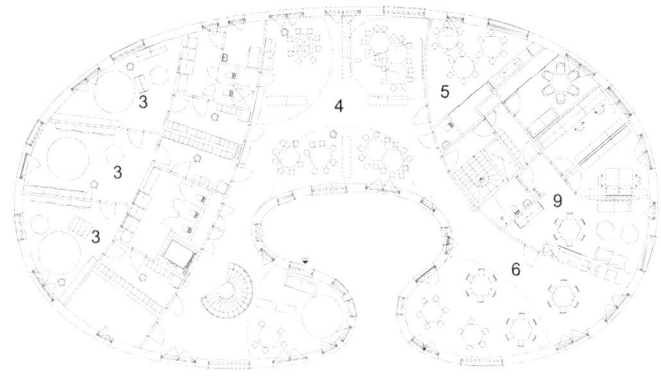

LEVEL 2

2 CLOAK ROOM 3 GROUP ROOM 4 COMMON SPACE
5 ATELIER 6 CANTEEN / ATELIER 9 OFFICE / ADMIN

kindergarten
taka-tuka-land

Location/
Hohenzollernring 93,
1358, Germany
Design/
Die Baupiloten

Photography/
Jan Bitter
(www.janbitter.de)
Area/
545 sqm

The original temporary structure of the kindergarten has been turned into an everlasting oak tree where lemonade grows and flows. The flow of lemonade has seven intervals where the children can enjoy it; for example, the large-scale windows where the midday sun turns the room into a glittering environment due to the crystals that have been mounted in the windows. Yellow is the dominant color of the building, both in the entryway and the corridors containing the lemonade gallery where the children can show their latest accomplishments to their parents. In the hall, the children's belongings are kept safe in lemon-colored cupboards. The architectural high point is the 'lemonade island' where the children are taller than the grown-ups. Its oblique surfaces invite every child to play and 'drown' in streams of yellow lemonade. In one of the rooms the stream of lemonade literally bursts through its boundary and floods into the garden. Metaphorically, Pippi Longstocking's old oak tree has been turned into an interactive façade. It has become an oblique climbing frame made of green oak wood covered by a yellow membrane with plenty of spaces to hide. The entire construction is protected against the elements by a transparent yellow membrane that sheds the inside with warm light.

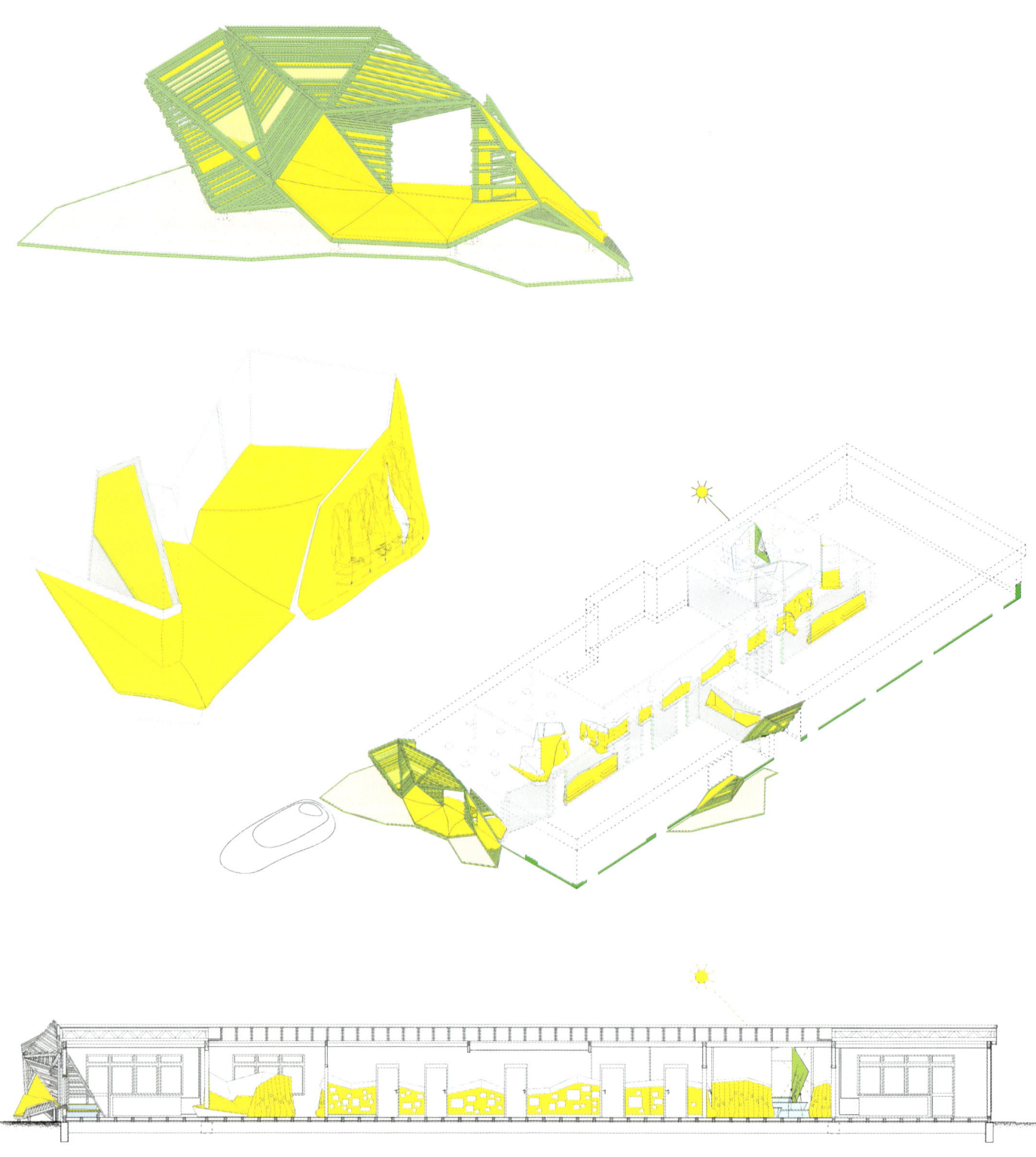

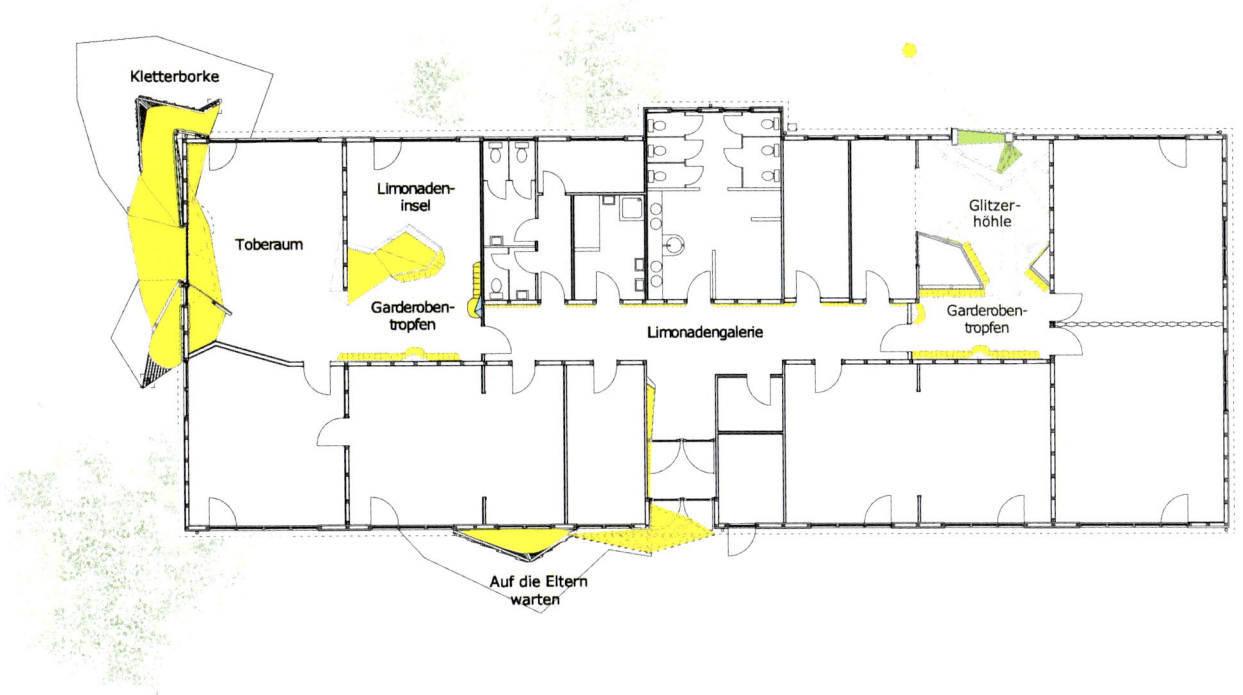

Kletterborke

Toberaum

Limonaden-insel

Garderoben-tropfen

Limonadengalerie

Glitzer-höhle

Garderoben-tropfen

Auf die Eltern warten

The Seven Stages of the Lemonade Tree

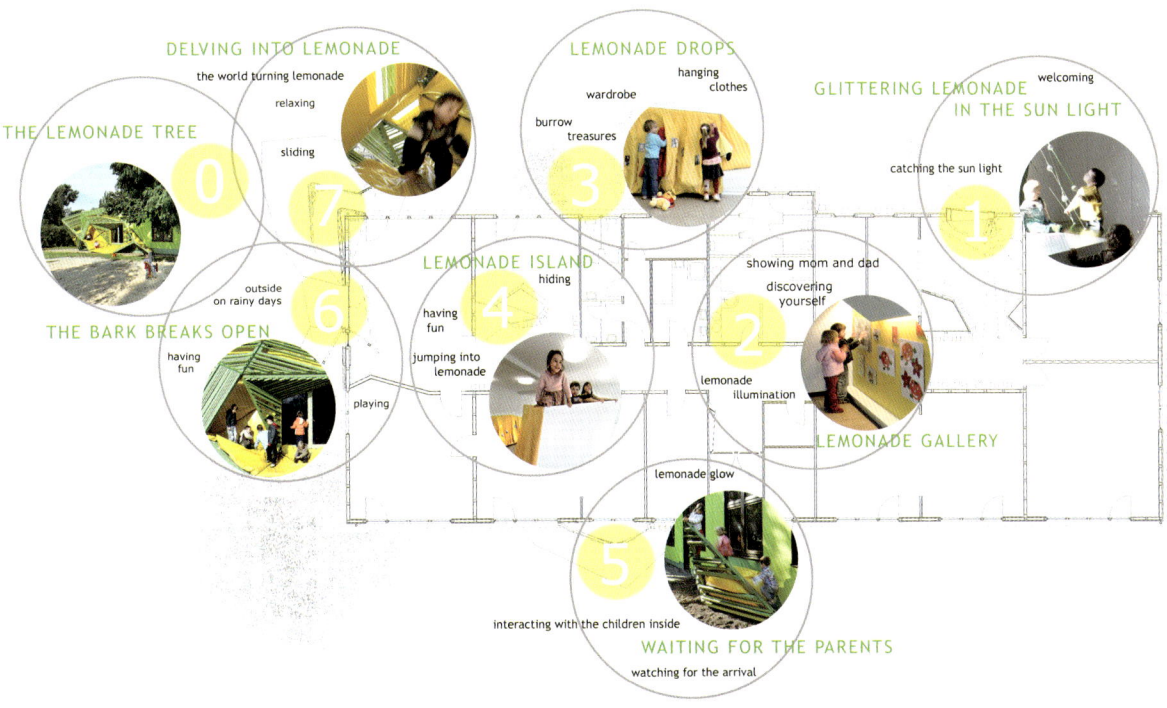

THE LEMONADE TREE
0

DELVING INTO LEMONADE
the world turning lemonade
relaxing
sliding
7

LEMONADE DROPS
hanging clothes
wardrobe
burrow treasures
3

GLITTERING LEMONADE IN THE SUN LIGHT
welcoming
catching the sun light
1

LEMONADE ISLAND
hiding
4
having fun
jumping into lemonade

showing mom and dad
discovering yourself
2
lemonade illumination

LEMONADE GALLERY

THE BARK BREAKS OPEN
having fun
6
outside on rainy days
playing

lemonade glow
5
interacting with the children inside

WAITING FOR THE PARENTS
watching for the arrival

new library for longford community school

Location/
Feltham, UK
Design/
Jonathan Clark
Architects

Photography/
Peter Cook
Area/
750 sqm

The structure for the new extension is formed entirely from Finnforest Kerto laminated veneered lumber panels which are created by overlapping and laminating 3mm thick veneers of spruce to produce a strong, durable material. An undisturbed grain is seen face on, while the build up of lamination layers is noticeable on the front, back and side faces. Kerto elements were cut, treated and stained to colors specified by Finnforest in Germany. After delivery to the site, the pieces were simply slotted together on the ground to be lifted into place. Steel shoe plates connect to the column base via vertical fin plates fitted into hidden saw cuts. As a result, the columns appear to simply rest on a single flat plate.

To the rear of the extension, timber beams are fixed to a steel frame provided to retain lateral stability in the existing building. The structure is completely external and exposed to the elements, which is unusual for this building material. After extensive research, the material was pressure impregnated so that it would be suitable for these conditions and be durable over an extended period of time. In between each fin are aluminum grating panels that provide more solar control as well as some structural stiffening for the external structure. Behind the structure is a two story panel of glazed curtain walling. The roof is a silver Trespa panel clad timber structure and is designed to give the impression of floating/sliding across the exposed timber roof beams.

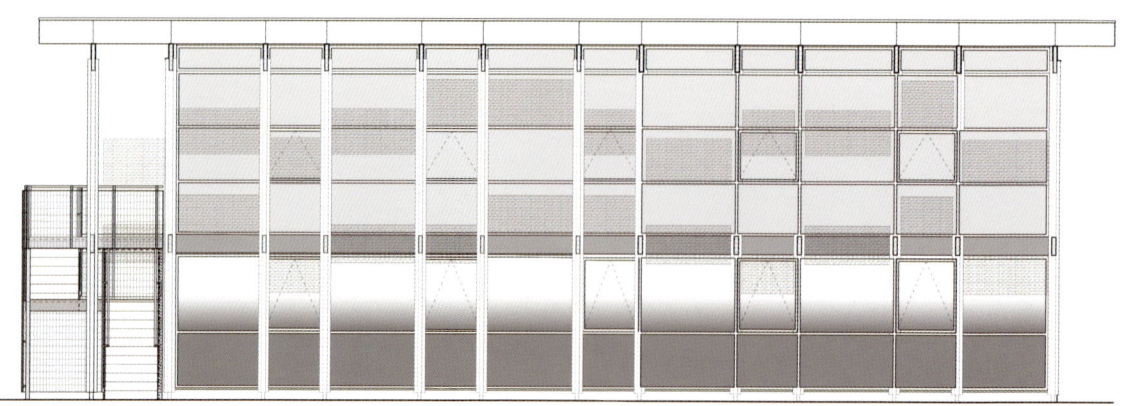

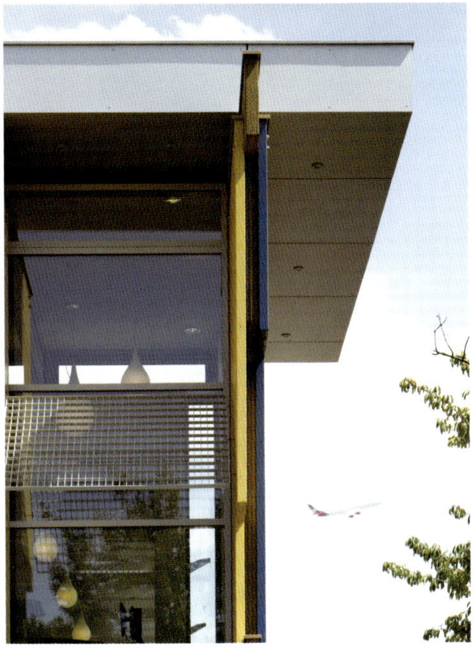

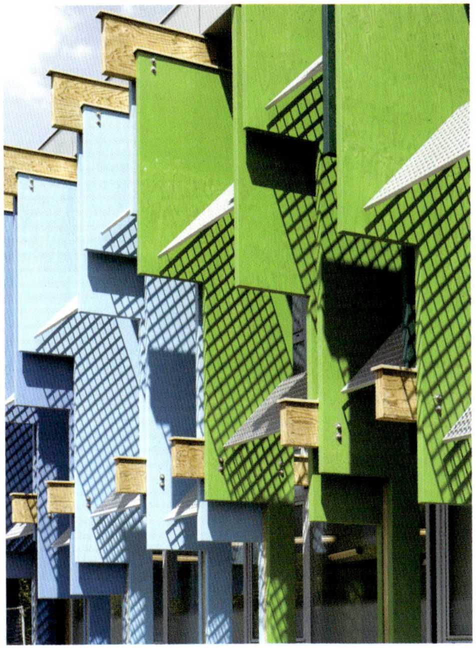

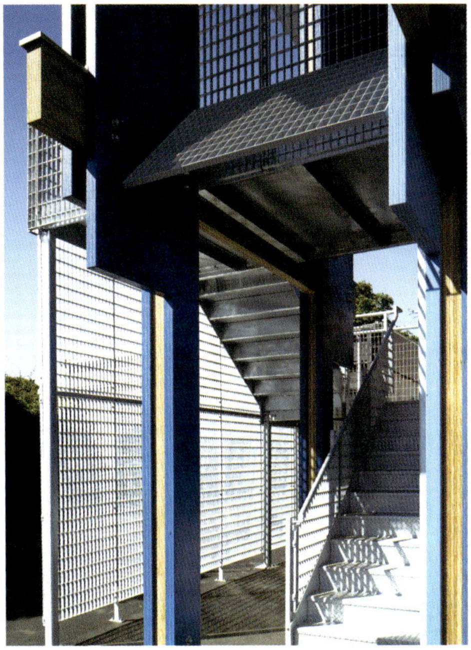

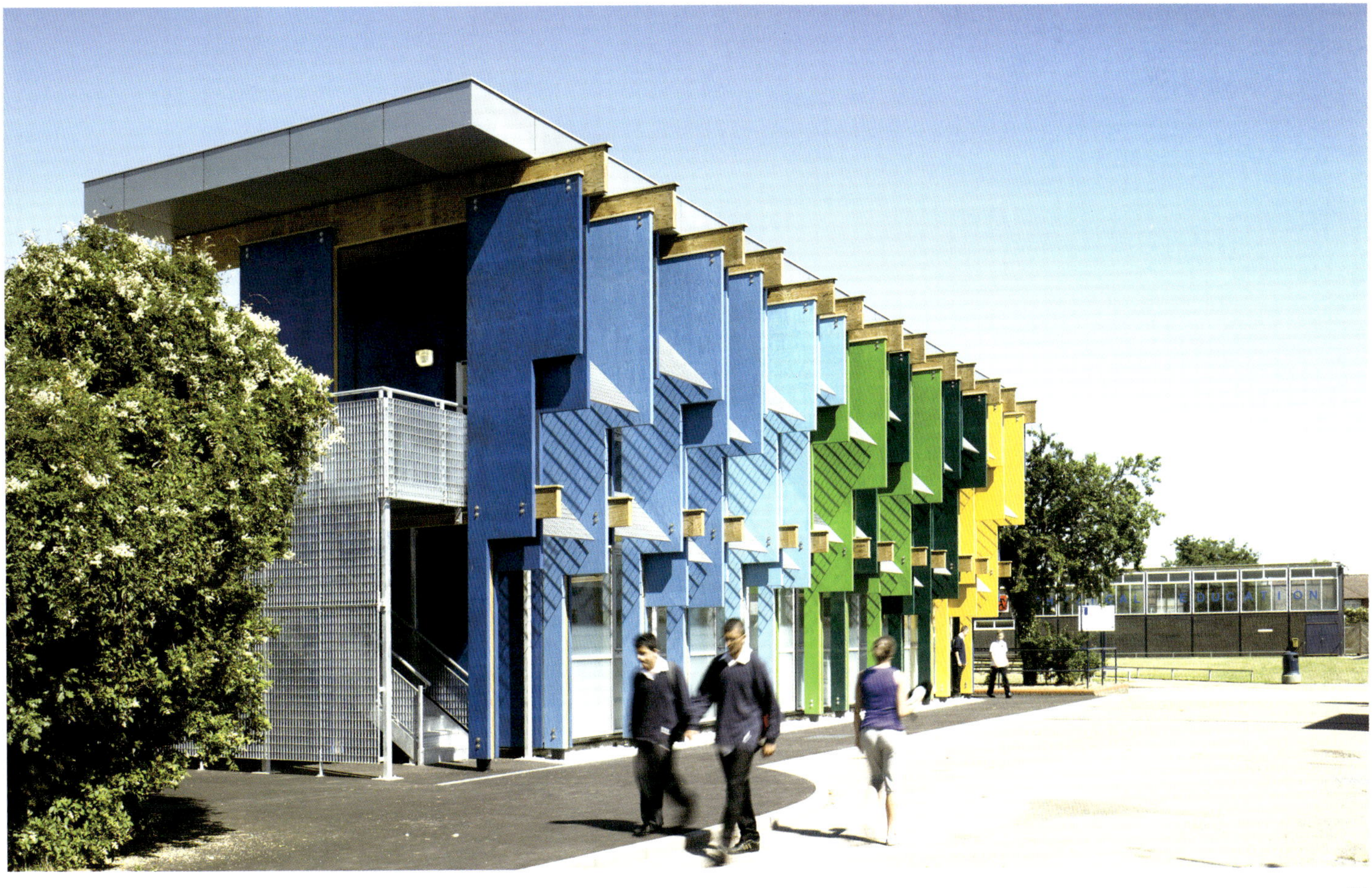

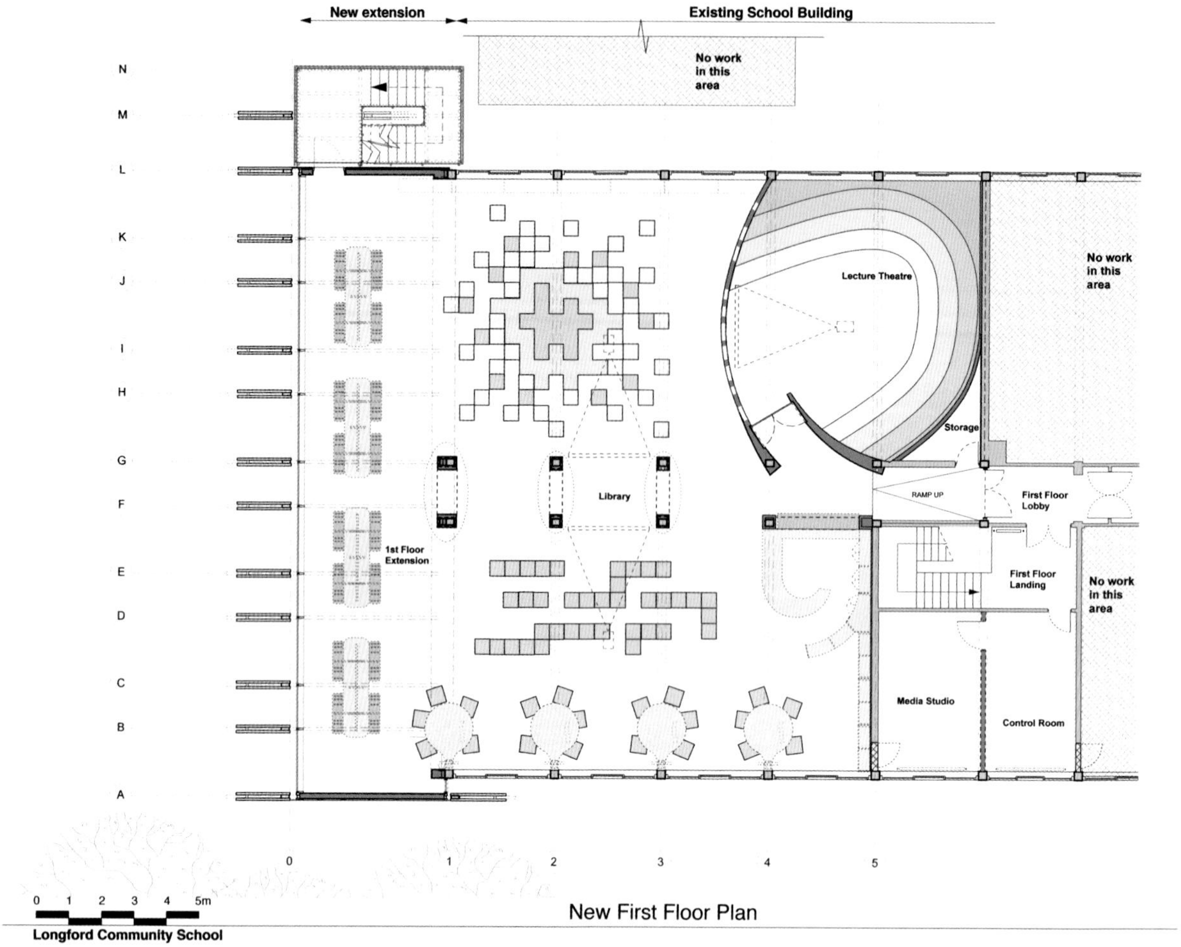

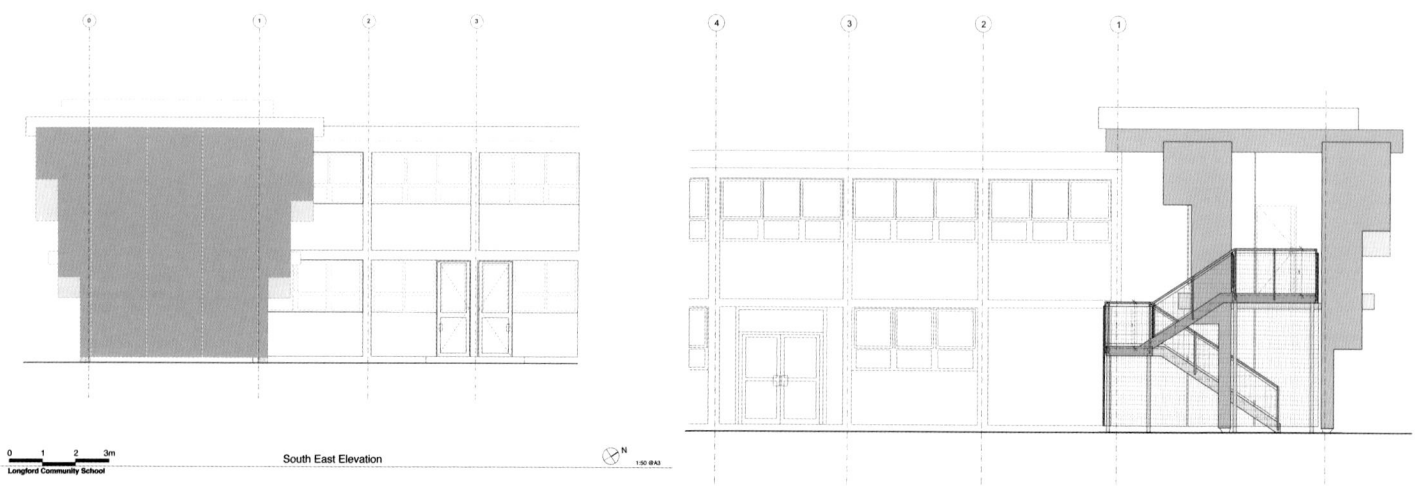

New extension   Existing School Building

No work in this area

N
M
L
K
J
I
H
G
F
E
D
C
B
A

Lecture Theatre

No work in this area

Storage

First Floor Lobby

RAMP UP

1st Floor Extension

Library

First Floor Landing

No work in this area

Media Studio

Control Room

0   1   2   3   4   5

New First Floor Plan

0 1 2 3 4 5m
Longford Community School

South East Elevation

0 1 2 3m
Longford Community School

N

1:50 @A3

096

kindergarten in rosales del canal

Location/
Zaragoza, Spain
Design/
MAGÉN ARQUITECTOS

Photography/
Jesús Granada
Area/
1,790.22 sqm

The basic unit of the school is the classroom. Its form responds both to the primary identification of the protective roof of the house and to the advantages of height and additional lighting in the classrooms. The shape of the classroom's roofing is repeated to cover larger spaces such as the multipurpose hall and the dining room.

The general configuration responds to clearly organizational criteria, placing the classrooms around the patio, with service spaces situated between them. The interior and exterior corridors are connected via a continuous outside porch. The lobby, the multipurpose hall and an administrative area comprised of a reception room, the teachers' lounge, and offices completes the functional program.

Systems based on light and dry construction were considered appropriate, due to the need to be finished as quickly as possible. The ventilated façade of phenol panels finished in natural wood and solar protection slats define the exterior shell of the buildings. The combination of horizontal and vertical wooden panels and colored boards forms an adventurous composition that introduces a playful air into the strict 1.20m x 2.40m modulation of the façade.

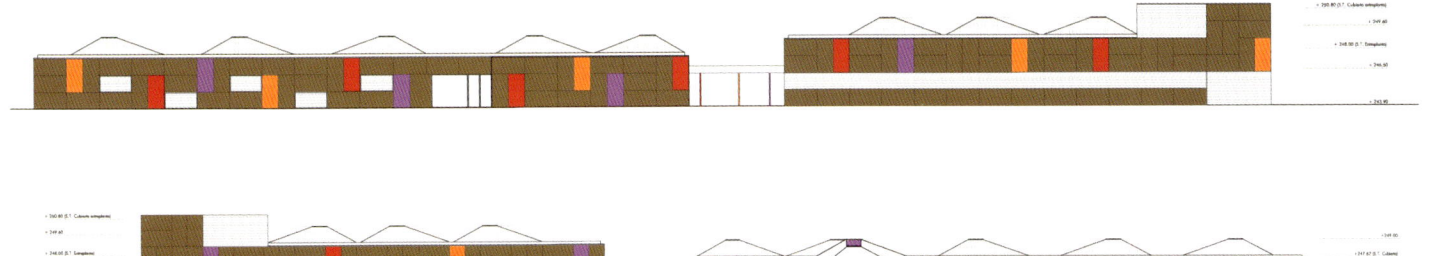

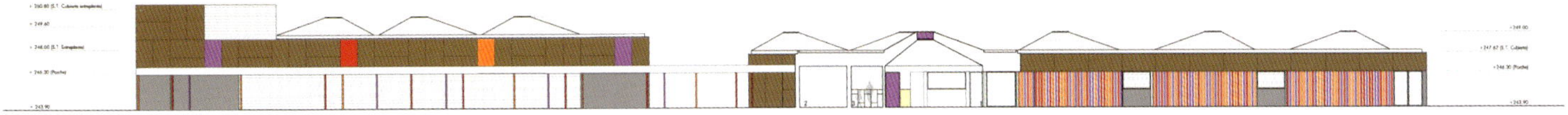

GROUND FLOOR PLAN / e 1:300

1 CLASSROOM
2 TOILETS
3 LOBBY
4 CORRIDOR
5 MULTIPURPOSE - HALL
6 RECEPTION
7 PRINCIPALSHIP
8 TEACHERS ROOM
9 TOILETS
10 STORAGE
11 TECHNICAL ROOMS
12 DINING-HALL
13 TOILETS
14 KITCHEN
15 LOCKER ROOM

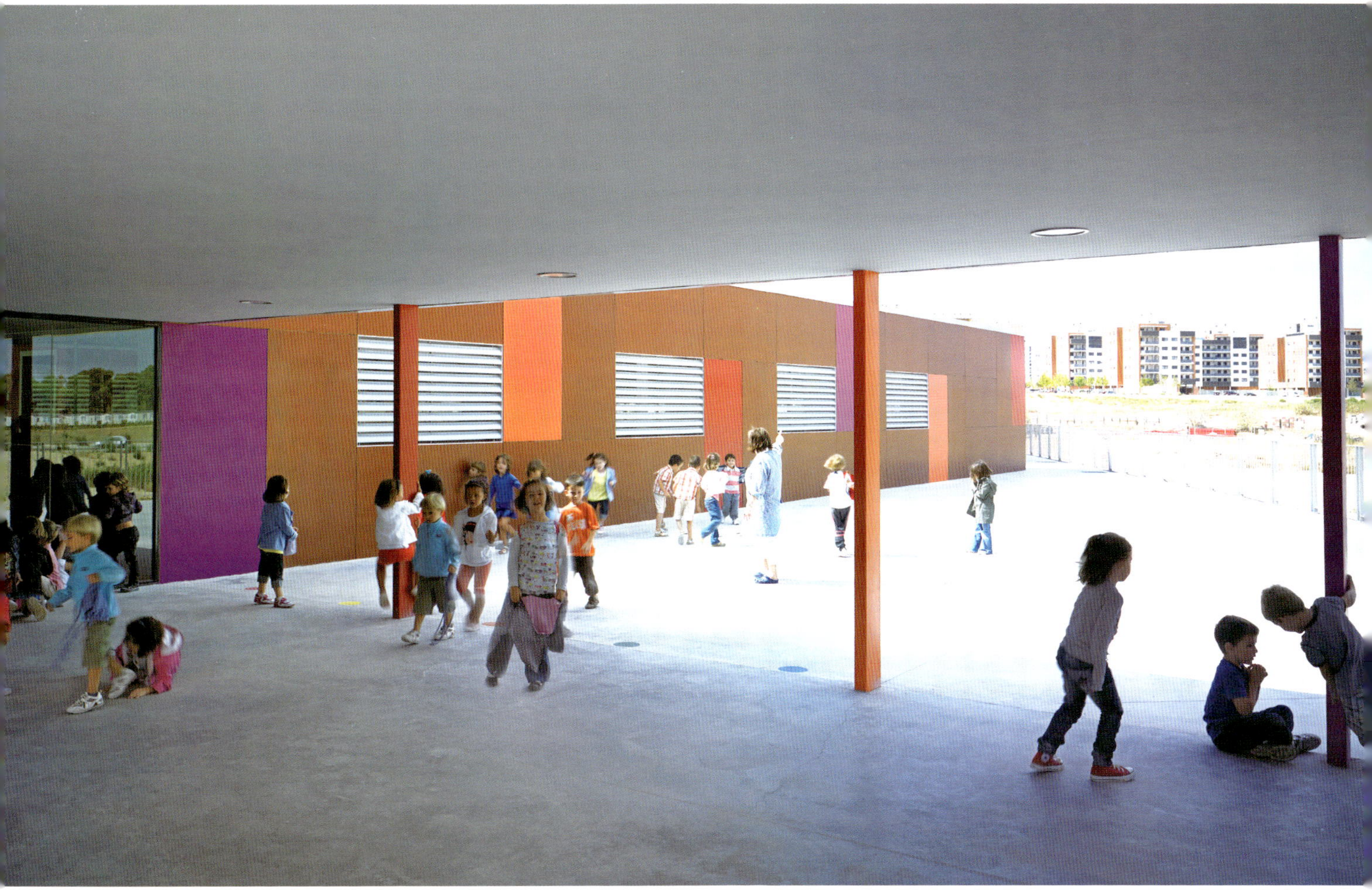

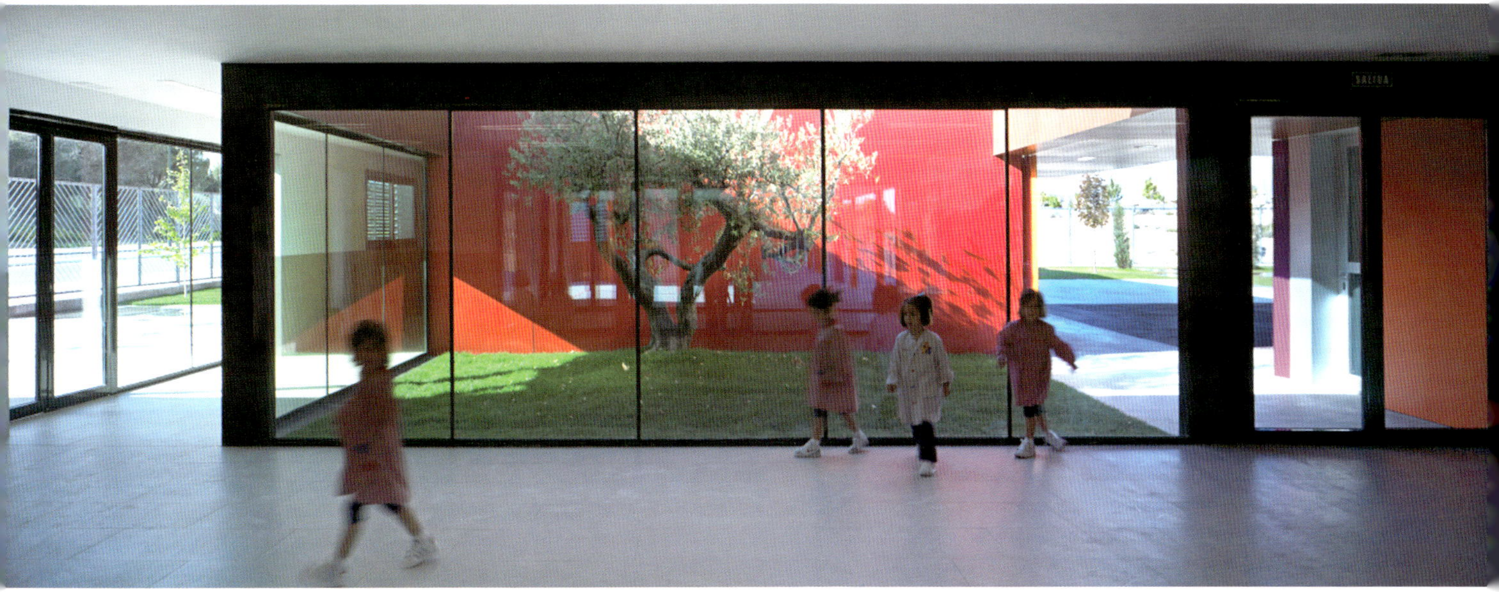

nursery school in pamplona

Location/
Pamplona, Navarra,
Spain
Design/
LARRAZ ARQUITECTOS

Photography/
Iñaki Bergera
Area/
1,519 sqm

The building is located within the NW side of the new neighborhood of Buztintxuri (Pamplona) within an area that includes three additional public buildings.

The main axis of the plot is on a north-south direction. The west-facing side of the building with the main entrance was originally disturbed by loud traffic noise from a neighboring traffic circle. The west façade was designed to act as a boundary to the adjacent plot.

Based upon the site circumstances, the architects decided to organize the building as a series of four parallel structures in which fully built and empty areas are alternated.

The organization of the inner space of the classrooms as well as the design of the furniture was designed to take into account both the children's and their educators' different perceptions of space.

On one hand, the children's activities are organized based upon several series of thematic 'corners' perfectly adapted to their scale within which they can develop different activities in a flexible way. Massive, undefined spaces were carefully avoided during the design and construction of the building. On the other hand, educators must have children under their visual control from any point in the classroom - and this was also taken into account when planning the space.

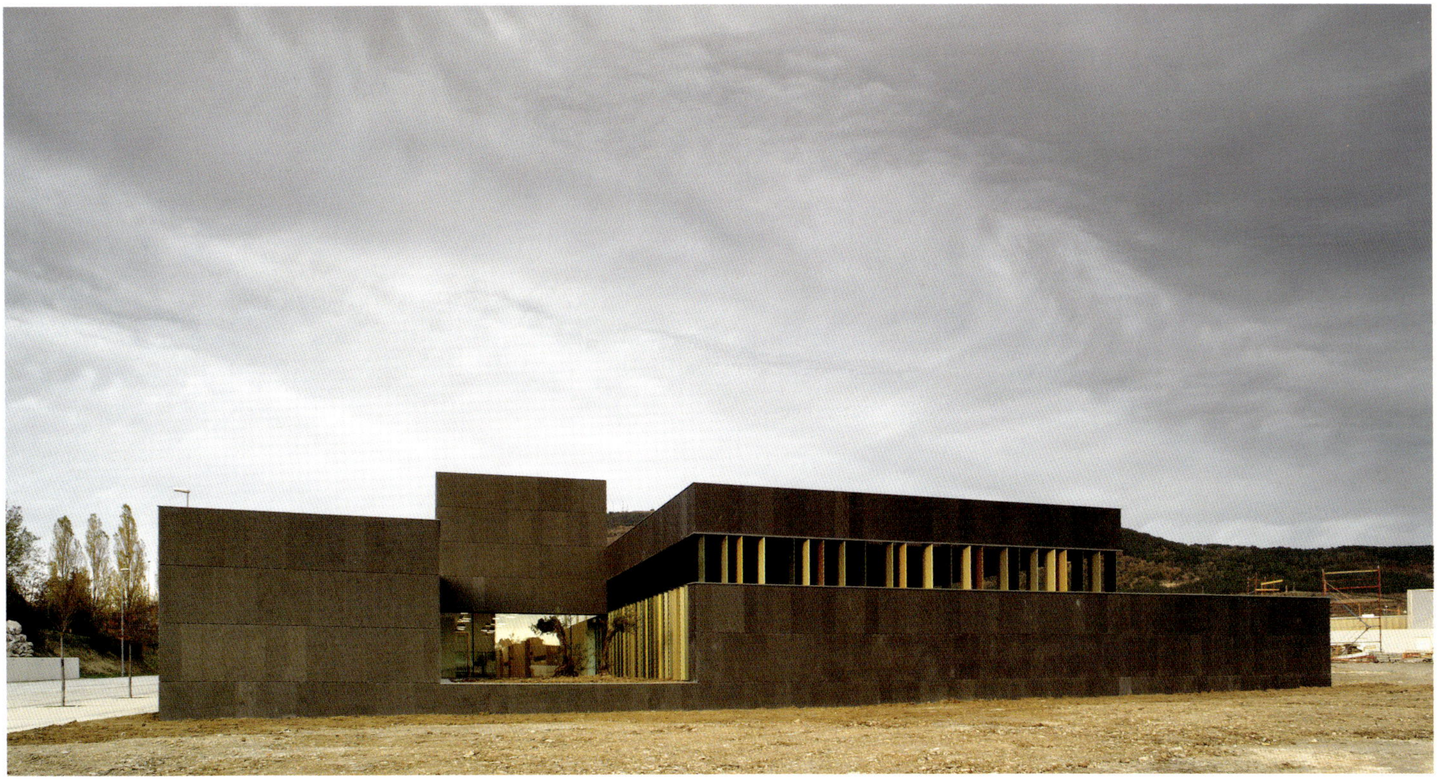
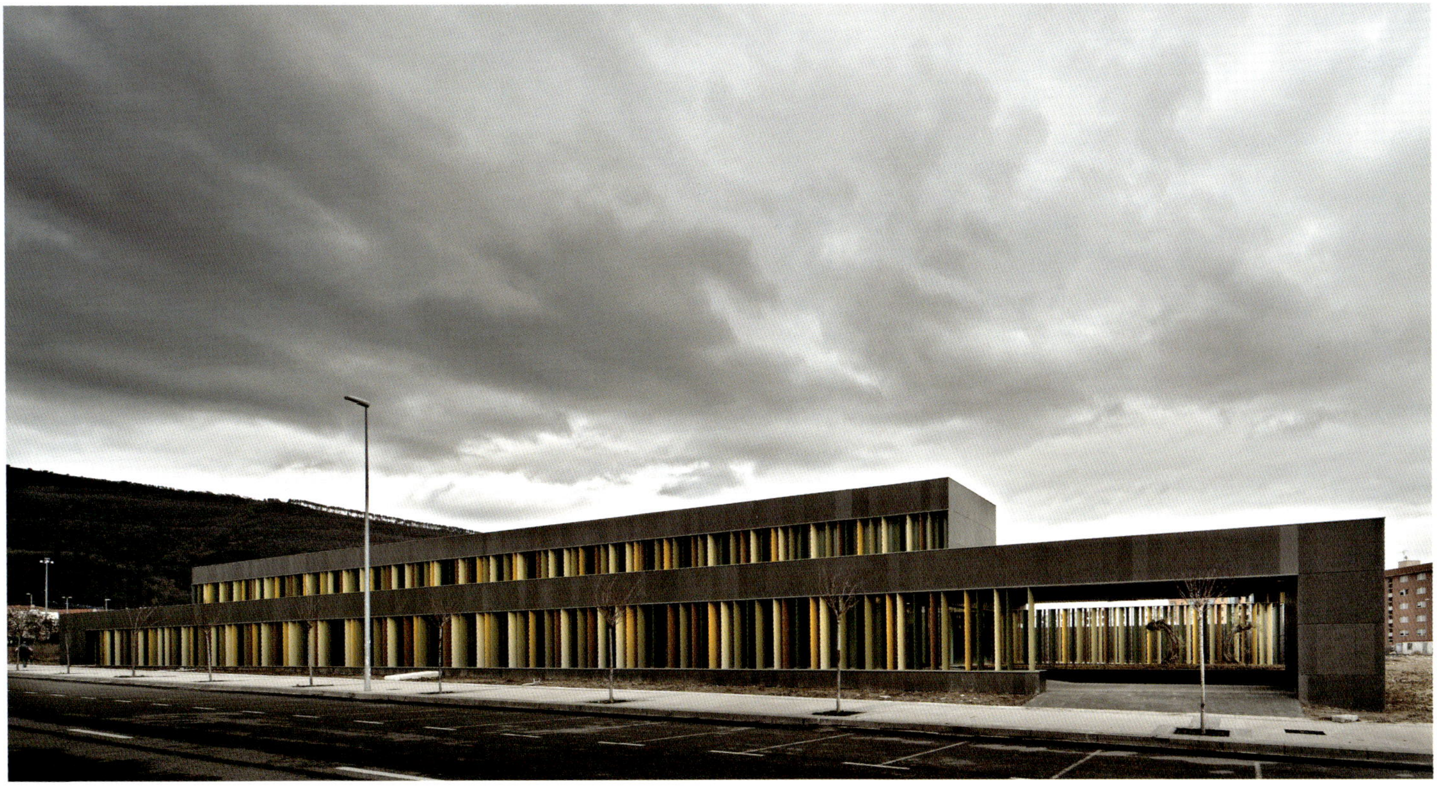

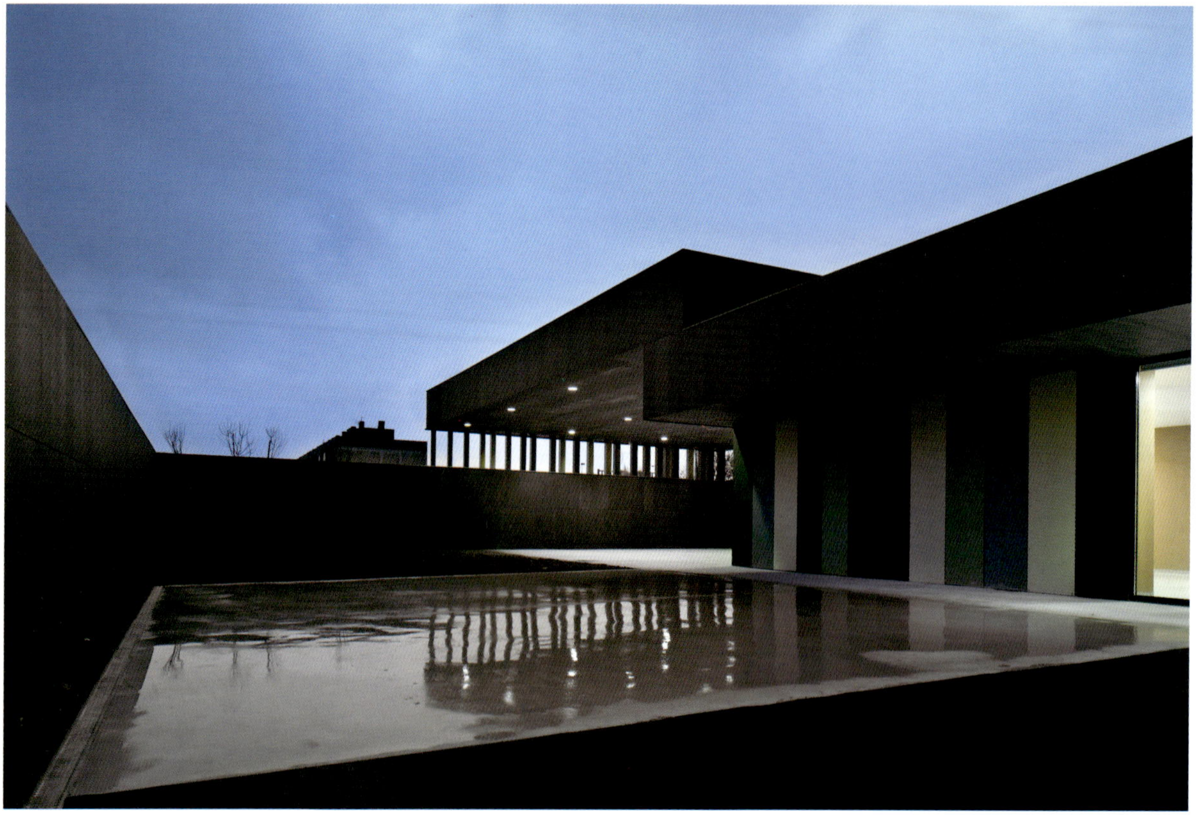

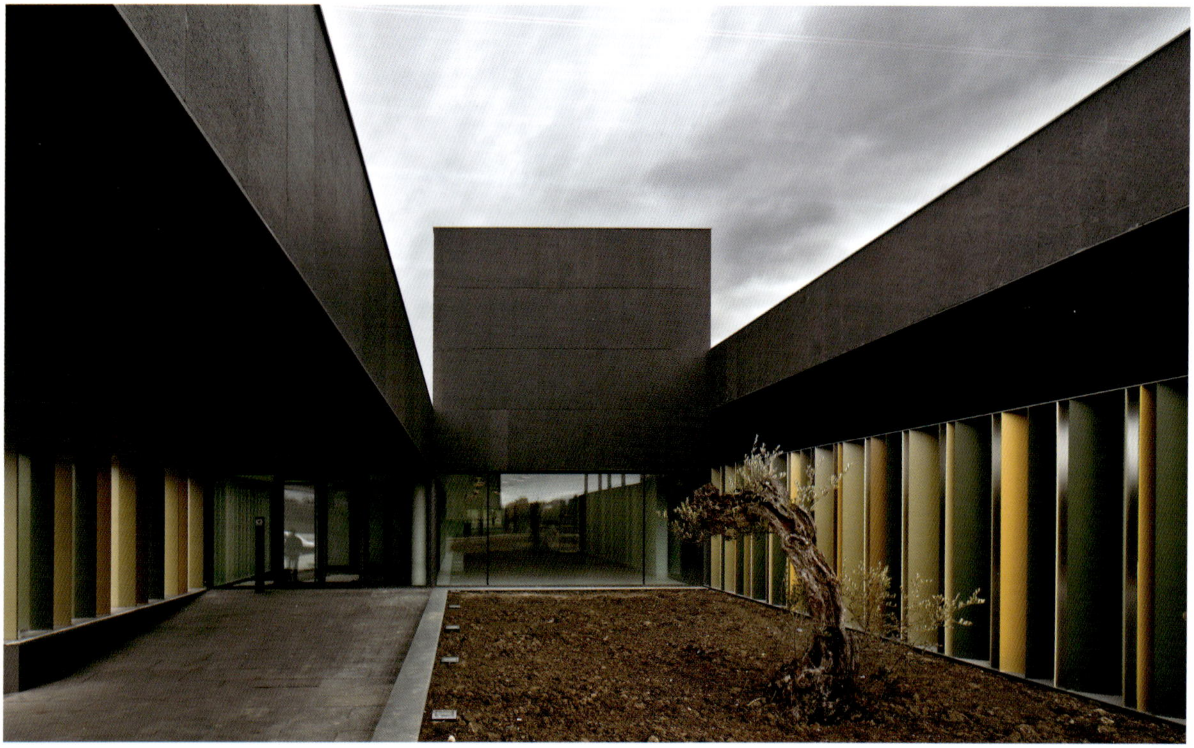

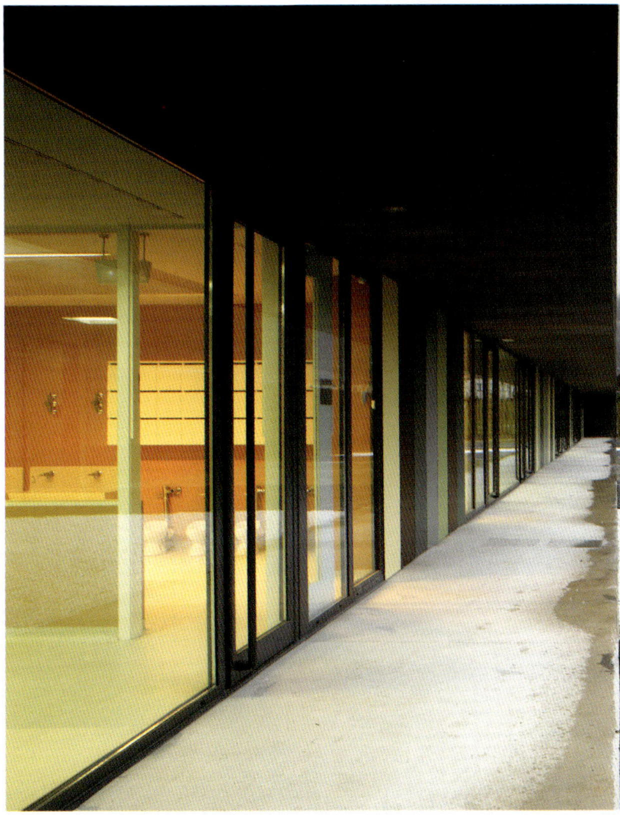

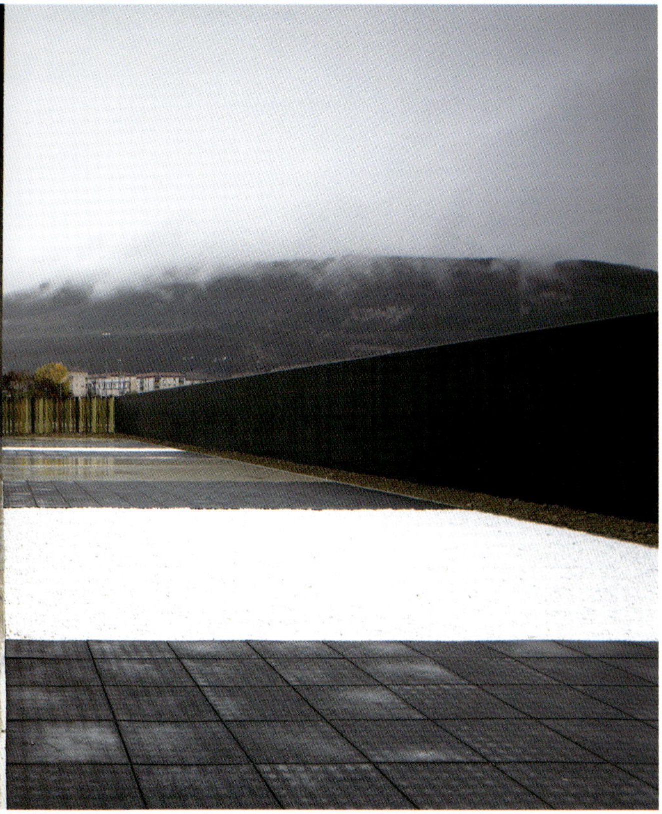

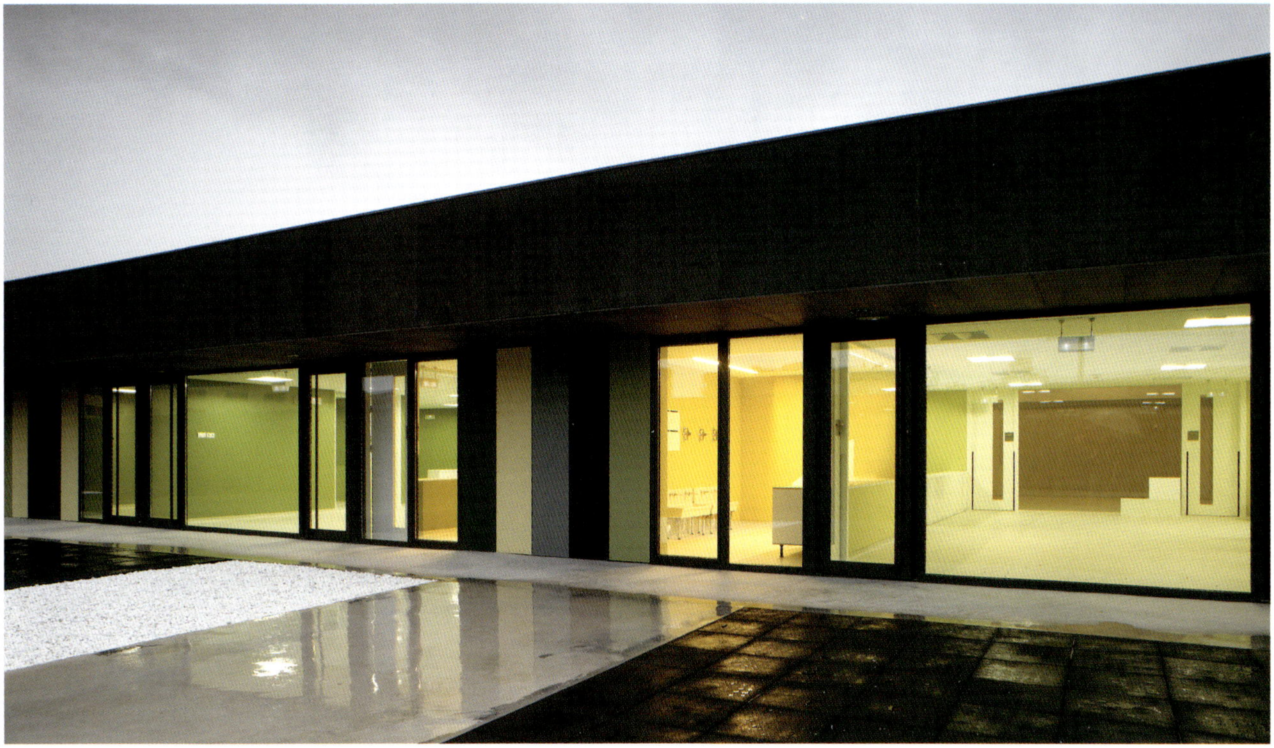

educational center in el chaparral, albolote

Location/
El Chaparral, Albolote, Granada, Spain

Design/
Alejandro Muñoz Miranda

Photography/
Javier Callejas
(javiercallejas@gmail.com)

Area/
915 sqm

The orientation of space makes the classroom's uncompressed glass cracks appear to tighten the diagonal space of the Southern corner of the building while adding large windows that allow light into an interior garden to the Northern side of the building. The glass fissures control light and are shaded in rainbow colors. They also introduce rainbow-colored light into dynamic areas of the corridors and reflect it onto the covered outside playground. Within the classroom, the glass is colorless so as to avoid a distraction to lessons.

Versatility also arises in the operation of classrooms by level of education (two classrooms are for younger children in their first or second year at the school and contain beds for naps, while two classrooms are for third and fourth year students and don't have napping areas). It is proposed that all classrooms co-existing within the same level results in more cooperative space for activities.

The design is inspired by the idea that all structures revolve around the exterior covered playground which is envisioned as the heart of the educational center. The playground is linked with all the classrooms by a continuous covered porch. Kitchen and dining areas, a gym, and administrative offices are also connected with the main building space by this garden corridor.

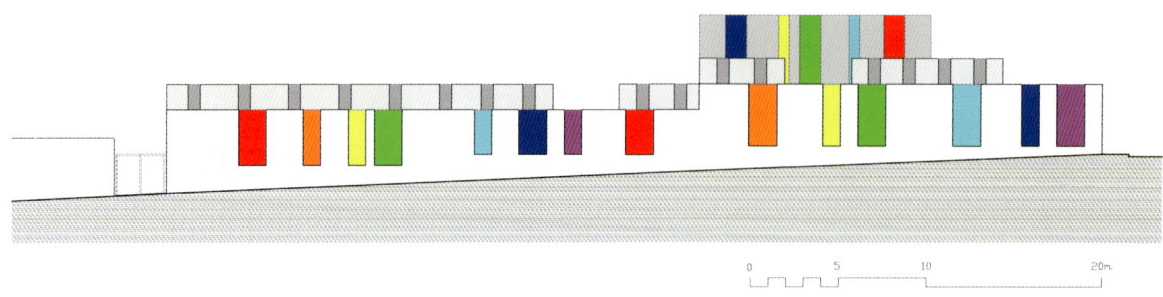

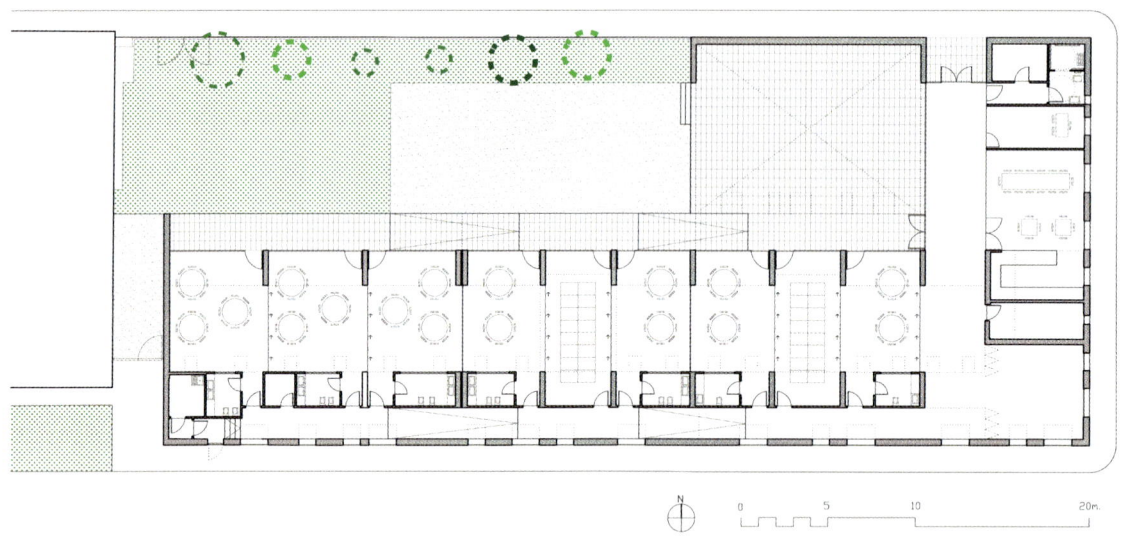

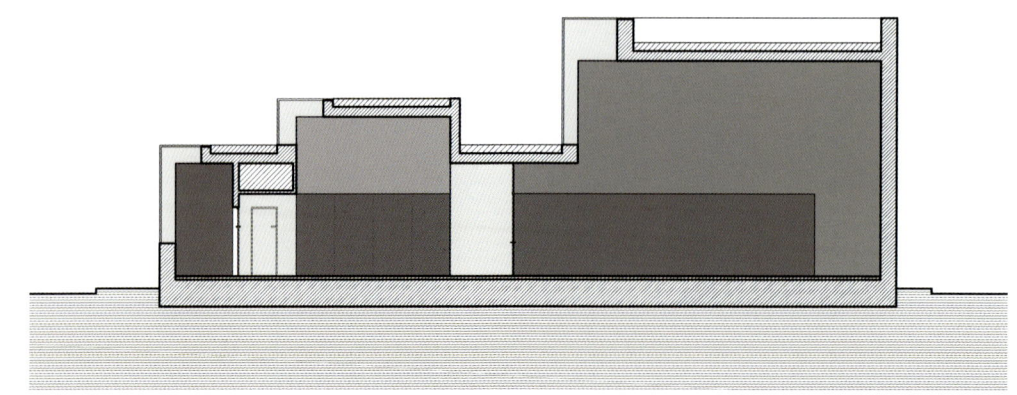

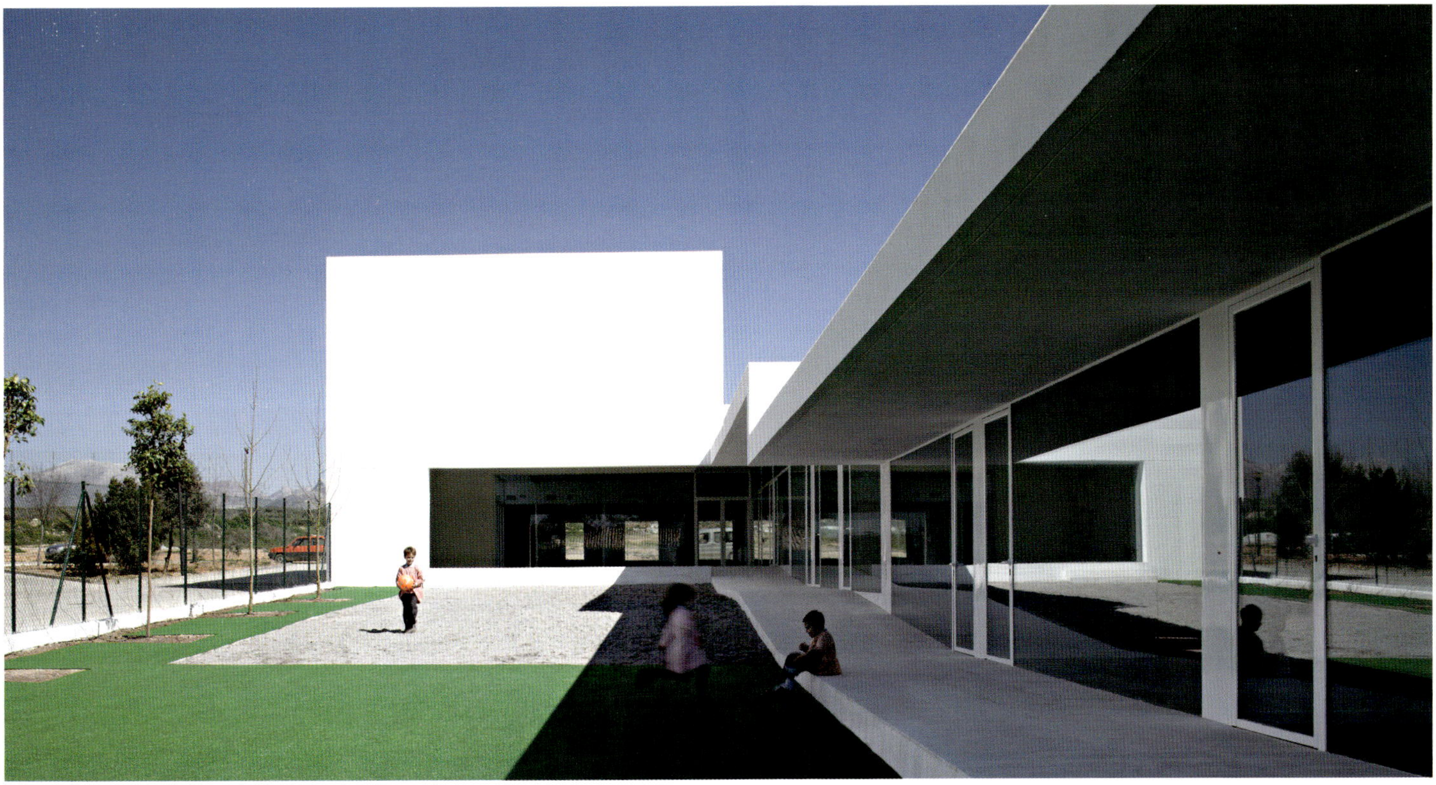

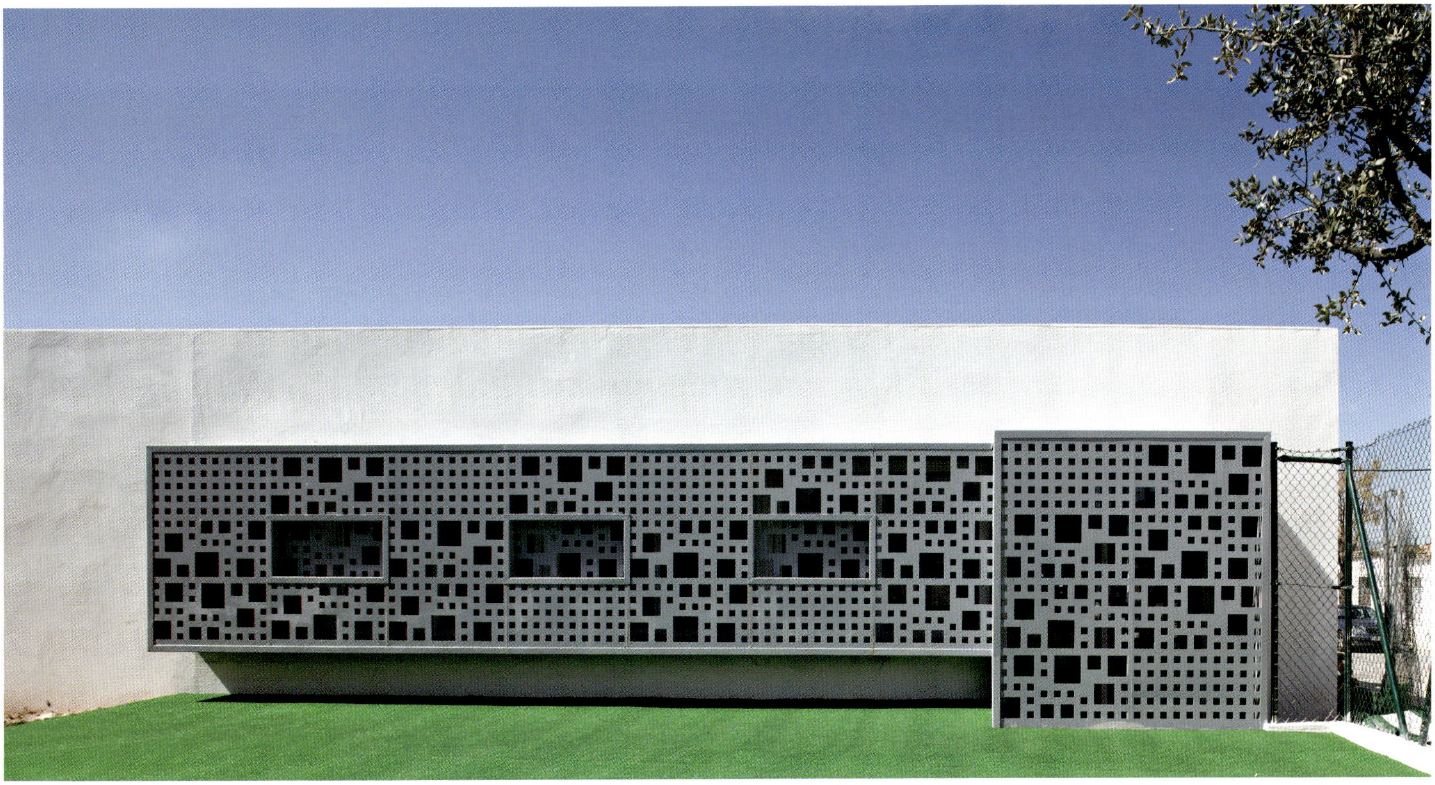

carl-bolle
elementary school

Location/
Waldenserstr. 20, 10551
Berlin, Germany
Design/
Die Baupiloten

Photography/
Jan Bitter
(www.janbitter.de)
Area/
241 sqm

Die Baupiloten invited the pupils to workshops in order to learn about their ideas and desires regarding the redesign of the school. The story of the "spy with the shimmering cloak" emerged from these workshops, eventually becoming the "storyboard" for the design of a spacious hallway that had previously been inaccessible.

In accordance with the school's own sports-oriented motto of "language and movement," the hallway was converted into a leisure area that encourages "exploratory learning." Through experiencing the architecture and newly created optical and acoustic space, the children can track down the "spy" while also learning about the process of scientific observation in a playful environment. They can move along climbing walls, observe space from different perspectives, or find some alone time in the various reading nooks. While the pupils helped develop the ideas for the space, Die Baupiloten were there to encourage their curiosity and exploratory spirit. The fixtures/installations appear as a snowy landscape within the building, both adorning and disguising the preexisting furnishings while simultaneously allowing parts of the original structure to shine through. Under the white surface, various parts of the installation shimmer red, blue, or green, delineating its different areas.

SPY IN THE SHIMMERING CLOAK

AFTERGLOW
Track down other kids. Feel the impression of coloured light and manipulate the space by yourself.

CODES
Develop codes to communicate with others. Get to know abstract forms of language.

COMPLEMENTARY COLOURS
Discover the colour wheel through complementary colours. Experience contrasting atmospheres.

FLASH-PUFFS
Set particles in motion through invisible and noiseless air streams and marvel at the haphazardly emerging flashes.

...ISCOPE
...e functionality ...scope by playing ... Question ...erceptions. Push

READING HATCHES
Retreat and concoct a plan, or just get away from everyday school life by reading a tricky detective story.

SPY CELL
Spy on other kids, become sensitized to the surrounding space, and sharpen the senses.

CRISSCROSSER
Rhomboidal openings serve as rungs and encourage the perception of one's own body.

SENSITIVE LISTENING
Activate sounds through motion and make music. Listen to music and eavesdrop on other kids.

LIGHT CONDUCTOR
Experiment with light and learn about the principles of light. Illuminate and uncover dark spaces.

RAINBOW SPECTRUM
Camouflage yourself with light and become invisible. Explore the colours of the light spectrum. Create additive and optical colour mixtures.

TWINKLING GATE
The kids are drawn in and catch a glimpse of the luminous hints and blurred silhouettes of the Spy World.

TWO-SIDEDNESS
Explore different perspectives. Experience changeability. Kids can sense and discover new worlds behind the appearance, allowing them to slip into new roles at will.

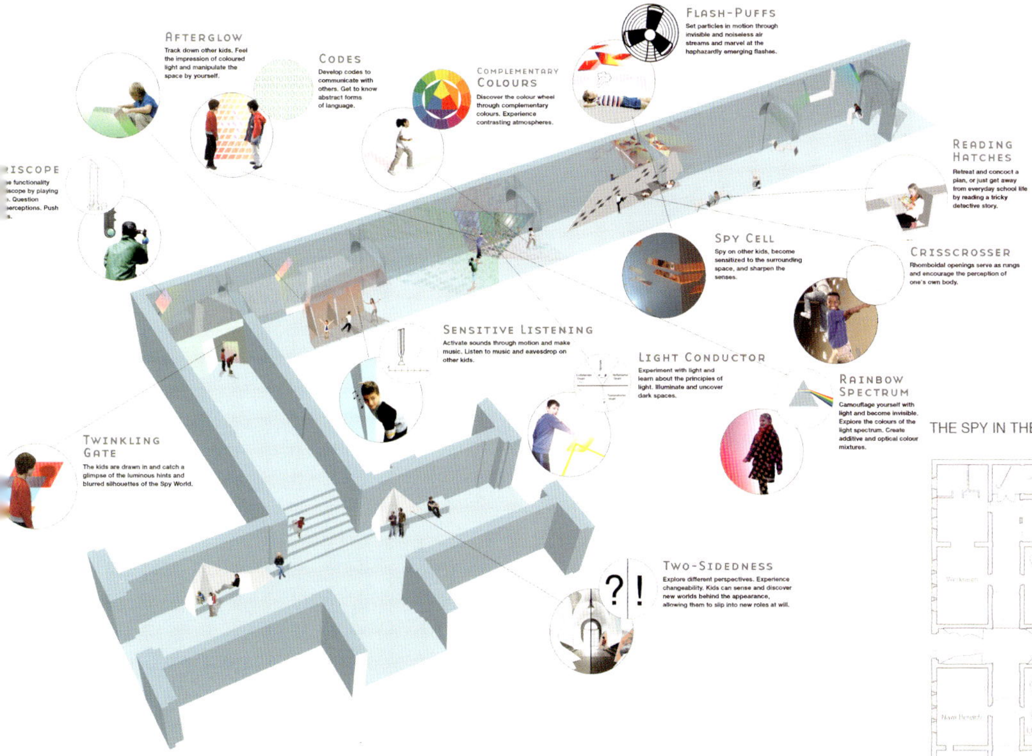

THE SPY IN THE SHIMMERING CLOAK

the spy floats in

he's beeing attracted by a mysterious glow

he gets frightened and begins to shimmer

he perks his ears

in disguise

He runs away, throws the children off his scent, and disappears.

sneaks

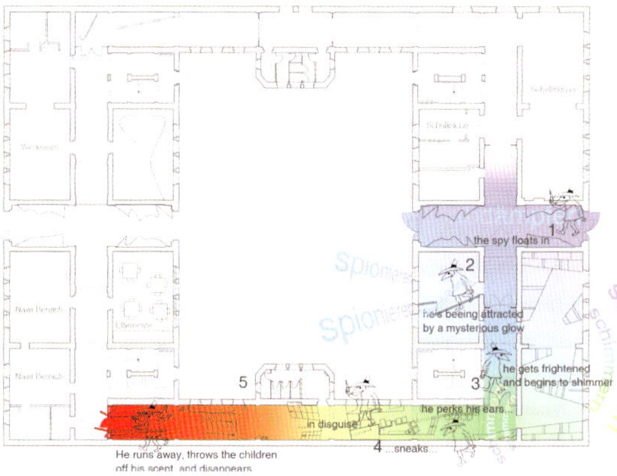

kindergarten rambuteau

Location/
Rue Rambuteau, Paris, France
Design/
Gaetan Le Penhuel Architectes

Photography/
Javier Callejas
Area/
1,177 sqm

A municipal kindergarten in Paris.

At the end of Rambuteau Street, the blue and red technical sheaths of the Pompidou Center mark the western border of the Marais area, a much protected neighborhood of Paris without many contemporary buildings. The project was carefully designed so that the architects would be given permission to build in a modern style within this area of traditional architecture. The building was designed vertically to preserve open views of the sky from its heights. On the ground floor, a planted garden contains a playground and obscures the view from neighboring buildings. The windows of the building are shaded by overhangs and the roof was planted with a hanging garden.

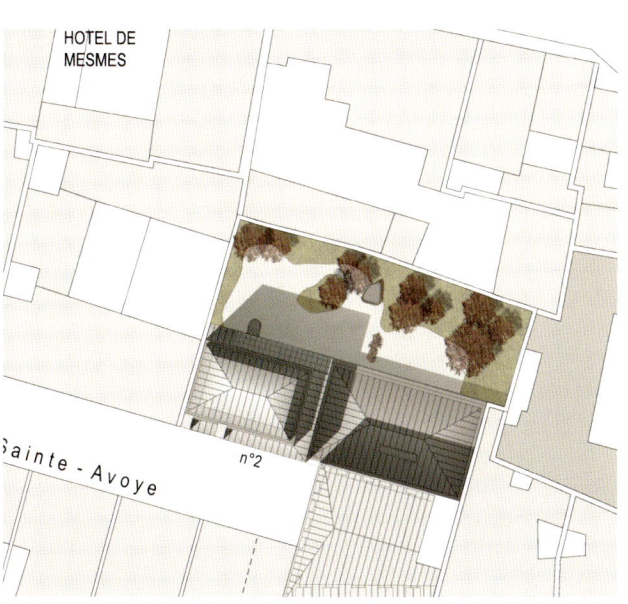

HOTEL DE
MESMES

n°2

Sainte - Avoye

passage sainte-avoye

rue rambuteau

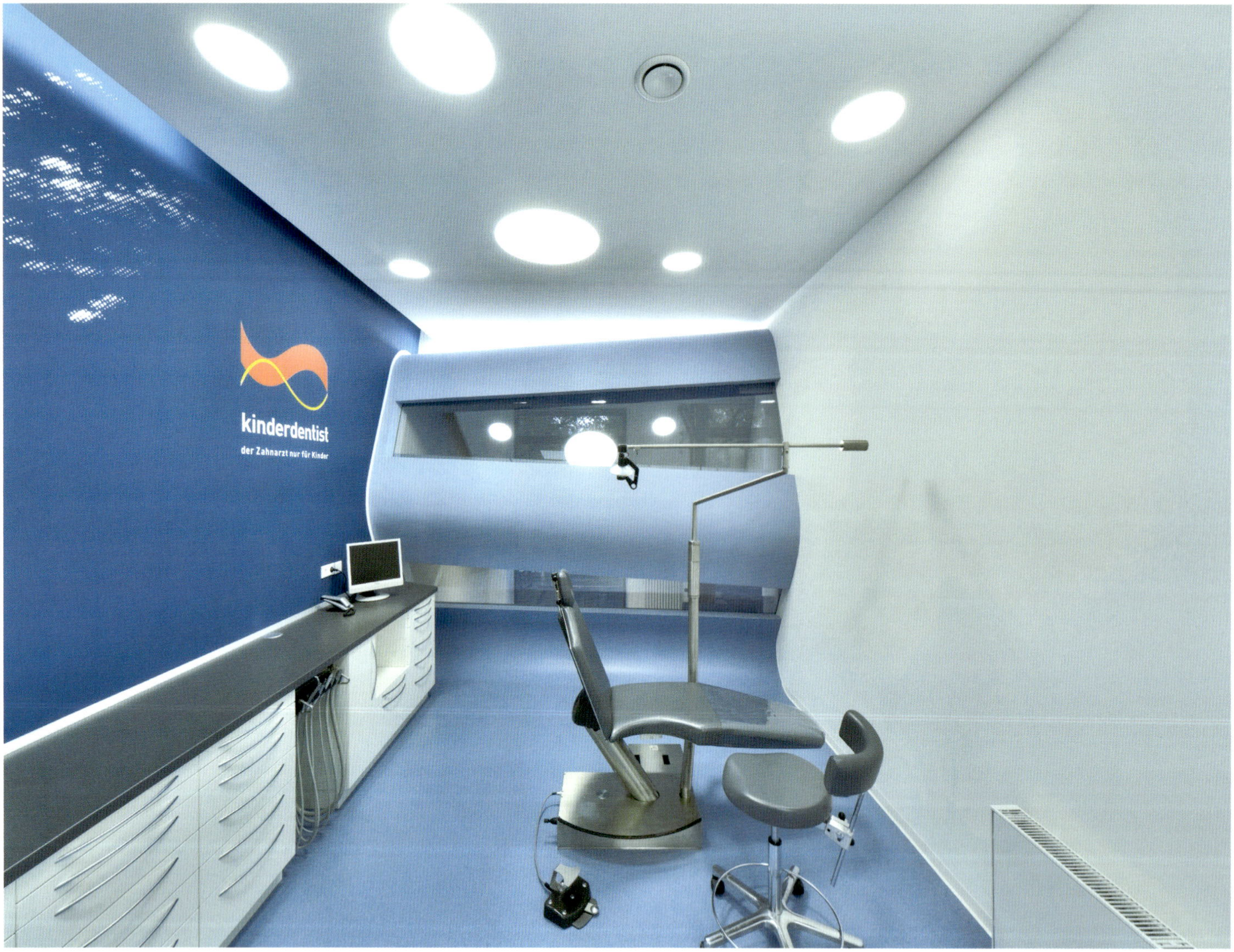

kinderdentist

Location/
Berlin, Germany
Design/
GRAFT

Photography/
andi albert
photographie
Area/
176.3 sqm

Kinderdentist, a dental clinic specialized in the treatment of young patients, was envisioned during a design process that focused on the opposite side of the spectrum: the indoor playground. GRAFT created an underground world that invites children to come in, play, and let their imagination run wild.

A 12-foot wave welcomes visitors from the outside world, carrying them directly to the reception counter. This wave, vibrant with patterns in different tones of blue, connects and reveals the upper and lower levels of the clinic. It invites you to the waiting room and reception in the lower level and opens up windows into the treatment rooms upstairs.

All areas follow the same theme of the underwater experience with their colors and architectural and spatial elements. Patterns of pixelated schools of fish connect all treatment rooms. The silver upholstery in the waiting rooms is reminiscent of submarines. The period of waiting, as well as the treatment itself, can be turned into a playful experience. In this way, childrens' attitude towards the usually feared dentist can be changed from an early age on. The young customers never have to leave the happy underwater world and can enjoy this completely new experience of a visit to the dentist.

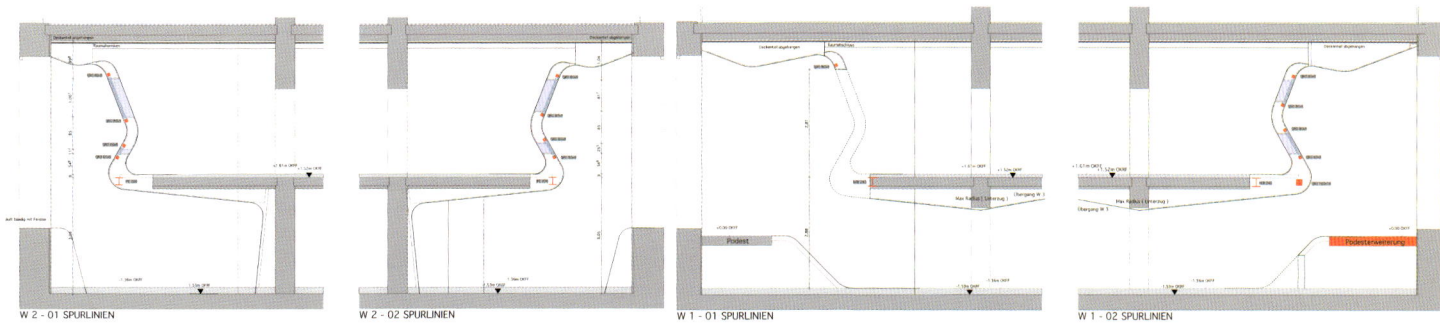

W 2 - 01 SPURLINIEN W 2 - 02 SPURLINIEN W 1 - 01 SPURLINIEN W 1 - 02 SPURLINIEN

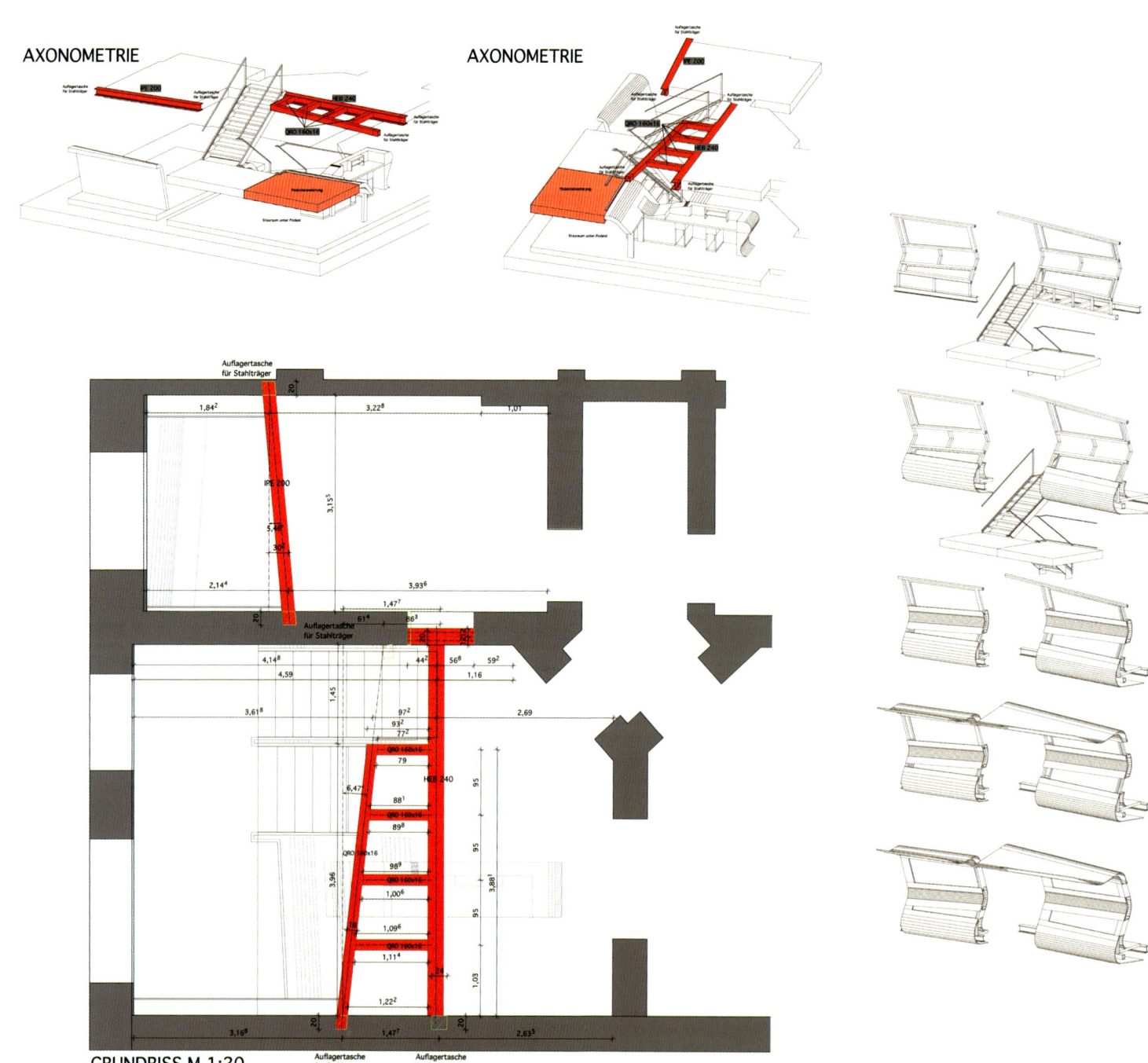

AXONOMETRIE

AXONOMETRIE

GRUNDRISS M 1:20

Auflagertasche
für Stahlträger

Auflagertasche
für Stahlträger

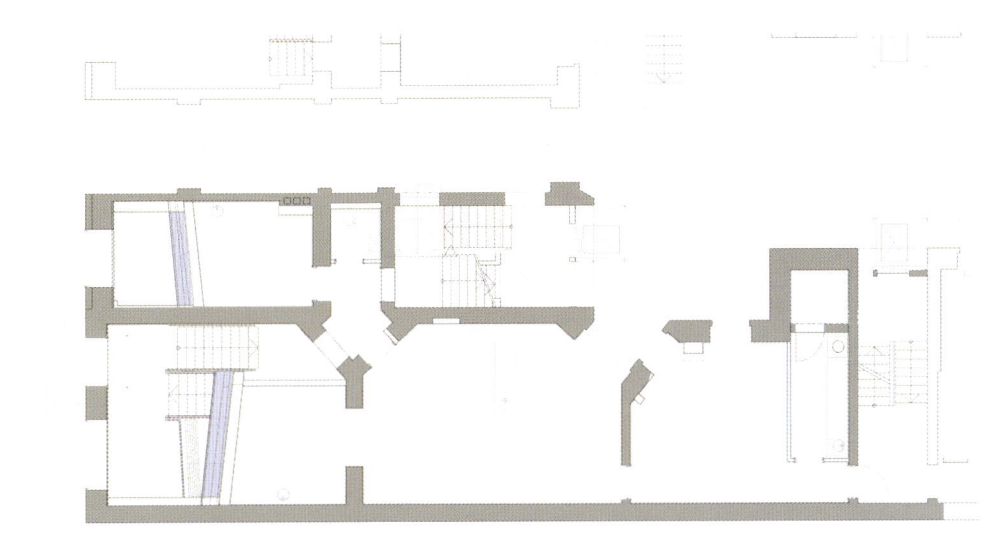

KOLLWITZSTRASSE

the nursery school in covolo di pederobba

Location/
Treviso, Italy
Design/
C+S Associati

Photography/
Alessandra Chemollo,
C+S Associati
Area/
900 sqm

Covolo nursery school forms an enclosure facing southeast and overlooking wheat fields and vineyards, embracing and allowing itself to be defined by the features of the landscape. A rough concrete wall was colored to match the surrounding landscape and treated with split aggregate to reflect light in a variable manner depending on its orientation. The wall opens to the south like the great arches of a portico barn typical of the region; the arches reveal the massive size of the structure. All of the spaces are visually connected to each other, just as children grow and learn by interacting with and relating to their schoolmates. Intervisibility is one of the main topics of the project.

The other main topic is the use of color conceived as a code. Colors are chosen to become a guide for children to move inside the spaces: yellow is the color for the youngest children, green guides the oldest, and purple is the color of the teachers. Blue corresponds to lessons dependent on age. Red is the color of the outside courtyards: it reflects the memory of the traditional barchesse. This "code of colors" makes the space a big didactic game within which children are able to move independently. All of the colors meet in the central square, which is a reworking of the traditional Venetian salon which is the main congregation space.

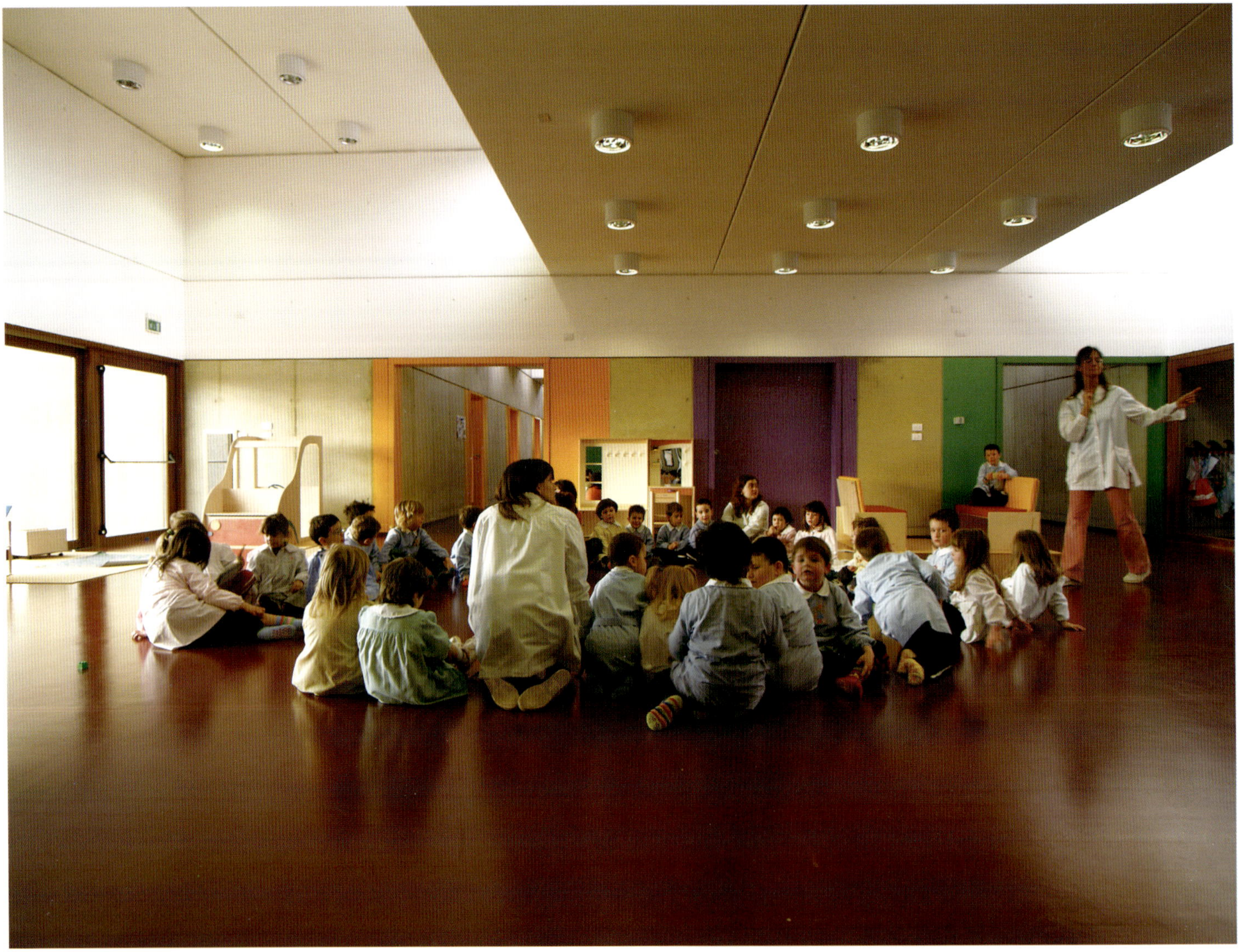

ponzano primary school

Location/
Ponzano Veneto, Italy
Design/
C+S Associati

Photography/
Alessandra Bello, Pietro Savorelli
Area/
4,102 sqm

Ponzano Primary School is designed for 375 children aged from 6 to 10. It has 15 classrooms and special workshop areas for art, music, computers, language and science, a gymnasium, a cafeteria, and a library. The classrooms where the children spend most of their time face southeast and southwest so as to improve their daylight exposure. Thanks to a judicious orientation, thick insulation, a green roof and sophisticated technologies (geothermal heating, photovoltaic panels, natural ventilation chimneys, and a building automation system), the school consumes only 3.6 kWh/m^3/year, reaching the Italian Class A+ efficiency rating with a building cost of only 1,030 euro/sqm including furniture; the building is proof that the very strong economic and functional requirements of an educational building are compatible with energy efficiency and high quality interior spaces.

Collective spaces are very important in the school design. All of the building spaces are gathered around a central square reminiscent of monastic cloisters. Within each building section, all of the spaces face each other and are reflected by the transparent, colorful walls. This complexity draws inspiration from the industrial districts of Veneto where people learn from each other by sharing and exchanging their experiences.

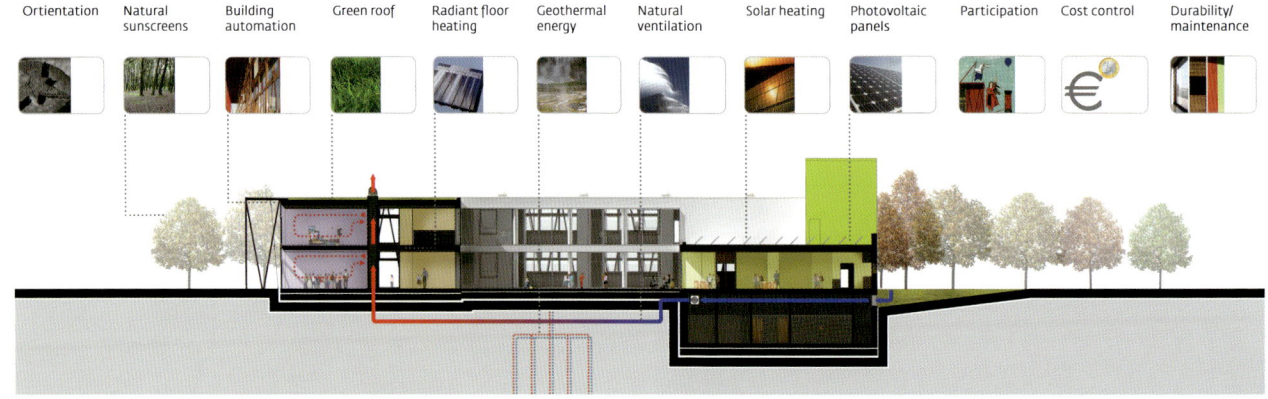

| Ortientation | Natural sunscreens | Building automation | Green roof | Radiant floor heating | Geothermal energy | Natural ventilation | Solar heating | Photovoltaic panels | Participation | Cost control | Durability/ maintenance |

Underground Plan 1:500
  1 Gymnasium
  2 Changing rooms

Ground floor Plan 1:500
  1 Entrance
  2 Central courtyard
  3 Teachers' room
  4 Laboratories
  5 Classrooms
  6 Canteen
  7 Gymnasium

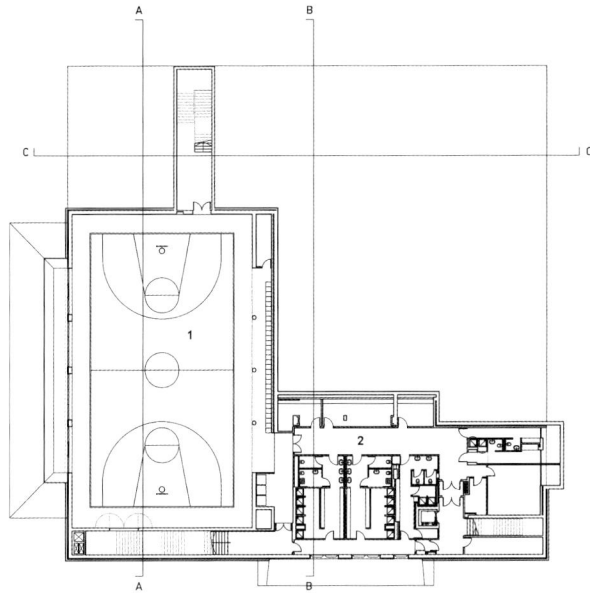

First floor Plan 1:500
  1 Classrooms
  2 Art classrooms
  3 Library
  4 Roof terrace
  5 Central courtyard

Roof Plan 1:500
  1 Green roof with ventilation chimneys
  2 Roof terrace
  3 Central courtyard

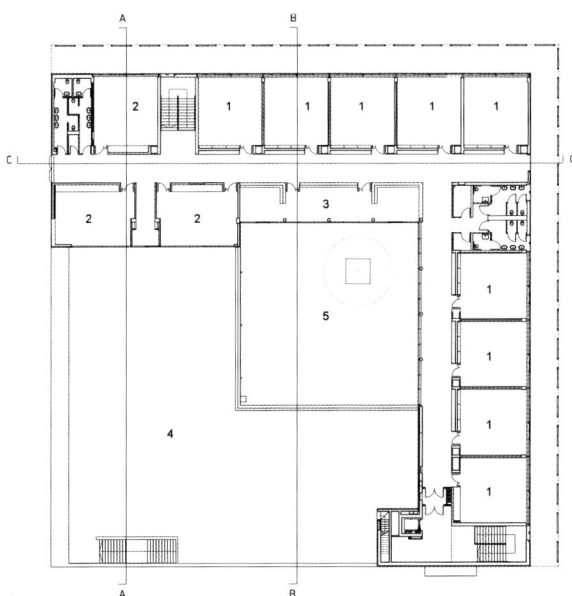

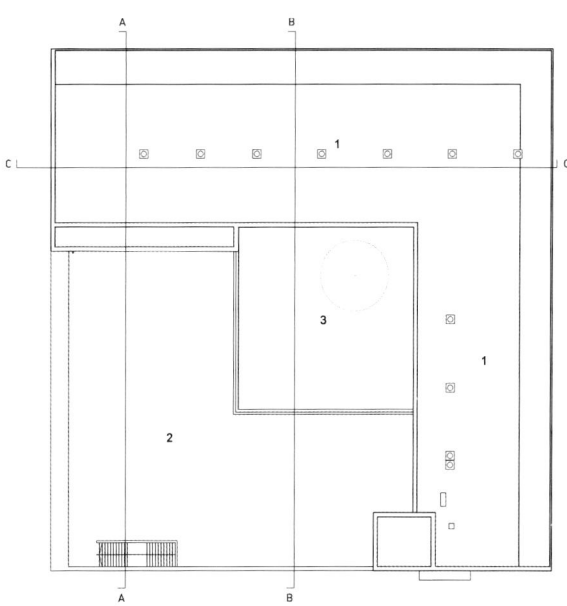

docet institute

Location/
Monterrey, Mexico
Design/
stación-ARquitectura
Arquitectos

Photography/
Ana Cecilia Garza
Villarreal
Area/
900 sqm

The building has a single "L" shaped footprint, with administrative services in one side of the structure and classrooms in the other. A large double height space with lots of light is what unites the two programs as the heart of the project. Family-oriented and extracurricular activities take place in this space, as well as festivities and meetings with parents. This space is strongly integrated with the adjacent courtyard with a playground visible through large windows.

The materiality of the project is simple and clear: a steel structure and walls made of concrete block, glass panels to cover large openings and an outer skin of perforated steel plate which helps to create shade for the exterior walls and cool the building. The designers chose to use a skin custom-made by a local manufacturer, instead of a prefabricated panel. This is the element that defines the image of the building. The front has smaller openings which allow light in but maintain building privacy.

The building is separated from the main street to avoid noise and the cars. A pedestrian and vehicular access route was introduced through a garden of trees that already existed on the site.

The façade of the building respects the idea that buildings should be found within the forest.

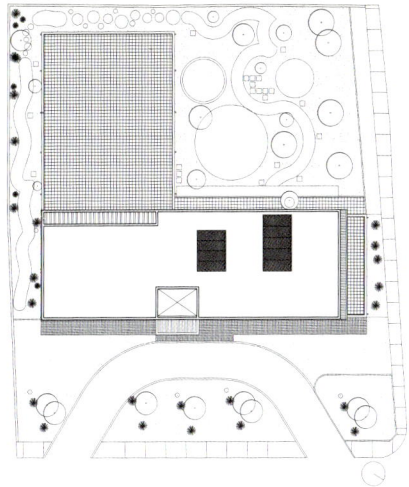

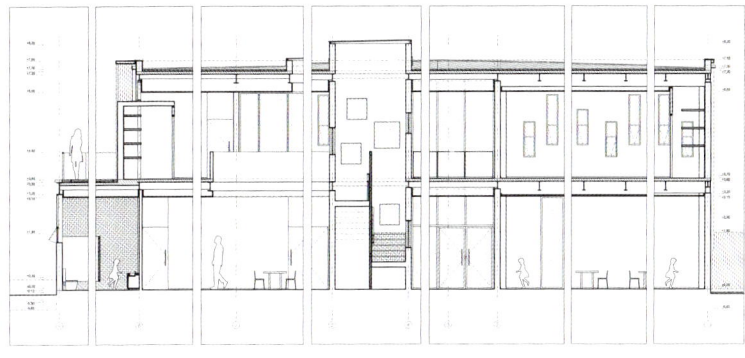

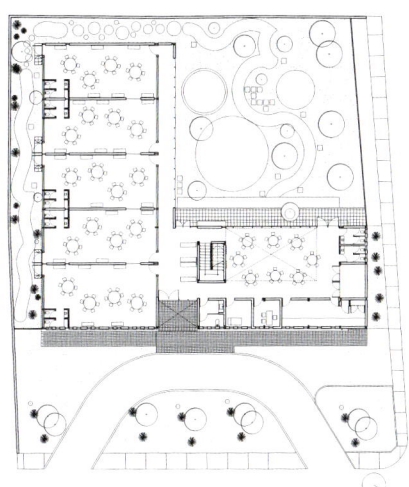

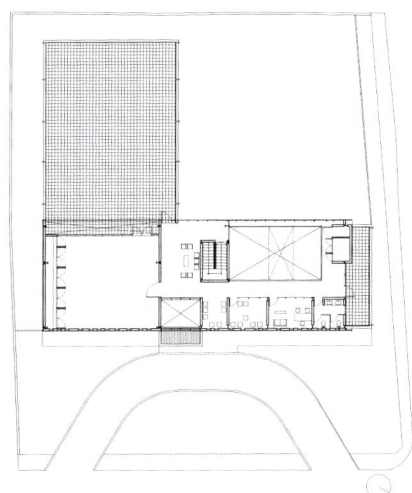

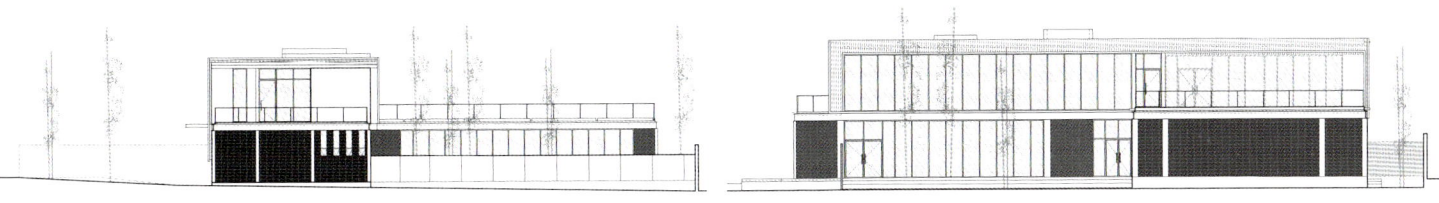

children's toy library

Location/
Bonneuil sur Marne,
France
Design/
LAN Architecture

Photography/
Jean-Marie Monthiers
Area/
380 sqm

The design of the Bonneuil-sur-Marne children's toy library resulted from an approach that aimed to simultaneously resolve a number of problems and develop new ideas. The project goals were:

- A new use for an existing building

- Design of a children's play area

- Creation of a small-scale public facility in a socially unstable area occupied by large housing complexes

- The difficulties of a very restricted budget (initially, the program simply called for a new interior layout)

LAN Architecture decided to design a building that had no sense of scale and which would appear timeless - a dense solid mass, an urban symbol standing out from its environment, a shell able to protect its contents.

The result is a volume that seems to have always existed and whose bunker-like appearance is reminiscent of a vernacular construction.

The design strategy was inspired by a medical logic of intervention. The creation of an additional freestanding skin allowed them to control the interfaces between exterior spaces and building and interior spaces, as well as meet the need for generous volumes.

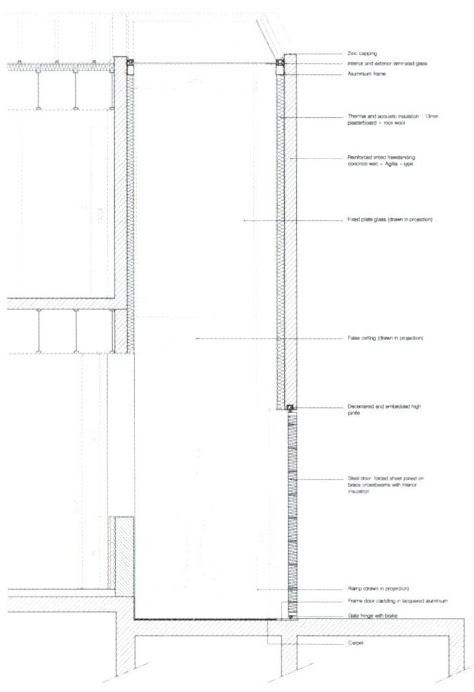

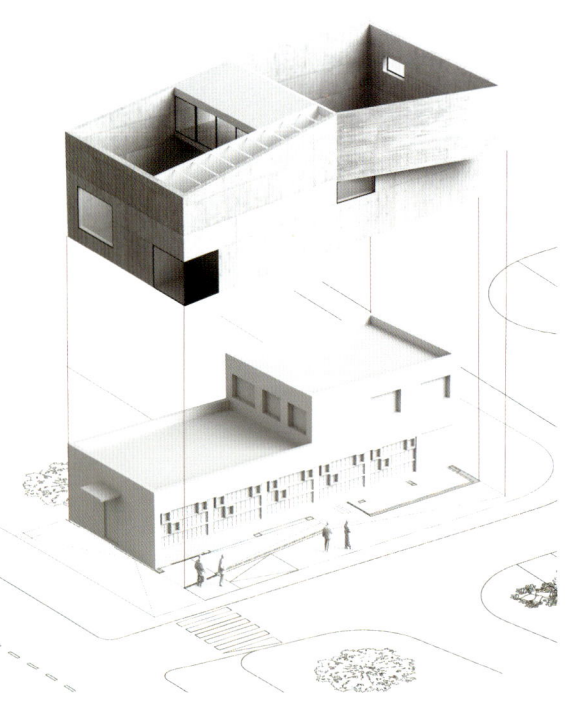

bubbletecture h

Location/
Sayo-cho, Hyogo Pref.,
Japan
Design/
Endo Shuhei Architect
Institute

Photography/
Yoshiharu Matsumura
Area/
968 sqm

The client requested that all people who visit the center, including residents of the Hyogo prefecture, be devoted to addressing global environmental concerns and be able to study and experience various approaches to problems within the site.

The architects' vision was to create a new architectural space that shared a point of contact with nature and the environment.

The site is on a steep slope on the north side of the forest. After integrating all functions, the client requested that the design correspond to the building function and structure. Two functions were built on parallel sites, one on flat land previously housing the old town road, and one on an elevated part of the site. The designers strongly believe in making use of limited flat land, to keep natural landforms as large as possible and minimize the impact of building construction on the natural environment. The form of the building is a rational shape connecting multiple functions within the site.

Site Plan S=1/400

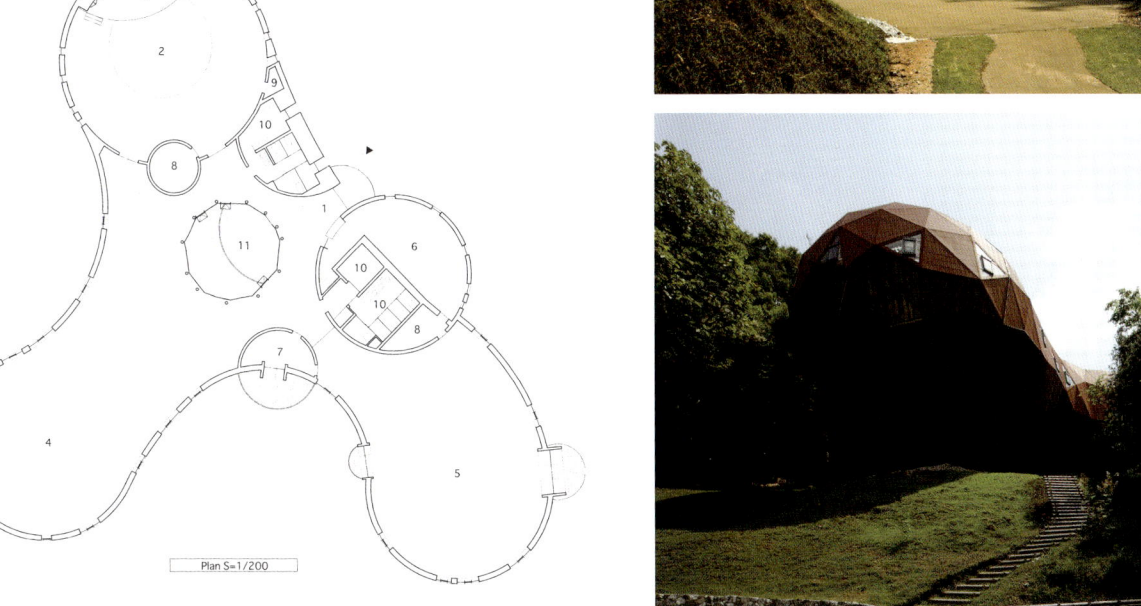

Plan S=1/200

155

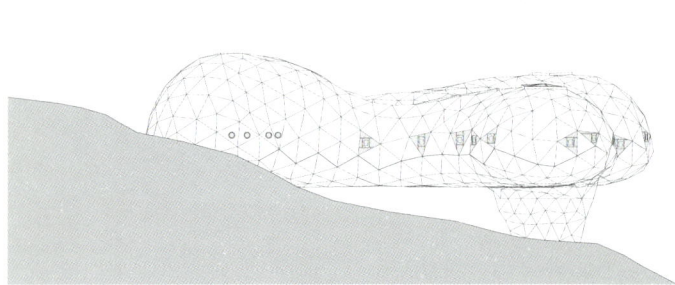

East elevation S=1/200

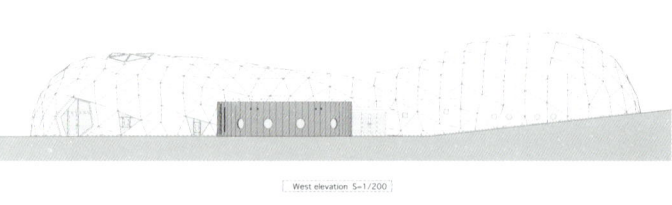

West elevation S=1/200

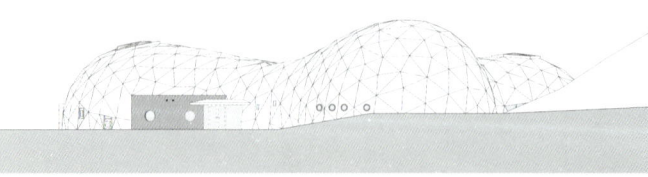

South elevation S=1/200

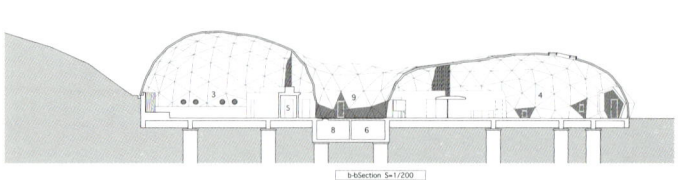

b-bSection S=1/200

bubbletecture m

Location/
Maihara-cho, Shiga Pref., Japan
Design/
Endo Shuhei Architect Institute

Photography/
Yoshiharu Matsumura
Area/
1,398 sqm

Bubbletecture M kindergarten is about 45 minutes away from Osaka by the Shinkansen train. The school's surrounded by a newly developed residential area. The structure consists of concrete boxes between each of the rooms and a wooden roof that ties them together. The shell-form roof is made of triangular continuous surfaces; its structural strength and geometrical consistency permit great freedom in designing of the necessary spaces. This structural system uses 2.5m wooden beams and hexagonal metal fittings that are factory-made and only assembled on the site. The integration of the wooden trusses and concrete boxes is geometrical but varied, creating a structure with a highly expressive effect.

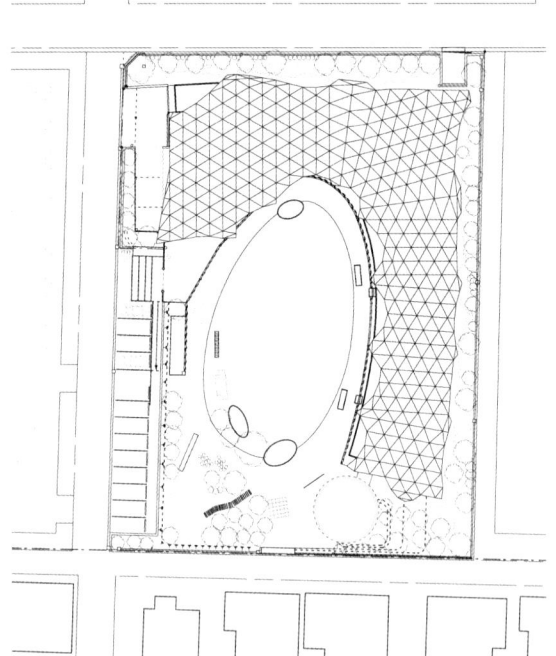

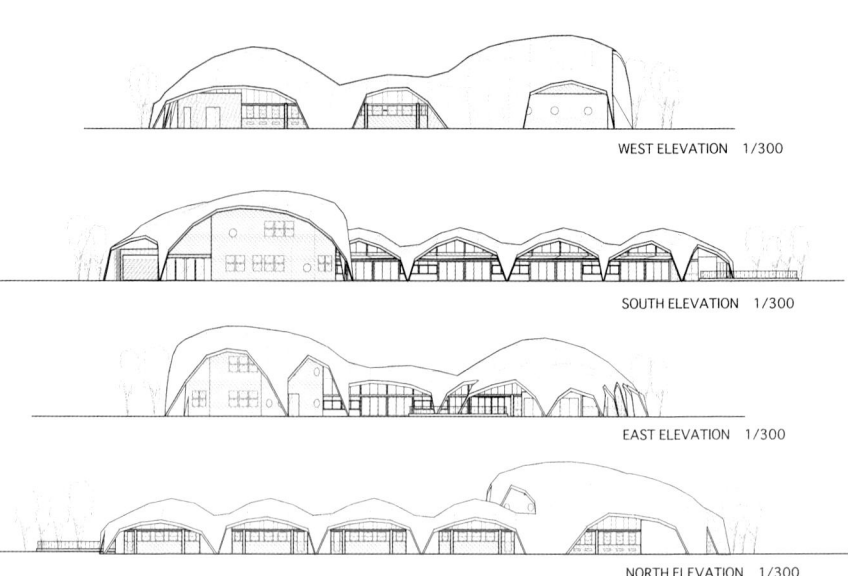

WEST ELEVATION 1/300

SOUTH ELEVATION 1/300

EAST ELEVATION 1/300

NORTH ELEVATION 1/300

1st Floor Plan 1/300

2nd Floor Plan 1/300

Photo by Iwan Baan

remez-arlozorov community campus

Location/
Tel Aviv, Israel
Design/
Mayslits Kassif
Architects

Photography/
Iwan Baan, Yuval Tebol,
Maor Roytman
Area/
3,000 sqm

The winning scheme by Mayslits Kassif Architects organized the compound's buildings, including an auditorium, gymnasium, residential tower, and education wing, around a public space which serves as the vital hub of the complex.

The first building that was erected in the complex is The Mina & Everard Goodman Educational Campus & Municipal Offices. The 100m long horizontal, serene structure of the education wing is juxtaposed with the lightly sloped site, enabling differentiation of scale and a series of terraced spaces accompanying the long building.

The dense plot and the tight public budget posed a challenge and led to a search for a feasible, yet inspiring, design. The kindergarten classrooms are, therefore, built on two levels that implement compact land use which creates an urban version of the familiar childcare programs.

A unique woven timber fabric separates the public space from the children's realm, creating a light filter and playful articulation of horizontal and linear space. This handcrafted system acts as a contemporary variation of the Tel-Avivian brise-soleil architectural tradition, which provides solar protection while enabling air flow through the façade.

Photo by Iwan Baan

Photo by Maor Roytman

Photo by Yuval Tebol

Photo by Iwan Baan

Photo by Yuval Tebol

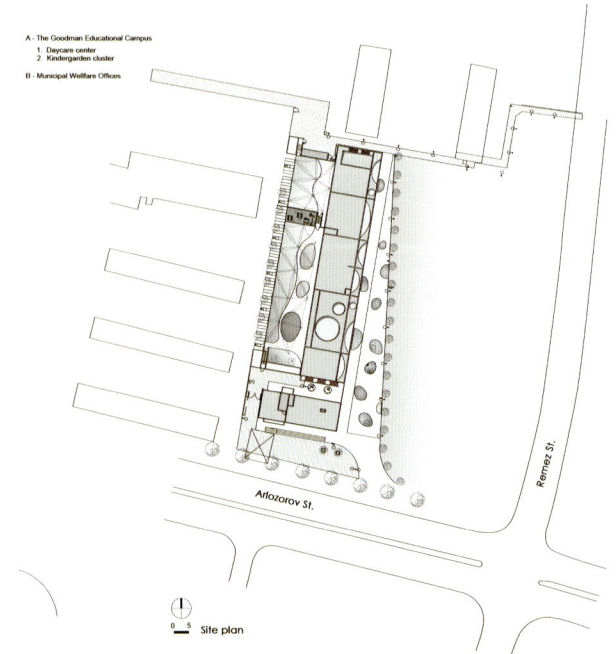

A - The Goodman Educational Campus
   1. Daycare center
   2. Kindergarden cluster

B - Municipal Wellfare Offices

Arlozorov St.

Remez St.

0 5

Site plan

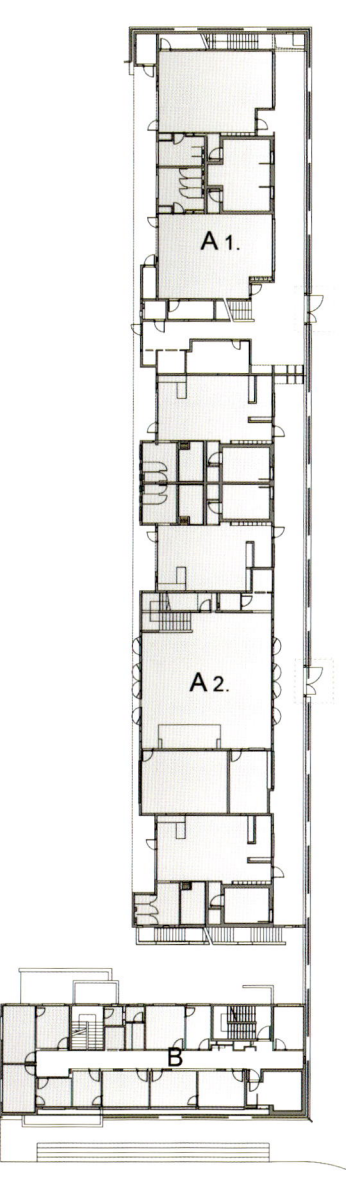

A 1.

A 2.

B

Photo by Yuval Tebol

segrt hlapic kindergarten

Location/
Sesvete, Zagreb,
Croatia
Design/
radionica arhitekture

Photography/
Boris Cvjetanovic
Area/
2,700 sqm

The 'rationalized landscape' is the result of a series of relations between 'natural' and 'artificial' elements which architects create by constructing or rearranging volumes. In its essence, the elegant gesture of enveloping a transformed slope by a curved trajectory means the radical equation of architecture and landscape in which each of the two elements also follows its own 'logic' as well as the 'logic' of the other element. The curved lane thus follows the inclination of the filled slope, so that all eight kindergartens and six nursery units have a corresponding outer space at the level of the encircled terrain, covered by a roof of deep, continuous eaves. It is important to stress that what the students encounter here is 'the first public area' many children are faced with and which unifies natural and urban properties. At the highest point of the 'ground floor' is the multi-purpose area of a stretched amphitheater. The rest of the building space houses everything from administrative offices to service facilities. The entire space focuses on the relation of 'artificial' and 'natural' architectural elements.

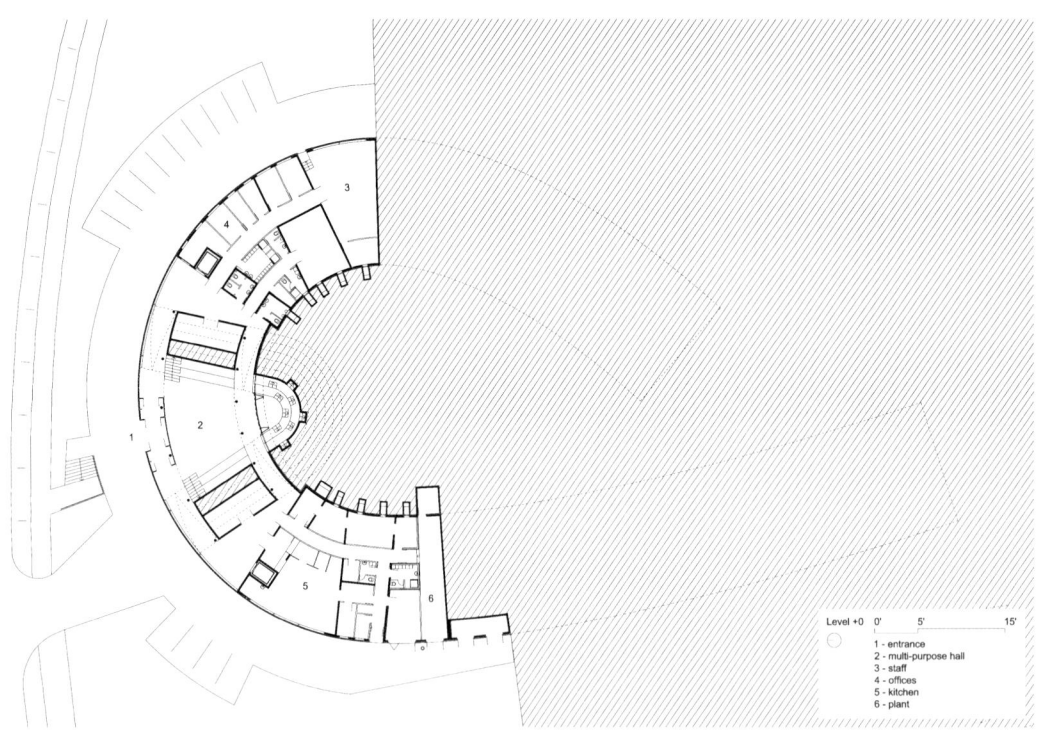

Level +0   0'   5'   15'

1 - entrance
2 - multi-purpose hall
3 - staff
4 - offices
5 - kitchen
6 - plant

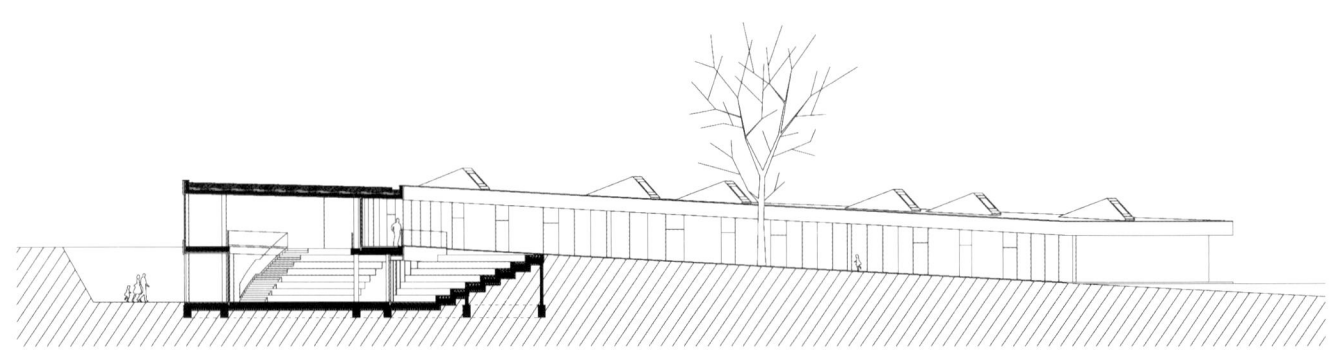

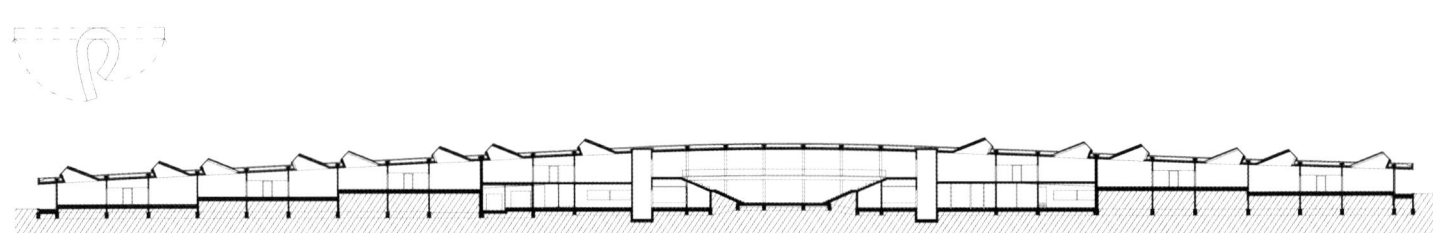

25 cradles nursery

Location/
Paris, France
Design/
RMDM Architects

Photography/
Grégoire Vieille
Area/
272 sqm

How can designers synthesize a contextual, functional and aesthetic work through architecture?

The confidential characteristic of the Passage des Tourelles in the XXth arrondissement of Paris led the architects to imagine an open building possessing a 'breathing area' located within the heart of a dense urban space.

The very particular presence of this nursery is expressed by a voluntarily marked architectural bias.

The school image is shaped by the meeting of two entities where typologies, materials and asserted colors produce a reading which is simple, plural and sequential at the same time.

The superposition of monolithic volumes of stone anchors the project at the level of the public space. The public wing houses all of the administration, technological, and service offices.

A second volume is located at the back of the lot which houses spaces for the children. This building is varnished, colorful, and asserts its presence through both complementary colors and the opposition of materials.

It is a place that asserts its temper by the dialogue and the interweaving of the architectures, or the material opposition and the color complementarity.

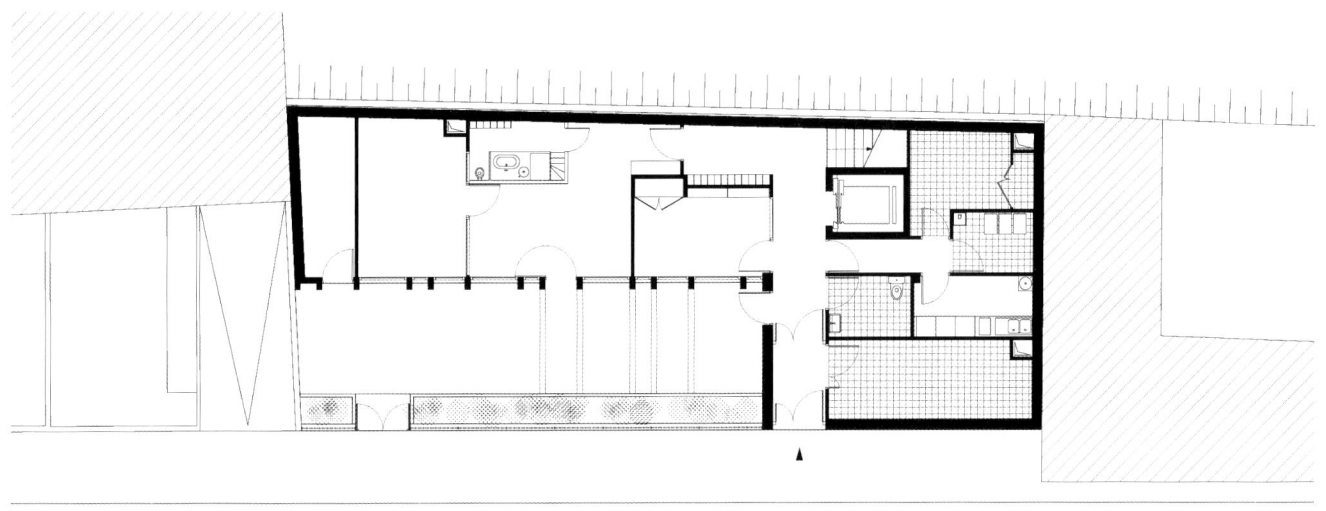

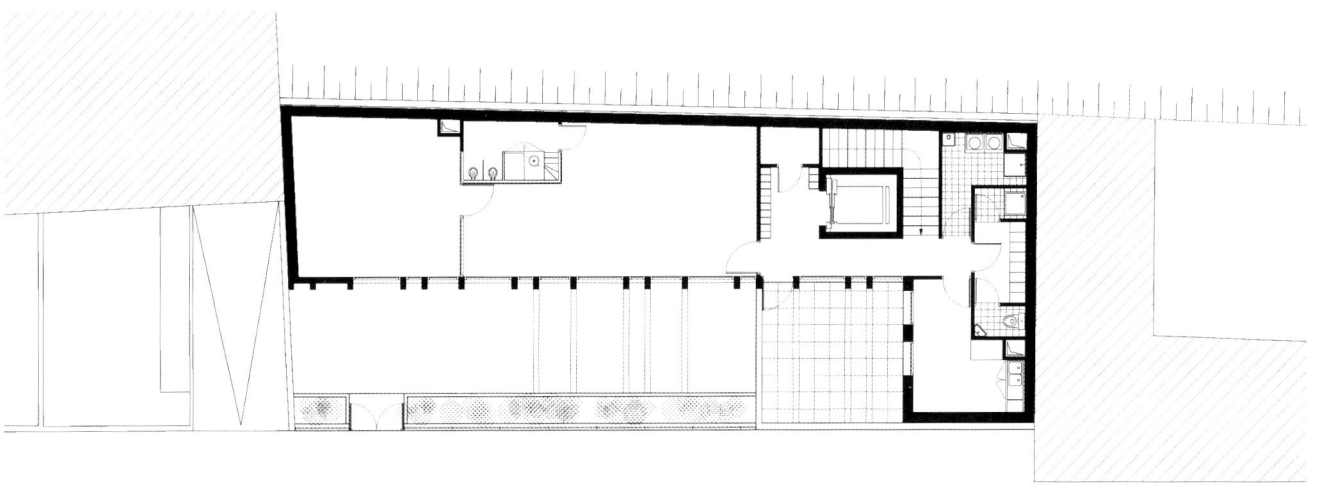

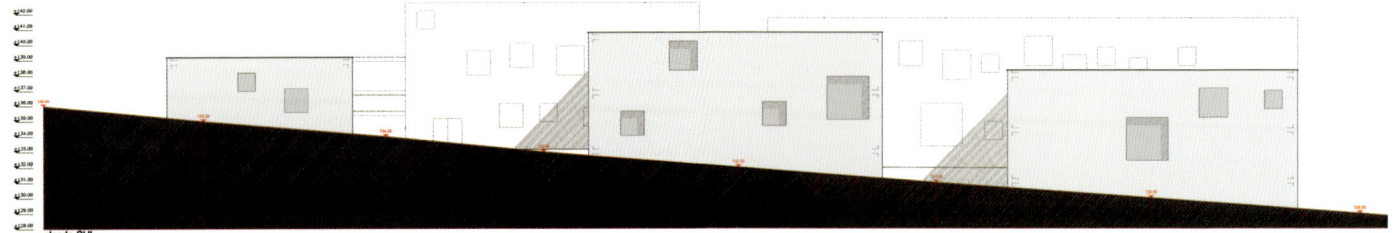

school center antas

Location/
Porto, Portugal
Design/
AVA Architects

Photography/
José Campos, arqf
Area/
2,645.26 sqm

The spatial and architectural design of the building housing the new Education Center Antas was formalized in several volumes, each containing part of the program in accordance with principles of internal organization, function, form and image, given the type of building and its specificity. The project concept took into account the morphology of the terrain, solar orientation, access and links to surrounding bodies. Great consideration was given to the relationship between outdoor spaces, between exterior and interior volumes, and between the interior spaces of the building itself. The objective was to formalize and realize a diverse environment through the creation of a building that is fragmented into several bodies interconnected with exterior spaces. The building aims to be an enclosed space of reduced relations with the urban surroundings.

alçado SUL

planta Piso -1

planta Piso 0

nursery monthey

Location/
Monthey, Switzerland
Design/
Bonnard Woeffray
architectes

Photography/
Hannes Henz
Area/
1,200 sqm

Monthey's new kindergarten is located in the town's Cinquantoux Park and replaces the former villa that had become obsolete. Conceived as a large house for children, the venue assumes an almost organic shape that merges with the wooded park and offers a range of interior spaces. Following the same logic is its composition of volumes topped by a roof composed of gently slanting sections.

The building can accommodate 180 or so children. It offers two floors arranged as six separate units. Each unit is divided into two spaces for activity and rest, with a bathroom in between. Each unit has a distinct character reflecting its position in the building; all benefit from different views of the park, and are bathed in sunlight in the morning or afternoon depending on the orientation.

The variety in position of the windows, all identical in size, contributes to a range of perceptions and facilitates visual contact for all ages.

While the construction is traditional, the exterior cladding is inspired by the world of childhood. The facades consist of timber slats finished in an array of toy-like colors, including pink, orange, red and green. Creating contrasting ambiences that are both happy and playful, the interior is composed of a rhythmic succession of colored floors and ceilings, with as many colors as there are units.

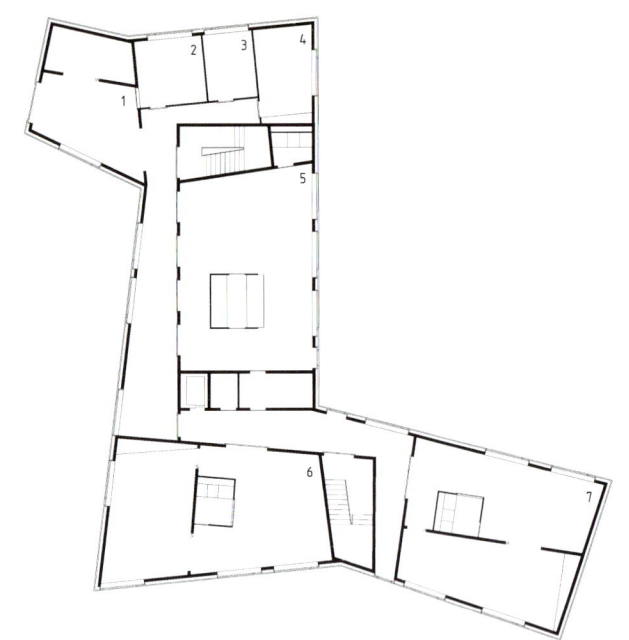

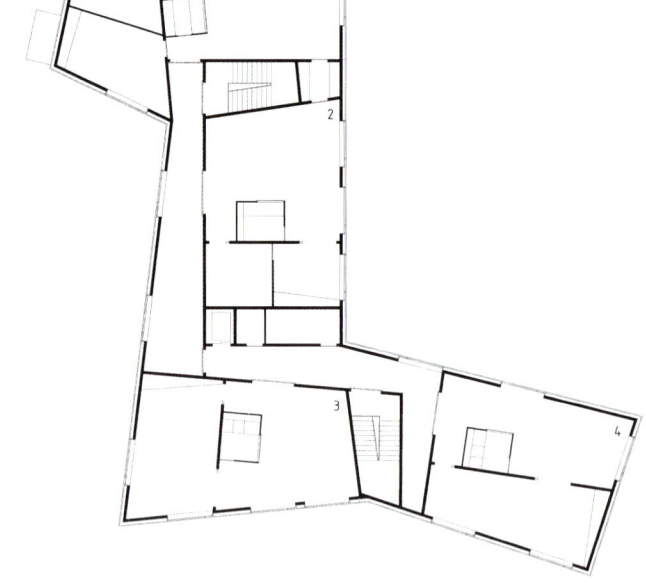

niveau rez-de-chaussée	ground floor
1 hall d'entrée	1 entrance
2 administration	2 administration
3 bureau directrice	3 directors office
4 salle conference	4 conference room
5 refectoire	5 dinning room
6 unité écoliers	6 pupils unit
7 unité mixte	7 mixed unit

5m   niv 0

étage	1.floor
1 unité 0-1	1 unit 0-1
2 unité 1-2	2 unit 1-2
3 unité 3-4	3 unit 3-4
4 unité 4-5	4 unit 4-5

5m   niv 1

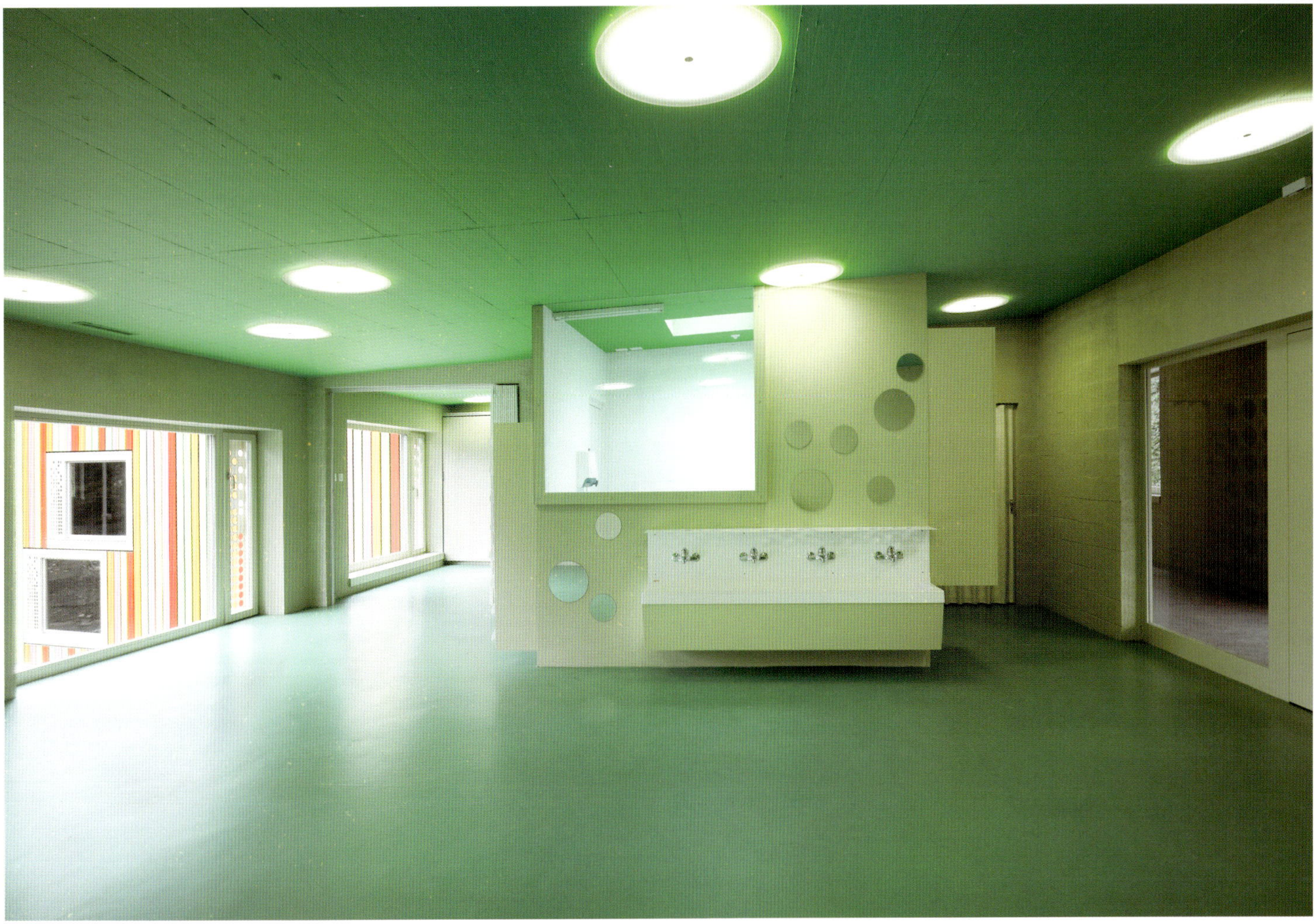

nursery in the park

Location/
Zaragoza, Spain
Design/
Santiago Carroquino
Architects & Grávalos
Di Monte Architects

Photography/
Jesús Granada
Area/
1,207.13 sqm

Located in Zaragoza within the up-to-date San Pablo Park and adjacent to both the Forest headquarters and the nearby river Ebro, the nursery is situated in the ideal environment to bring children closer to teaching.

The façades that generate the building volume clearly respond to the building function and the site's possibilities. The housing and office areas are closed off, while the classrooms are completely opened up to the park which they face.

The façade of the classrooms, which faces the green zone, presents an abstract composition, ordered by vertical stripes and perforated by torn and narrow hollows (such as tree trunks), suggesting a relationship of cohesion with the surrounding environment. From the inside of the building, the vertical hollows create light and space very similar to that found in a natural forest. The façade materials sieve the light that is filtered through green polycarbonate sheets, allowing maximum internal light levels while avoiding dazzling light.

The building lets children take center stage. The classrooms vary in proportion to the different stages, allowing the setting of different appropriations of space depending on the various courses. All measurements are based on both children's interaction with the space and the practical needs of teachers; for example, fixed lower windows are designed for children, while windows at an adult height can be opened when needed.

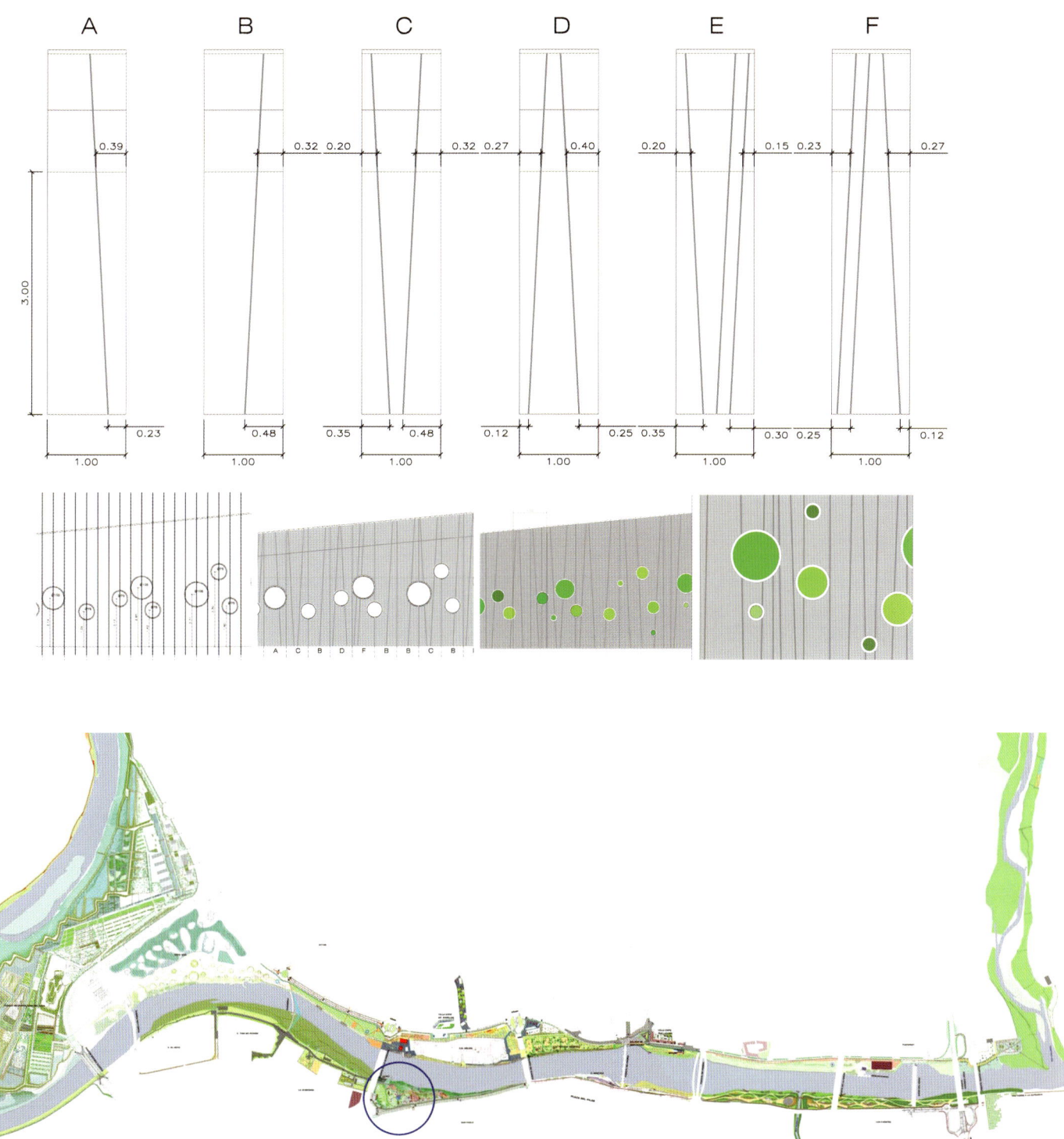

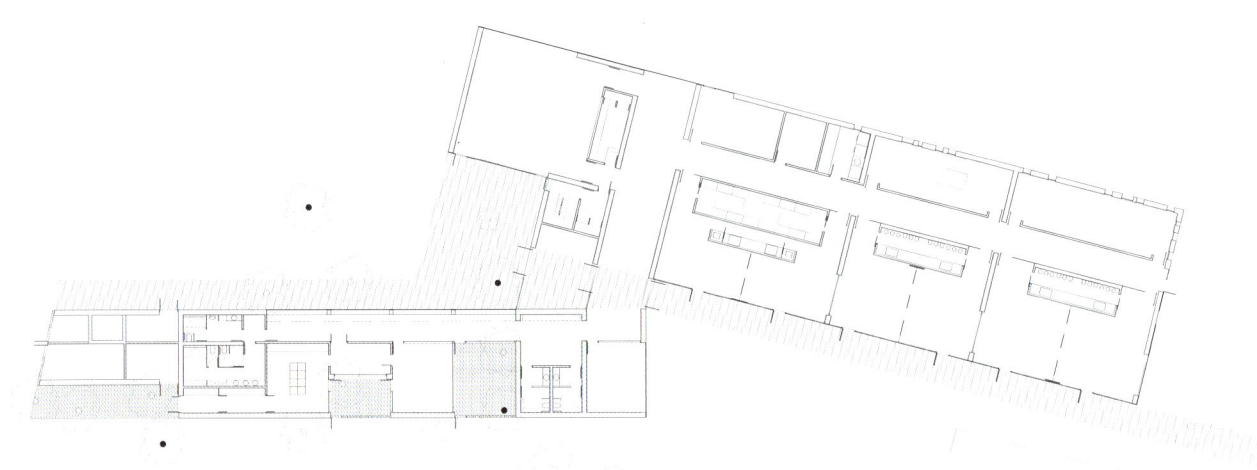

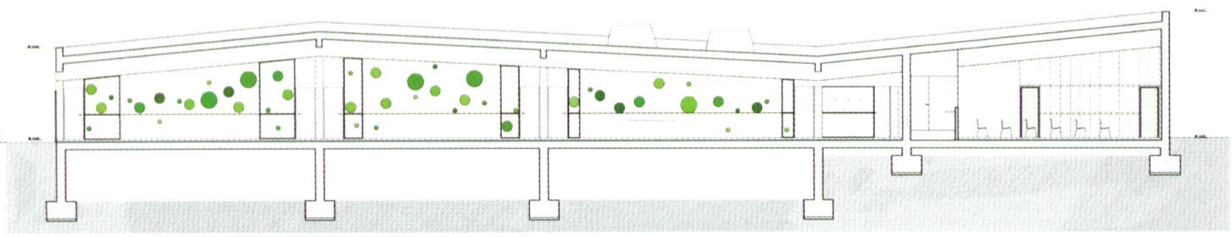

SECCION 1

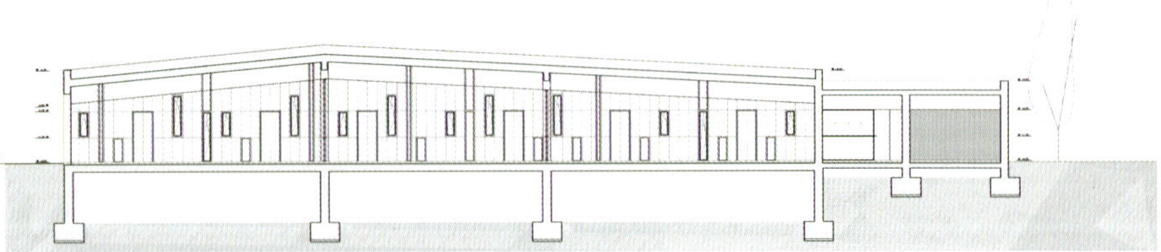

SECCION 2

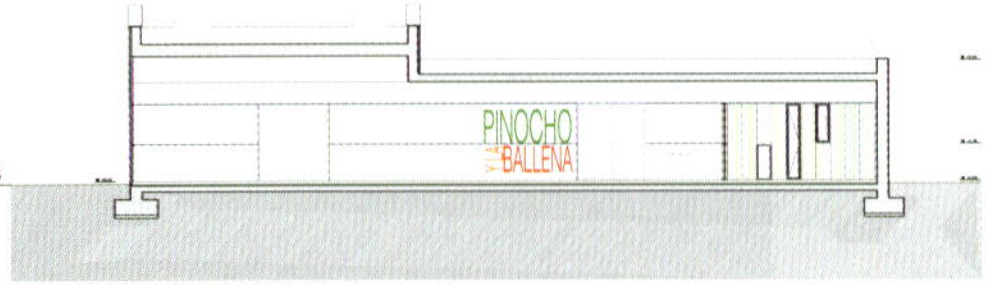

SECCION 3

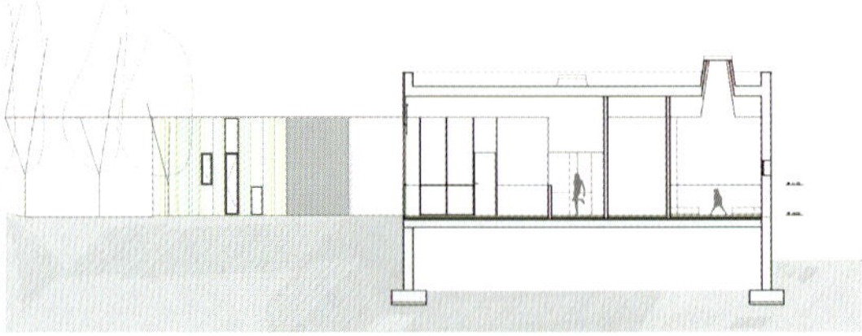

PINOCHO y la BALLENA

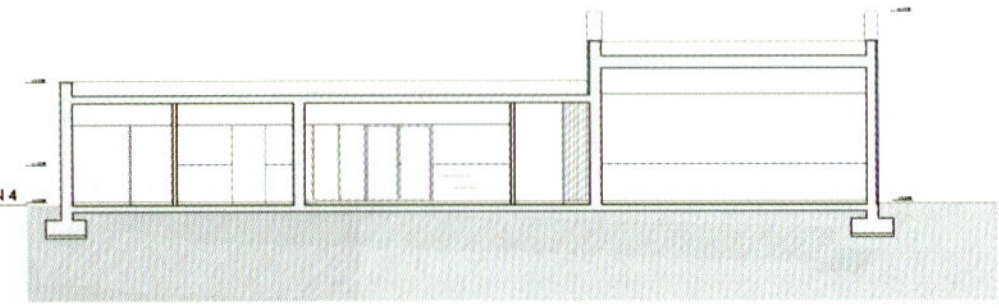

SECCION 4

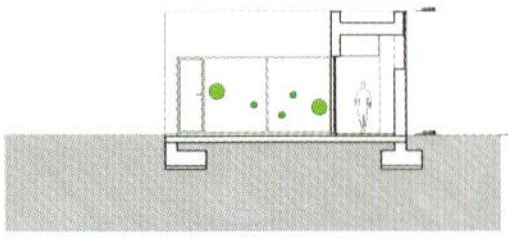

SECCION 6

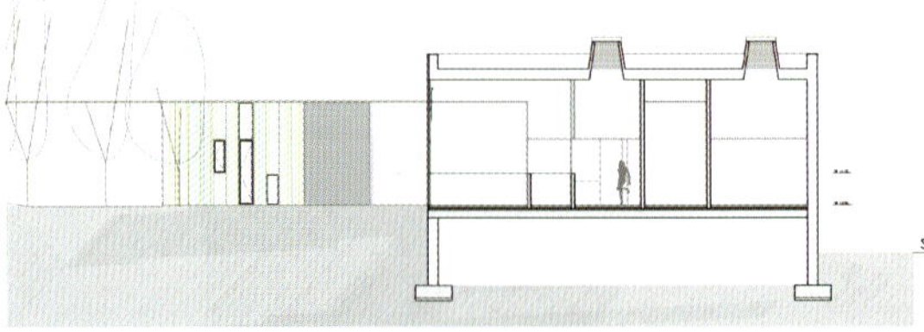

SECCION 7

SECCION 8

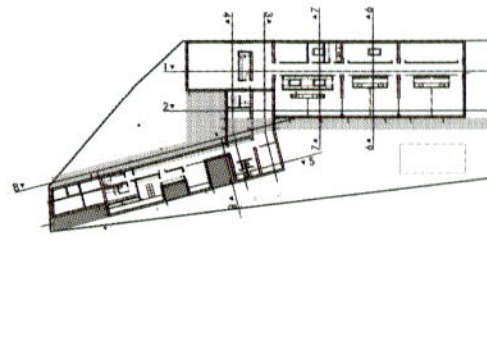

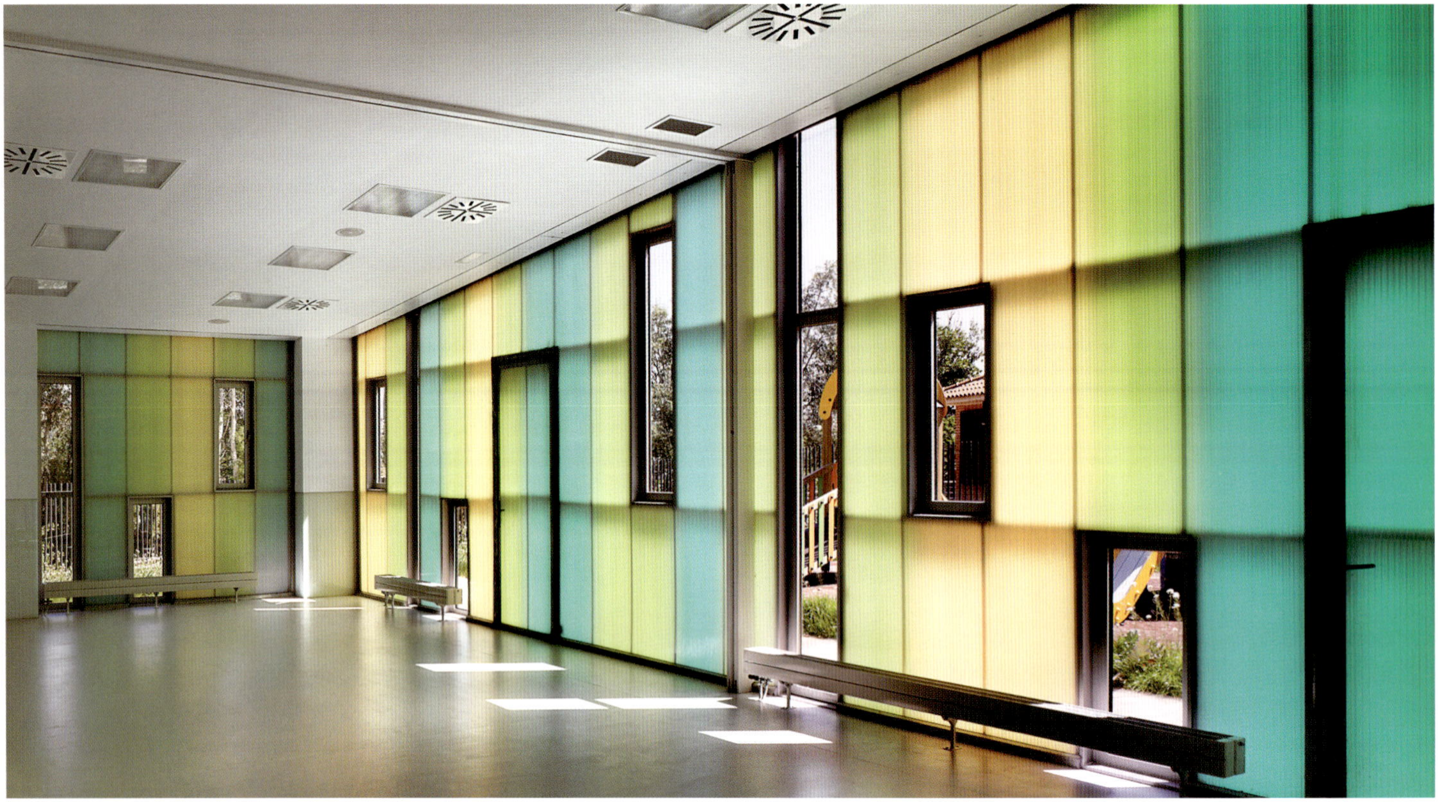

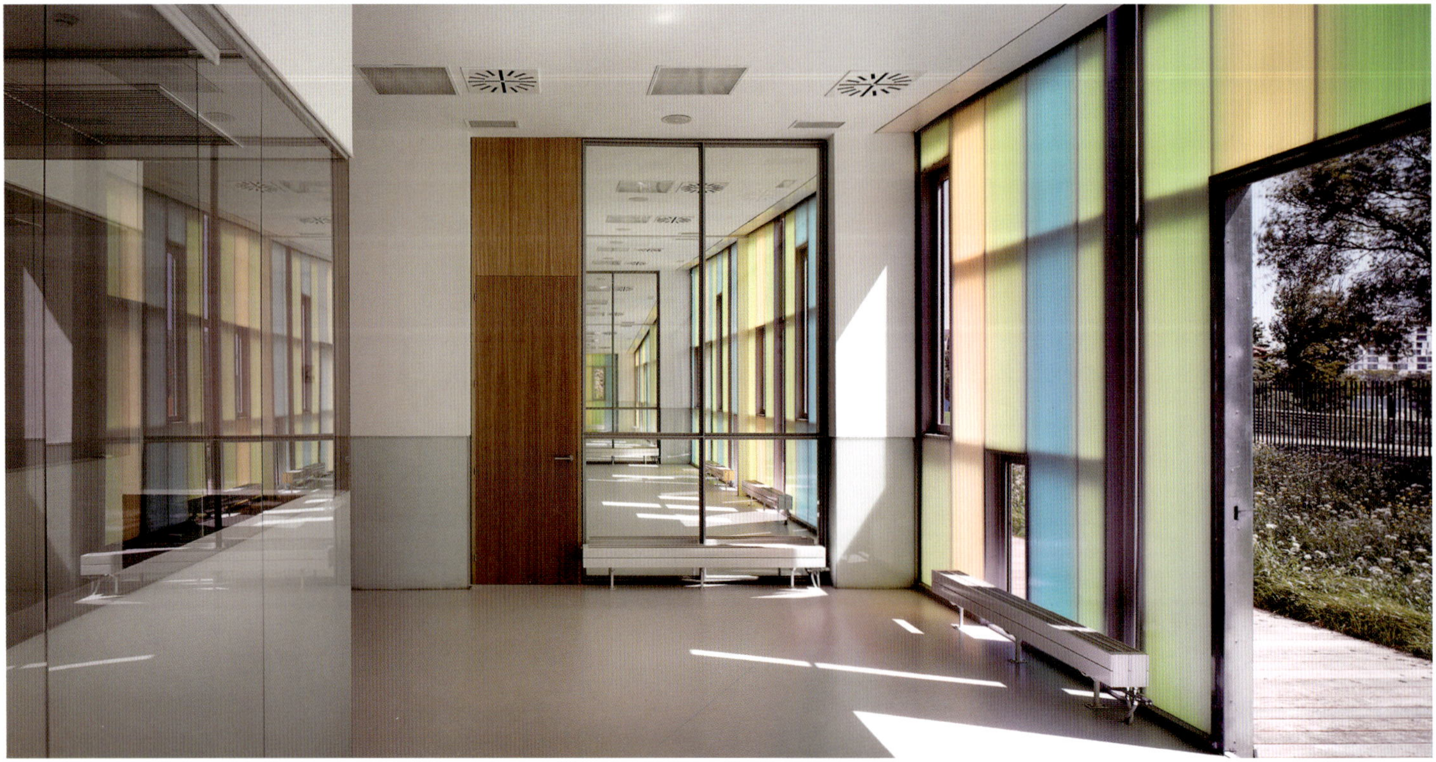

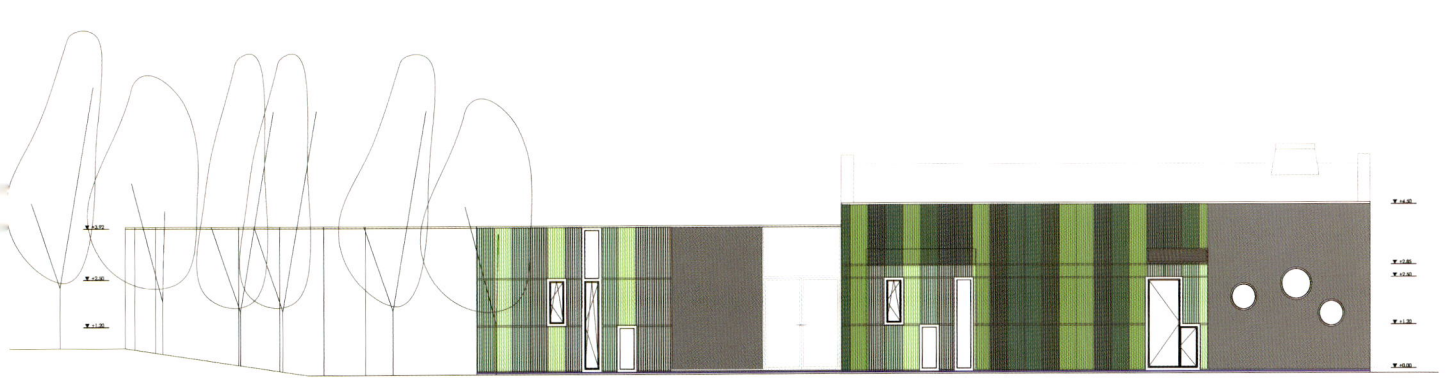

kindergarten 'barbapapà'

Location/
Comune de Vignola,
MO, Italy
Design/
ccd studio

Photography/
Fabio Mantovani
Area/
1,158 sqm

The project of Kindergarten 'Barbapapà' was originally imagined as a design response to a competition for project financing proposed by Vignola's muncipality in 2006. The program consisted of an educational space for 60 children divided into four classrooms. The area is located on the border of urban development, up a hill from the city and not too far from the historical center. The natural environment required careful assessments aimed at preserving this atypical part of the landscape in the Emilia Romagna region. The project aimed to be an architectural expression of mature consciousness about the building's sustainable themes, recognizing the value of positive relationships with one's surroundings. The architectural project aims to express this principal theme in every aspect in order to convey the importance of sustainability to all of the building's young visitors.

A vegetable garden was introduced on a raised level to create protected spaces for children and reduce the visual impact of the volume. An entrance was created from the hillside instead of the urban street.

The green deck ensures good thermal insulation and the preservation of environmental comfort through terrain on top of the wooden roof structure.

Natural resources also allow daily needs to be satisfied. Glass openings are used along the entire length of the façade to filter sunlight into the space at different times of the day in order to heat the interior.

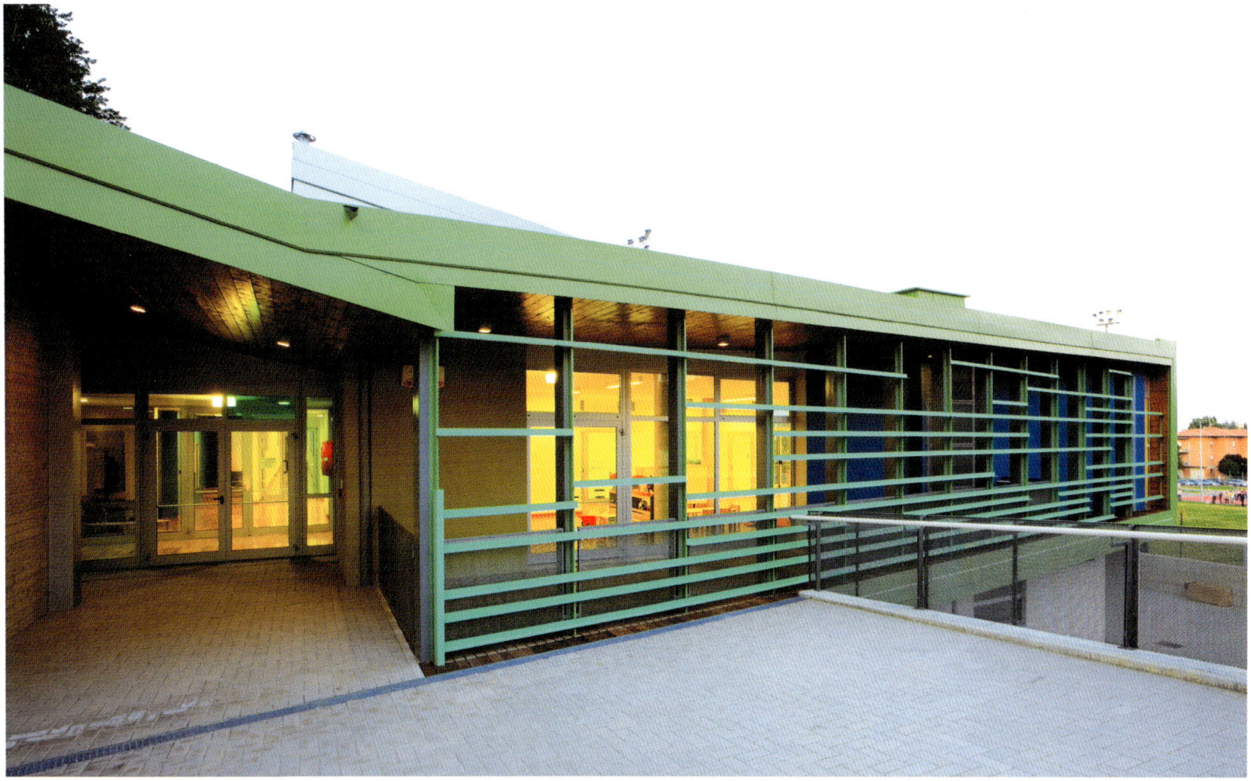

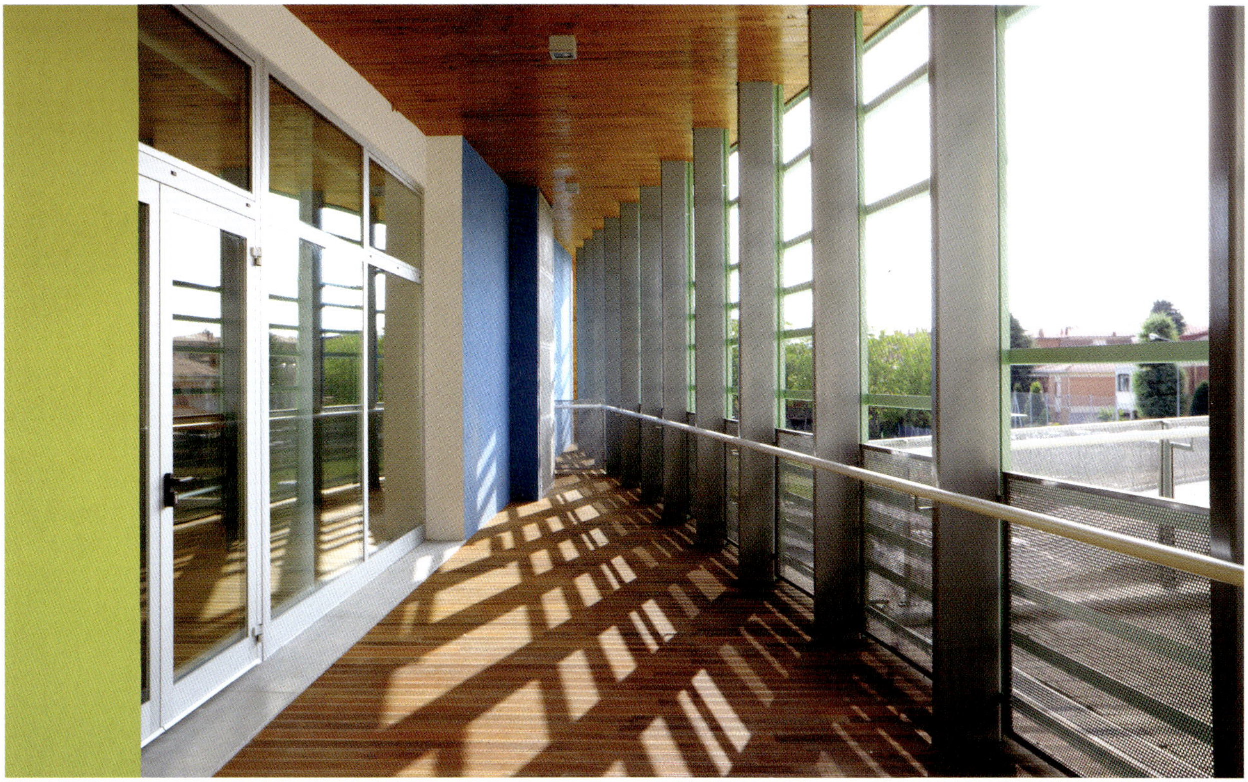

1 ingresso pubblico   5 area sosta camion derrate   9 area esterna pavimentata   13 teatro naturale
2 ingresso addetti   6 deposito passeggini   10 area sabbia   14 giardino di fiori
3 parcheggio pubblico   7 collettori solari e fotovoltaico   11 orti   15 vegetazione autoctona
4 parcheggio privato   8 tetto verde   12 giochi

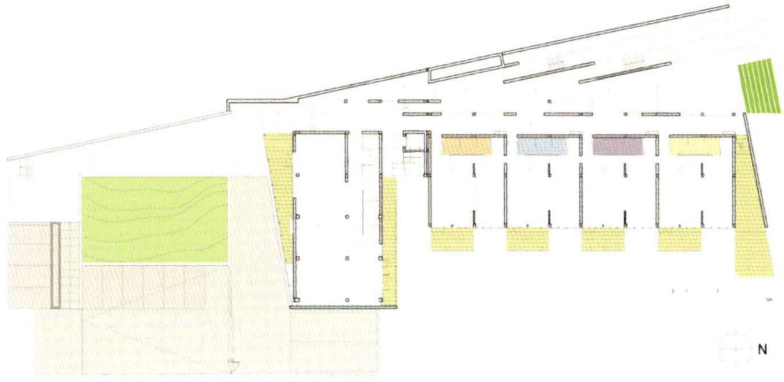

PIANTA LIVELLO 0

1 percorso esterno   5 servizi igienici   9 laboratorio
2 ingresso   6 centro bambini e genitori   10 sezione
3 attesa genitori   7 scale / ascensore   11 teatro naturale
4 ufficio   8 spazio comune   12 uscita d'mergenza

N

riciclo delle acque piovane

copertura con manto vegetale

raffrescamento naturale

bagni della sezione

pavimento a pannelli radianti

irrigazione con acqua piovana di recupero

sonde geotermiche

collettori solari e pannelli fotovoltaici

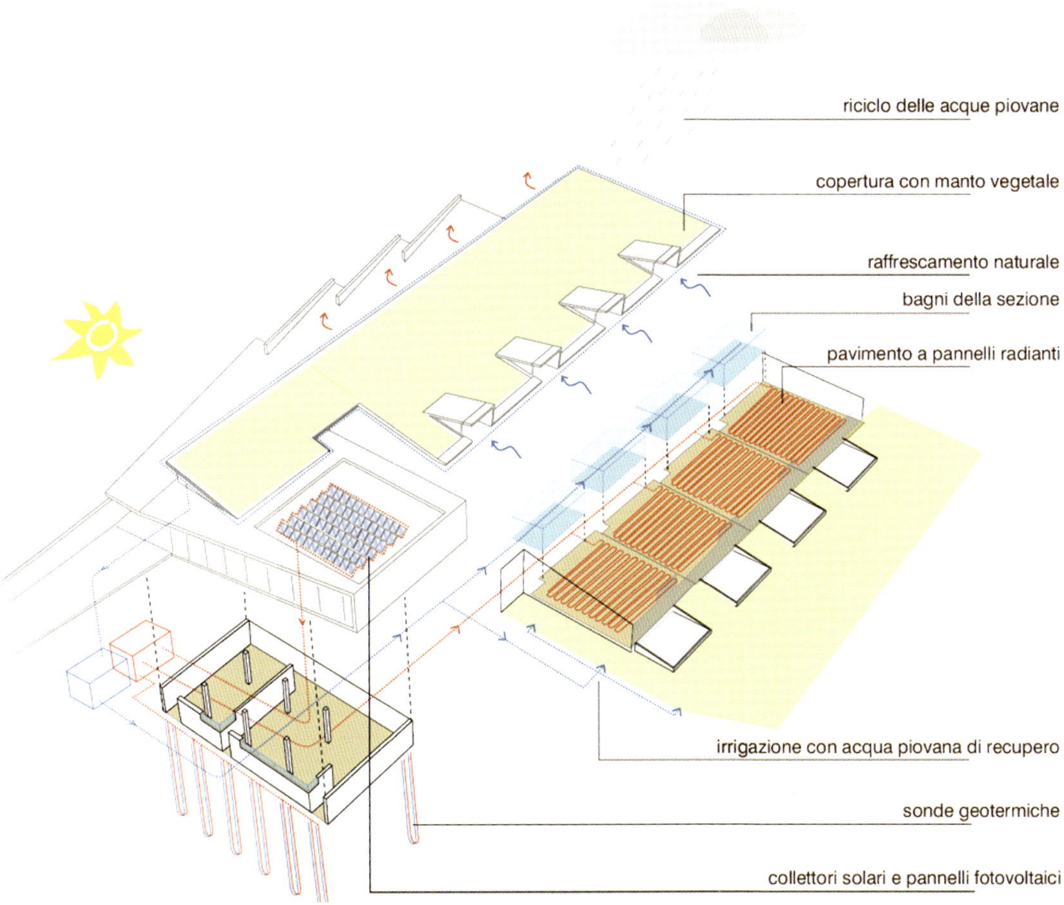

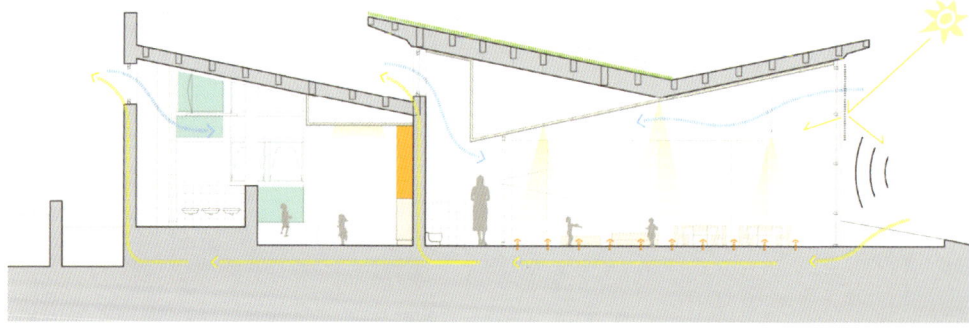

ventilazione naturale
fondazione areata
riscaldamento a pavimento
ventilazione naturale
ventilazione controllo radiazione solare
vetrata acustica

kindergarden school in areatza

Location/
Areatza, Spain
Design/
IA+B arkitektura taldea

Photography/
Aitor Ortiz
Area/
234 sqm

The kindergarten school in Areatza was designed in response to a series of project challenges. The first challenge was to create spaces which combined privacy with a need for gentle spaces and views. Second, the spaces needed to introduce pleasing natural light without overexposing the children.

Architecturally, these priorities led us to generate a single and strong volume, finished in wood and possessing a layout where all amenities look south and towards the road and sidewalk, while classrooms face north into the building's lot. Therefore, while the classrooms receive even and constant light, the amenities act as a filter which protect the children within. Moreover, all the spaces are designed on the scale of children, with several openings and windows at the floor level. Visual contact is maintained between the exterior gardens and inner spaces of the building. The polyvalent area faces north and south, opening itself up to the site and allowing greater visual control of the exterior private spaces.

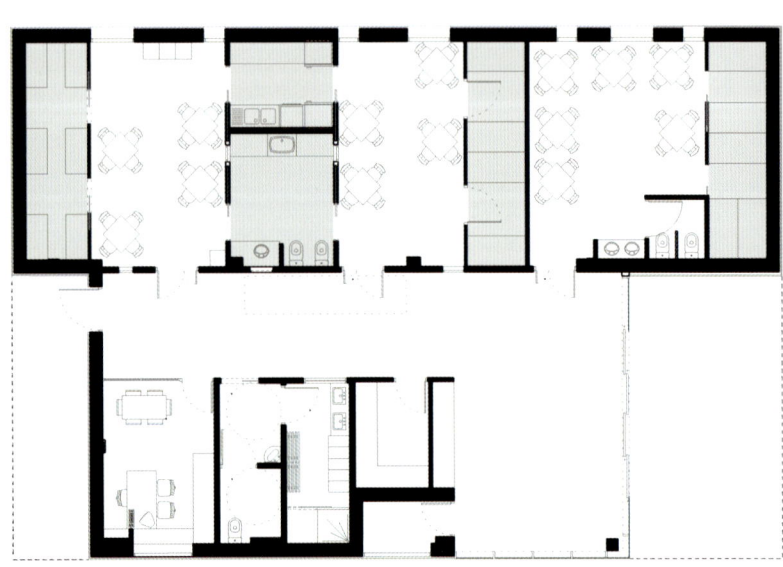

oslo international school

Location/
Oslo, Norway
Design/
Jarmund/Vigsnæs AS
Architects

Photography/
Ivan Brodey
Area/
3,900 sqm new
structure, 3,300 sqm
refurbishment

Oslo International School is a private school of approximately 500 children from more than 50 different nations, with divided reception, kindergarten, primary, and secondary school spaces.

The school is based on traditional use of classrooms combined with special facilities for advanced studies.

The primary goal of the building project was to upgrade existing areas, replace temporary structures and establish new educational areas for specific needs. The project was divided into three building phases to allow continuous use of the school during the construction period.

The existing structure from the 1960s was worn down, but had obvious architectonic qualities. The organization on one level provides an easy orientation, good natural lighting and close contact with the outdoors.

The new structure gently transforms the easy organization within a limited budget, and tries to keep the inherent qualities. The new mechanical systems are placed on the roof.

With reference to the qualities of the old structure, the new buildings are organized around three new atriums suitable for play and recreation for the different groups of children.

The existing atrium is established as the quiet garden with white gravel, benches and greenery suited for quiet play and conversation. Two large existing oaks are preserved.

The atrium in phase two has a rubber floor suitable for the youngest childrens' play. The westward-facing open school yard will be used for sports activities.

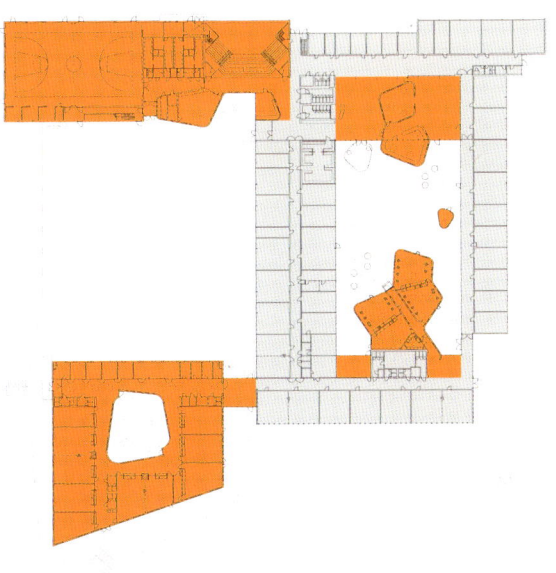

OSLO INTERNATIONAL SCHOOL

PHASE 1

PHASE 2

PHASE 3

RENOVATION

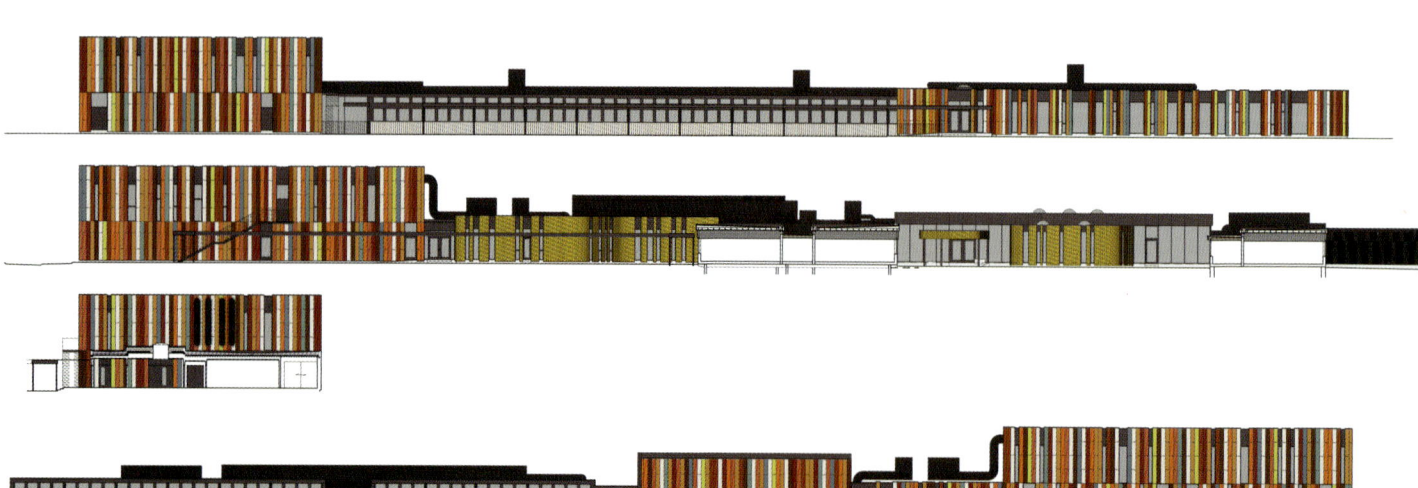

skanderborggade
day-care centre

Location/
Copenhagen, Denmark

Design/
Dorte Mandrup
Arkitekter ApS

Photography/
Jens Markus Lindhe

Area/
555 sqm

The building design is the result of planning regulations and the need for the greatest possible connection between outdoor grounds areas and the roof, as well as a desire to take optimal advantage of the site's orientation in relation to the sun throughout the day. The building consists of two planes which extend to the boundaries of the site. One plane forms the ground terrain plane covering the contaminated ground, while a second forms the roof. The ground terrain surface is folded upwards in such a way that it forms a hill or slope between the ground and roof. The path of the summer sun from northeast to northwest traces the cut of the slope. The slope angle offers the best sun exposure to both the slope and the courtyard from the south and west. Underneath the slope an unheated space is formed where a forest of columns is used for swings and other forms of play, whether the weather is cold or wet. Two other light wells cut into the roof plane ensuring daylight and a variety of outdoor space in conjunction with the other rooms of the building.

Day-care Center Skanderborggade - West facade towards Skanderborggade 1:100

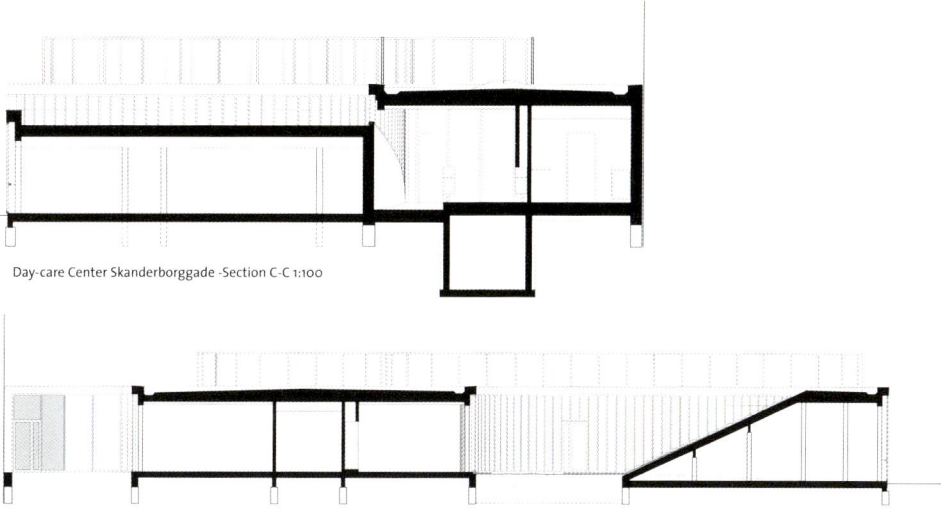

Day-care Center Skanderborggade -Section C-C 1:100

Day-care Center Skanderborggade · Section D-D 1:100

ensemble bloemershof

Location/
Dieren, the Netherlands
Design/
Bekkering Adams
architecten

Photography/
DigiDaan
Area/
3,130 sqm

The ensemble is conceptually designed as a frozen forest, with an open and transparent ground floor with concrete columns as tree trunks, filled in with glass and natural stone accents crowned with an upper elevation with slender wooden slats as a 'leafy canopy' hovering above the ground floor. The clear selection of materials provides a strong architectural identity.

The interiors are light and transparent and offer an optimal functionality to their users, with a generous central hall and cafeteria area and a diversity of classrooms and workshops for the vocational school, a high tower with vistas to the eating area and classrooms, and spacious gym facilities.

Sustainability plays a key role in the project. Besides an optimal inner climate, sustainable and future-proof materialization and spatial logistics, the building was designed with the newest sustainable installation technologies.

The project Bloemershof is the first building in the Netherlands where concrete core activation by means of air is applied – the so-called 'Concretecool' system. It uses the natural accumulating qualities of concrete to realize a school with the highest degree of ecological ventilation and cooling standards.

The roof surface of the school is provided with a solar energy system by means of Photovoltaic cells, and a daylight regulation system was implemented to increase efficiency and reduce energy costs.

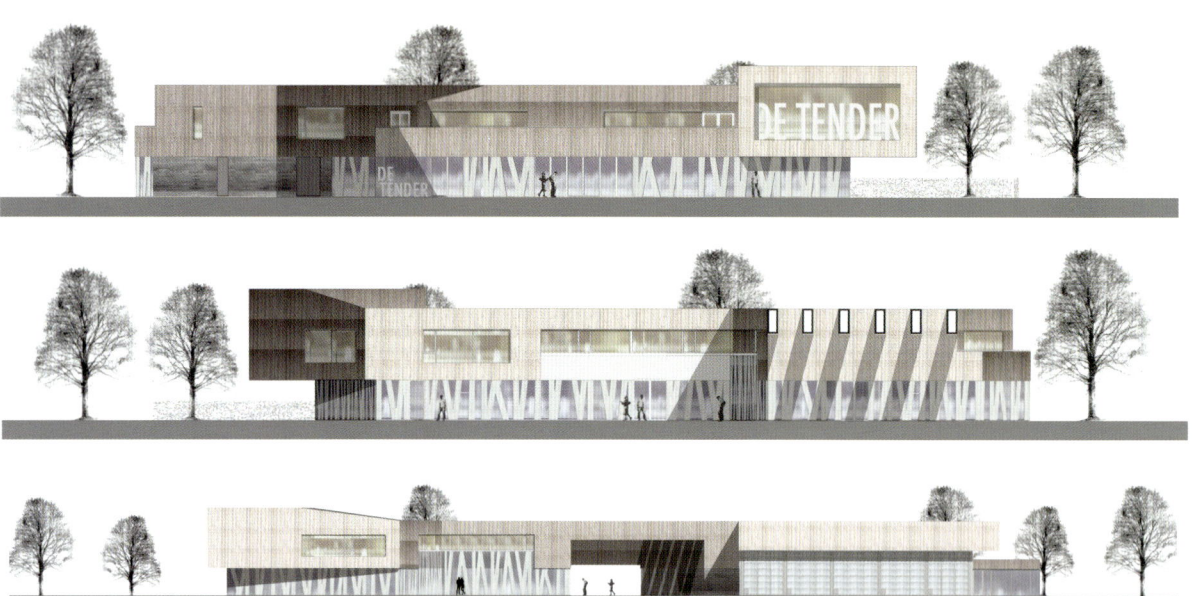

day-care center, naestvedgade

Location/
Copenhagen, Denmark

Design/
Dorte Mandrup
Arkitekter ApS

Photography/
Jens Markus Lindhe

Area/
1,000 sqm

The project consists of two main elements, the prism and the frame, which are tied together by the middle building and the roof terrace. The prism shape is determined by the intention to create a minimum of shadow on the west-facing outdoor areas of the neighboring housing estate. At the same time, it creates the best possible outdoor areas for the users of the day care center. The motif of the prism is a gardening greenhouse. It creates a precise yet transparent boundary between the motif of the prism and the garden itself. The prism is constructed by two independent elements, the roof and the inner climate protection. An incision in the prism was made in the building to create access to the roof terrace.

The frame contains the building facilities, the kitchen, the administration offices, and the staff room. The motif of the frame is the precisely defined border between the controlled natures of the garden bed in contrast with the wild character of the garden itself. The roof of the frame is densely covered with tall grass that over the course of time will grow into a dense jungle.

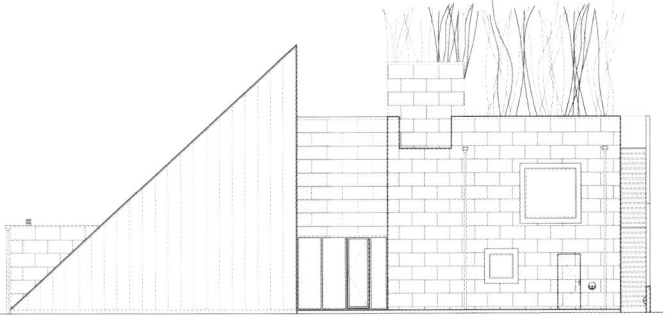

North facade 1:200

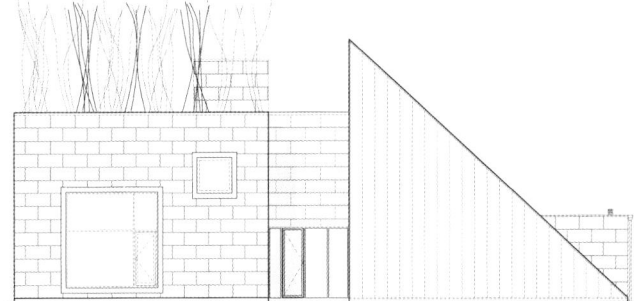

South facade 1:200

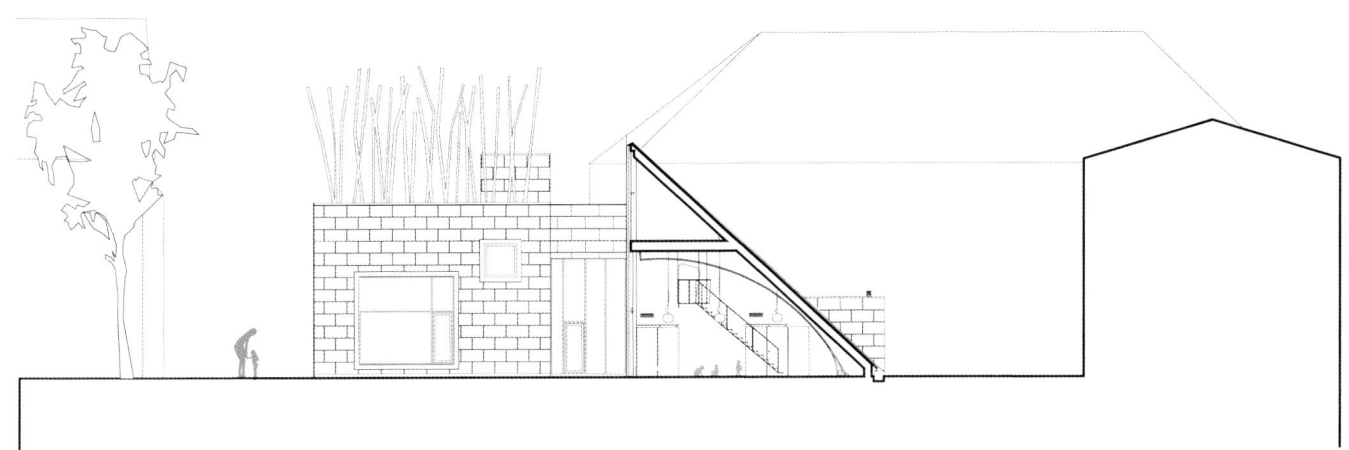

Day-care Centre, Naestvedgade - Cross section 1:200

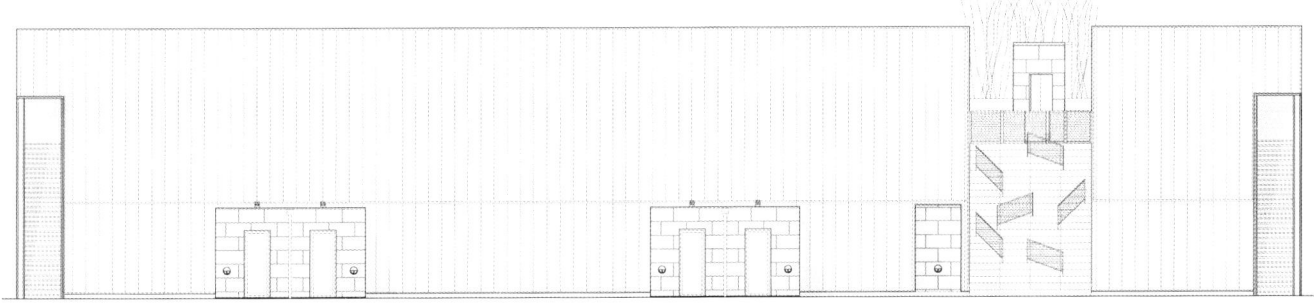

East facade 1:200

Day-care Centre, Naestvedgade - Elevations 1:200

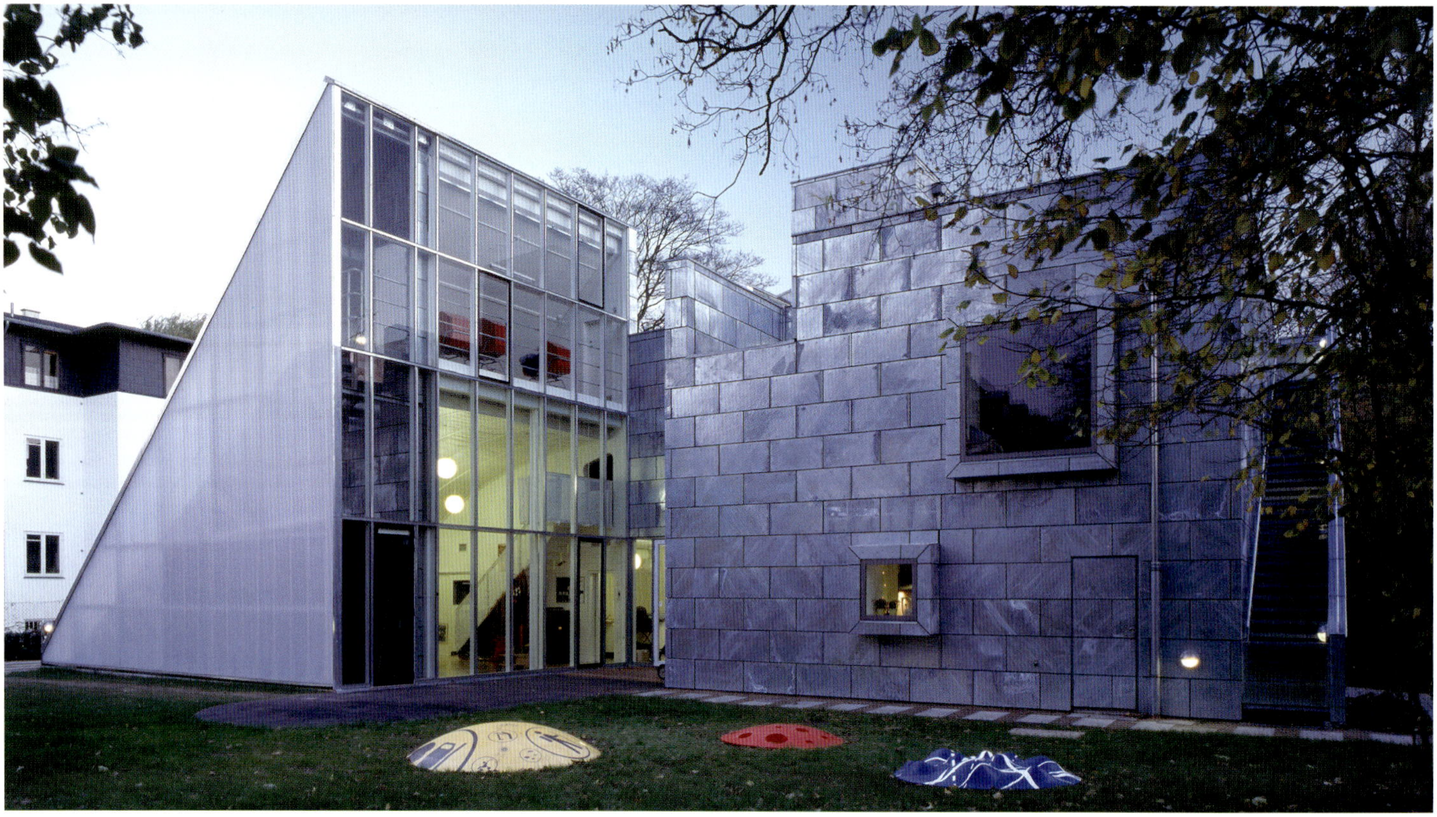

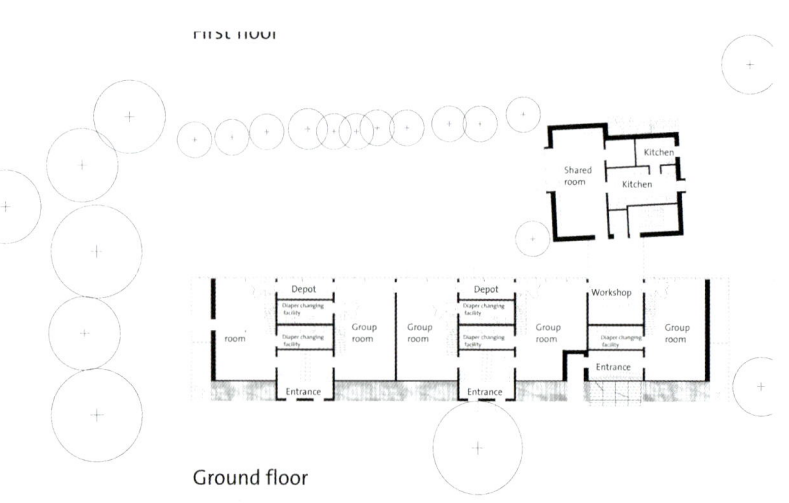

First floor

Shared room

Kitchen

Kitchen

Depot

Diaper changing facility

Group room

Group room

Depot

Diaper changing facility

Group room

Group room

Workshop

Diaper changing facility

Group room

room

Entrance

Entrance

Entrance

Ground floor

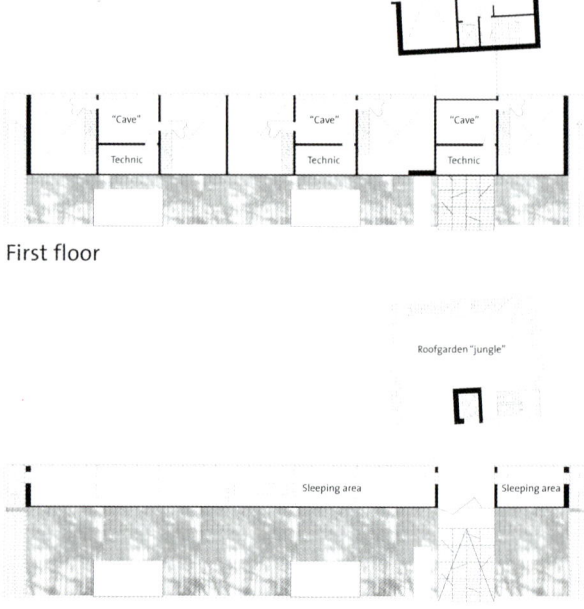

Office | Staff room

"Cave"

Technic

"Cave"

Technic

"Cave"

Technic

First floor

Roofgarden "jungle"

Sleeping area

Sleeping area

Second floor

youth recreation & culture center gersonsvej

Location/
Hellerup, Copenhagen,
Denmark
Design/
Dorte Mandrup
Arkitekter ApS & CEBRA

Photography/
Adam Mørk
Area/
2,600 sqm

To express the complexity of the program under one roof, the building is designed as a space that unifies the recreation and leisure activities of three connected houses. Inspired by the surrounding villa, the building design downscales the large volume of the gym to the scale of the area.

There is a dynamic synergy between the villas and throughout the house, where sports and leisure are directly intertwined, both physically and mentally. Indoor and outdoor spaces were merged in relation to the center's activities, with all ground level activities designed to have direct access to the garden or courtyard.

The terminology of the building recognizes classic house spaces such as the entrance hall, dining room, atelier, living room, terrace, garden and attic. Through the use of color, light and surfaces, varying moods emerge in a series of rooms. Each room is created with its own special character which calls for specific technical, acoustic, material, and spatial decisions.

The ambition was to create a hangout for children, recalling Pippi Longstocking's famous imagined "Villa Villakilla" more than any real world institution.

SKATE PARK   GARDEN   GREEN BAFFLE   GERSONSVEJ

SOUTH ELEVATION

GERSONSVEJ   FORECOURT   SKATE PARK   RAILWAY

MOTOR COORDINATION   REHEARSAL

WARDROBE   TERRACE   DANCE HALL

HEART

CROSS SECTION

tokyo baby café

Location/
Tokyo, Japan
Design/
nendo

Photography/
Jimmy Cohrssen
Area/
205 sqm

The design of a "parent's and child's cafe" was envisioned in Tokyo's Omotesando as a space for parents to enjoy being out and about with small children, without worrying about strangers around them. The café is fully stocked with picture books and toys, and includes a playroom, private rooms and separate spaces for nursing and changing diapers. Wide aisles make it easy to move around with a stroller, and light switches and door handles are placed high up to keep children from using them.

The café is designed to be enjoyed by two very different sizes of users: parents and small children. The interior plays on this difference in scale and the difference in how adults and children see. Take a table - adults live their lives aware of tabletops and the objects placed on top of them, but children see the table's underside. A table's leg can look like pillars, and the underside of the table is like a roof to a child. The cafe's "absolutely huge" and "absolutely tiny" furnishings play with these two different perspectives: that of the adult and that of the child.

A nursing sofa becomes a playroom when blown up on a massive scale, and a diaper-changing table is reinvented when shrunk to miniscule proportions. Big windows pair with small ones, and big light bulbs contrast with small ones. The floorboards vary in size, and the undersides of tables, where parents' eyes don't reach, hide pictures of baby animals and their parents. Parents and babies of all different animal types can be found throughout the café, waiting for human visitors and their children.

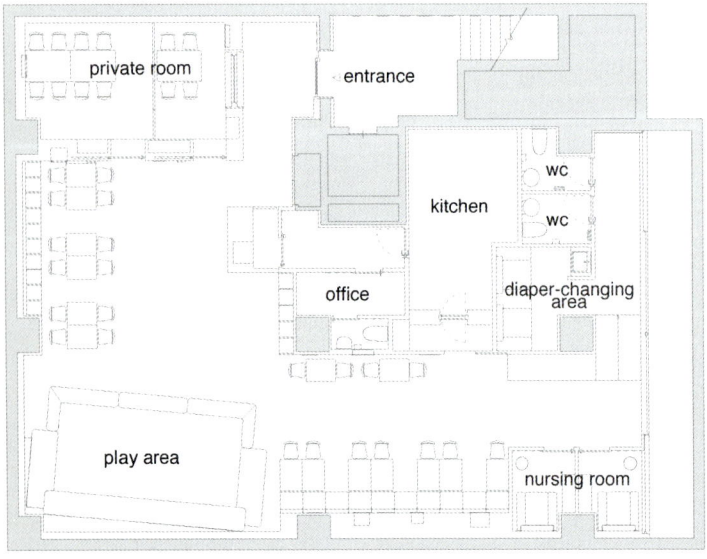

kid's republic in shanghai

Location/
Shanghai, China
Design/
SAKO Architects

Photography/
Zhong Hai SHEN
Area/
105 sqm

On the first floor, bookcases are arranged on a full wall. The bookcases have different widths, depths, and thicknesses and were made by using boards from a variety of trees. Some of these wooden pieces protrude or withdraw, forming a solid, tactile structure. There are also bookcases made out of hollow logs, while flourishing leaves grow out of the floor. Visitors truly feel absorbed in the space when sunshine reflects in these leaves. The ceiling is composed of logs, with branches interspersed at equal distances so that passersby see the tree trunks' outer rings through the building's glass windows.

When the visitor steps up to the second floor, an activity space covered with rough bark appears. The interior is a pure white space with irregular round holes in the ceiling. The ground is of a different height as the space is used as a stage and auditorium. The floor is covered with colorful carpet on which children can lie and read peacefully. An office area is located adjacent to the activity space, and holds office desks inlaid with log sections that extend to the wall surface. The bathroom signals a complete change of style, with all surfaces finished in stainless steel. The round lighting forms are reflected in the stainless steel finishes and create a safe haven for visitors.

1F plan

scale 1:100

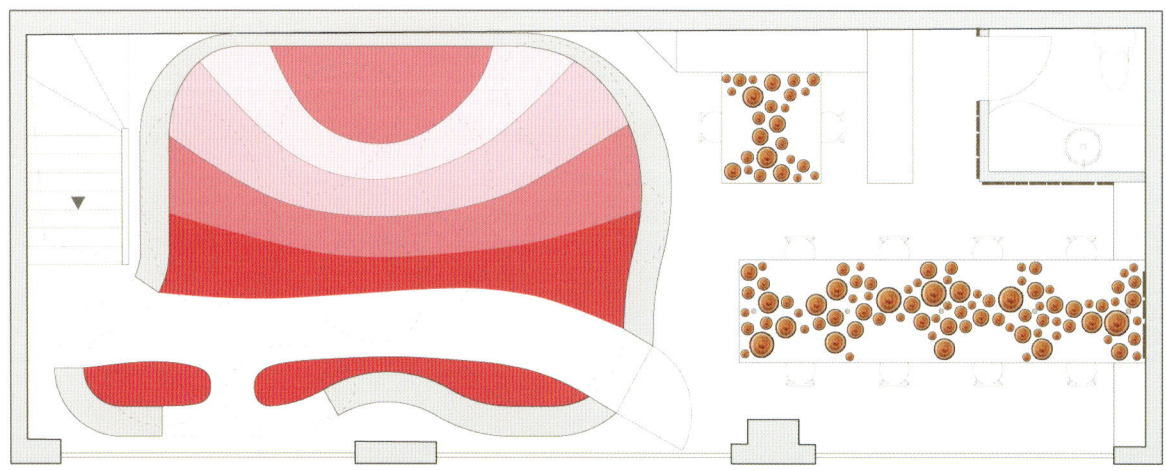

2F plan

scale 1:100

jellybeans children's boutique

Location/
Springfield, MO, US
Design/
sharon taylor designs/
Pickwick House

Photography/
Nathalie Bearden of
nathaliebearden.com
Area/
2,400 sqft

The idea was to create a store unlike any other we had ever seen. The owner, Meghan Chambers, wanted to encourage playfulness, style, and sophistication.

The designer believes in reinventing things - reusing, recycling, and finding beauty in the not so pretty things. Flea markets are where she starts in the design process. Uncovering a tattered, unappreciated treasure and then helping it dress itself up to go to the ball is how she approaches projects. The visual message of Jellybeans is inviting, unique, adventurous, stylish, hip, and sophisticated.

The designer finds inspiration from all over - from tearing pages out of her favorite interior design magazines, her old Cookie magazines, old maps and globes, and royalty. The color scheme was chosen from a beautifully illustrated vintage children's book.

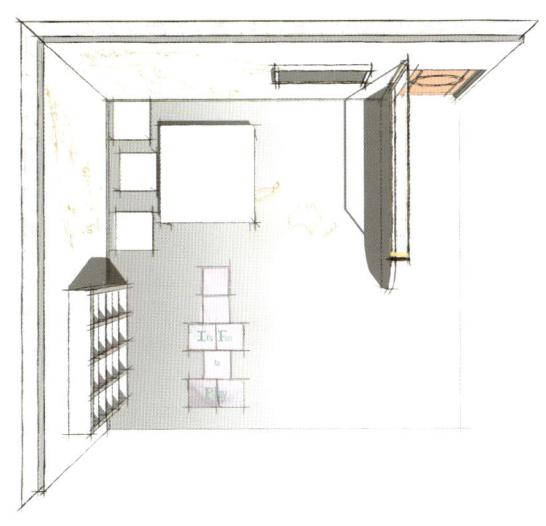

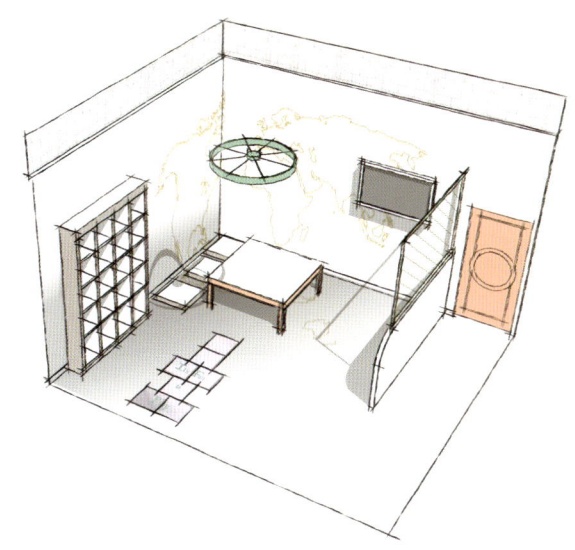

Let the GREAT world spin ON at... JELLYBEANS!

cenerino

Location/
Bassano (VI), Italy
Design/
Andrea Tognon
Architecture

Photography/
Cristia Guizzo
Area/
120 sqm

Impressed by the sight of a high-end, multi-brand boutique designed by Andrea Tognon Architecture, Vittorio Cenere contacted the design firm on his own behalf. He asked Tognon to develop a concept for Cenerino, a children's fashion shop. Having decided to approach the project from an adult perspective, the designer rejected the standard 'retail playground' with toys and games for kids in favor of a child's world interpreted as a sophisticated, design-filled realm that appeals to grown-ups as well. The interior is an installation of components that recall individual childhood sensations. Tognon raised the level of the pavement and used a low ramp at the entrance to lend importance to small objects and to draw attention to the aspect of growing. Out-of-proportion pieces of furniture and folding screens hint at the game of hide-and-seek. The combination of light shining through rose-shaded windows and walls of a pale blue hue creates a fantastical atmosphere.

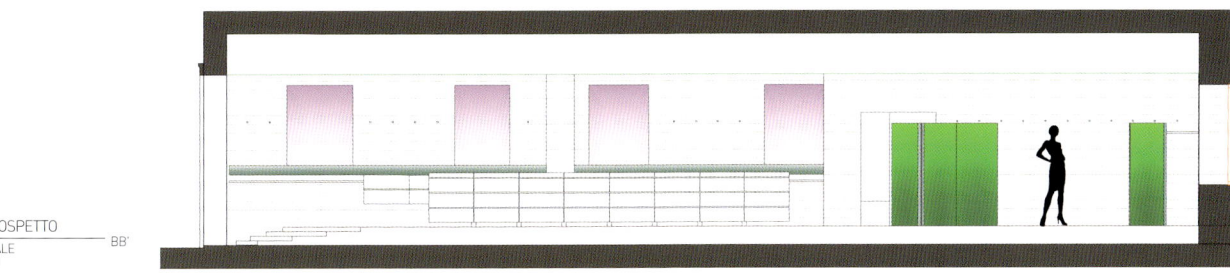

PROSPETTO BB'
SCALE
1:50

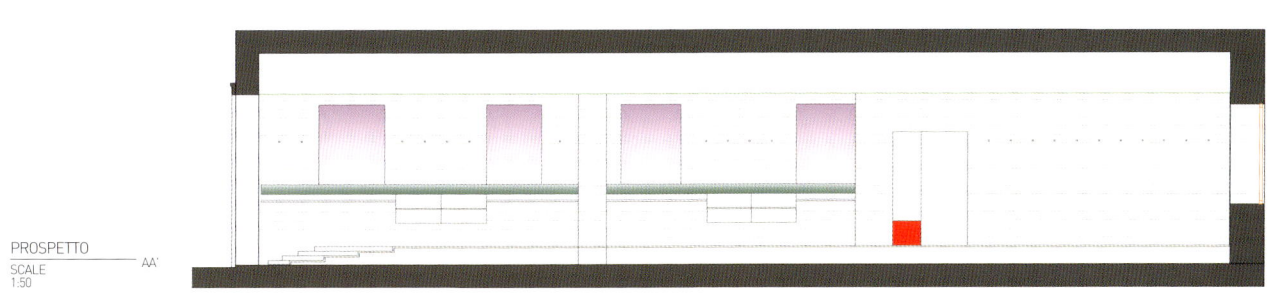

PROSPETTO AA'
SCALE
1:50

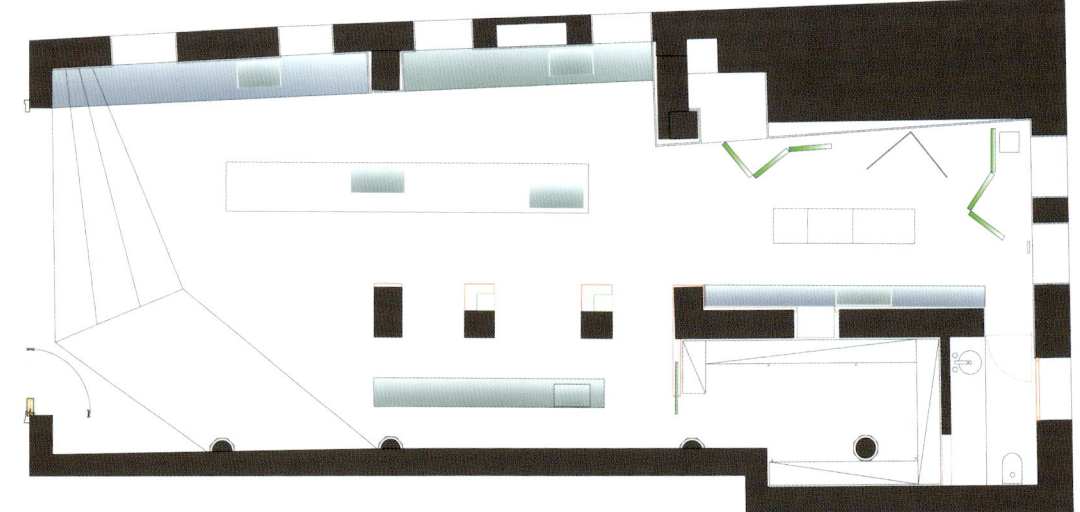

PINTA

SCALE
1:50

mon petit

Location/
Escaldes-Engordany,
Andorra
Design/
MIQUEL MERCE
ARCHITECT +
MSBESTUDI-TALLER

Photography/
Miquel Merce
Arquitecte
Area/
90 sqm

The project is more than a store. Here, the customer brings the product, making it complicit in a new concept where fashion and marketing become both necessity and reality. This opens up endless possibilities for volume and size of the products on display. The first challenge of the design was flexibility - the designers wanted to merchandise both large and small items without having to constantly reorganize the space. The second challenge was complexity: it was important that the space presents only the most unusual and striking children's products in unique ways.

The architects wanted to create a sculptural space that is both useful and critical of the times in which we live. They imagined a sustainable interpretation of the idea 'less is more.' The solution was a space formed through the repetition of reusable elements within a sculptural rhythm beyond a commercial discourse. The idea was to bring spectators into an architectural world where elegance and sustainability go hand in hand, where necessity and art mingle, and where things have many uses. The end purpose is not interior design or decoration, but a lasting change in our society, our ways of thinking and seeing, and a change in our architectural understanding.

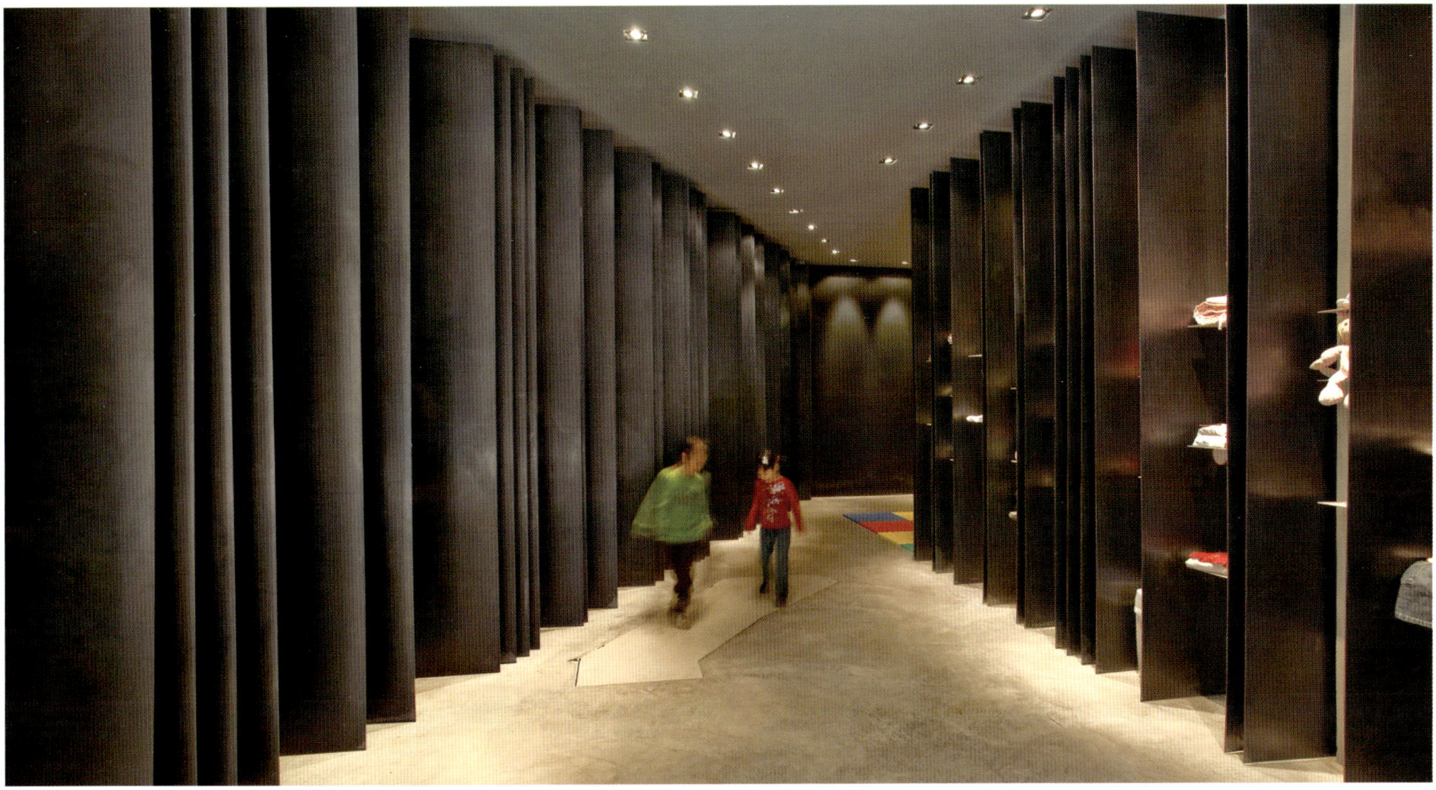

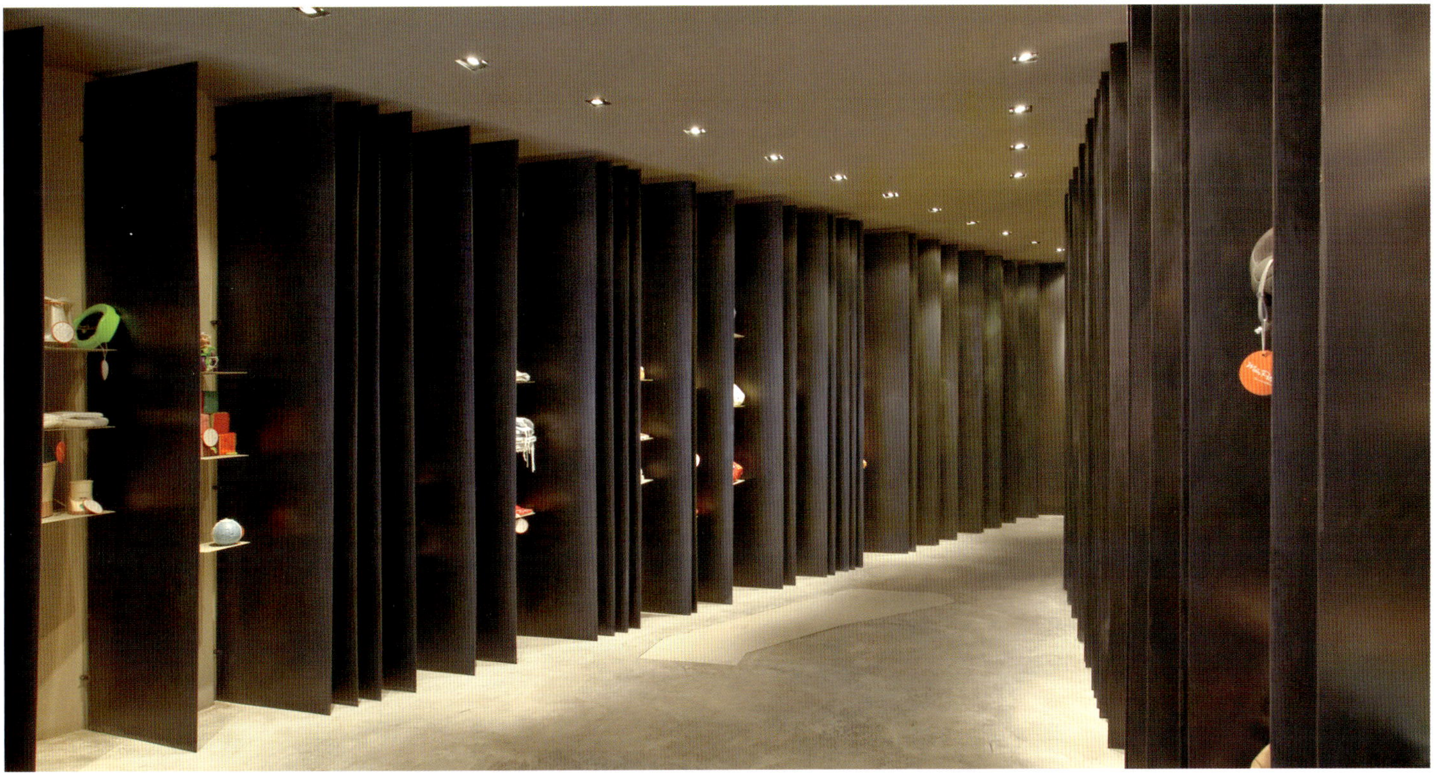

primetime nursery school

Location/
Sao Paulo, Brazil
Design/
studio mk27

Photography/
Nelson Kon
Area/
870.75 sqm

This project is the first Brazilian nursery developed from a program specifically aimed at children aged from zero to three years, based on an exclusive educational concept.

The focus of the project was to incorporate the specificities of this program, seeking adequate creative solutions.

The priority was to conceive of an abstract non-stereotypical space with a playful character that would meet the functional demands of the numerous procedures involved.

Circulation is achieved through ramps. The use of friendly materials, such as the soft floor and operational ergonomics, was fundamental in creating a safe and comfortable environment within which children can explore, learn, and play.

The technical team involved adhered to this same orientation, offering ideal solutions for the best air and water quality, floor heating and balanced lighting.

The landscaping was carefully conceived to guarantee safe interaction for the children.

In addition to using natural materials, the colors yellow, orange and red were selected to create a stimulating atmosphere.

NORTHEAST FACADE
scale 1:200

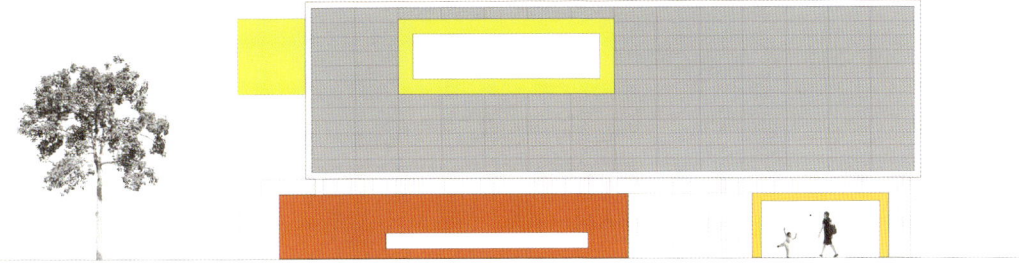

NORTHWEST FACADE
scale 1:200

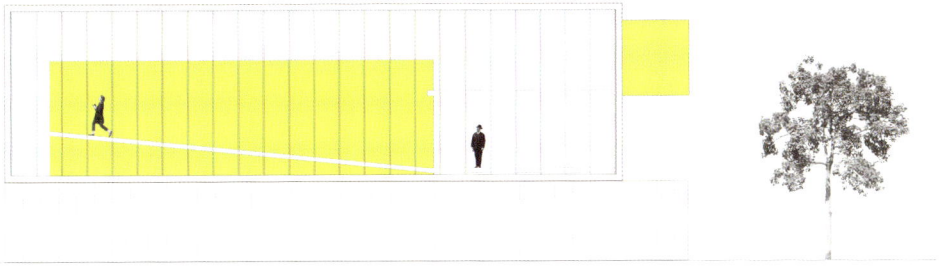

SOUTHEAST FACADE
scale 1:200

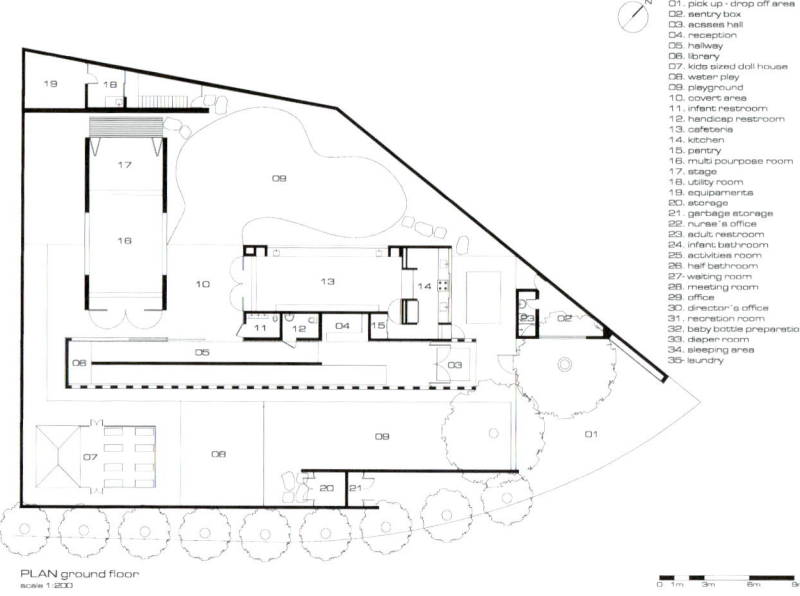

01. pick up - drop off area
02. sentry box
03. access hall
04. reception
05. hallway
06. library
07. kids sized doll house
08. water play
09. playground
10. covert area
11. infant restroom
12. handicap restroom
13. cafeteria
14. kitchen
15. pantry
16. multi pourpose room
17. stage
18. utility room
19. equipaments
20. storage
21. garbage storage
22. nurse's office
23. adult restroom
24. infant bathroom
25. activities room
26. half bathroom
27. waiting room
28. meeting room
29. office
30. director's office
31. recreation room
32. baby bottle preparation
33. diaper room
34. sleeping area
35. laundry

PLAN ground floor
scale 1:200

0 1m   3m   6m   9m

bailly school complex

Location/
Saint-Denis, France
Design/
Mikou Design Studio

Photography/
Florian Kleinefenn
Area/
7,000 sqm

The school complex is aligned on the rue de Bailly like a 'building wall' on one level which is hollowed out and inverted to form the esplanade for the entrance. The esplanade is designed like a space of hospitality and is protected and covered by a playful light shelter. Its brick base is extended in the building interior by a brick path which functions as an interspace area with access to both learning areas and the recreation center. The body of the building as seen from the rue de Bailly shows a glazed screen printed façade which protects the privacy of the children, while interior gardens have transparency into the building space. Each schoolyard is extended visually one level higher by a sloped garden which is made accessible by a ramp connected with the schoolyard. The garden space is important for classrooms on the higher levels and enables children to get fresh air between lessons. As a two level building, the roof was designed using a brightly colored palette so that it is visible to children from the street and to the surrounding high buildings.

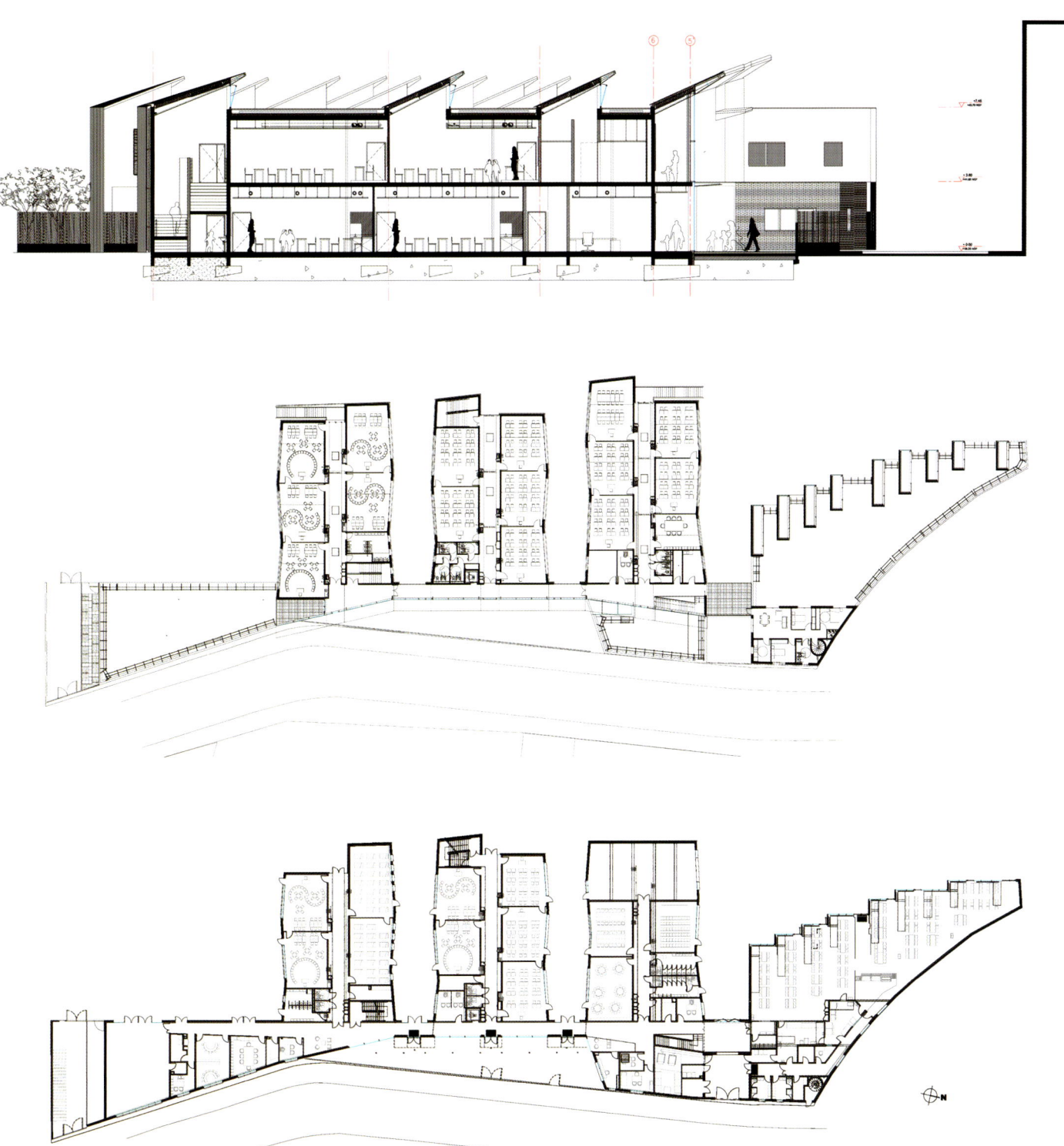

dragen children's house

Location/
Sanderum, Odense,
Denmark
Design/
C. F. Møller Architects

Photography/
Uffe Johansen
Area/
1,100 sqm

This integrated kindergarten is one of the first in Denmark to be built and certified as a passive house, which means that its energy consumption, and thereby its CO_2 footprint, has been drastically reduced. The project largely uses materials with the Nordic Swan Ecolabel, certifying a minimal environmental impact.

The low energy consumption is achieved via increased insulation, dense constructions, well-regulated ventilation and highly efficient heat recycling. The building is so well insulated that the children's activities can cause the temperature in the rooms to rise.

The actual construction process was carried out in as sustainable a manner as possible. Environmentally harmful materials were rejected, while the energy consumption involved in the building process was minimized by utilizing prefabricated elements with brief assembly times.

The fundamental architectural concept is a simple and clear geometric form on two levels, with the children's areas located in the well-lit southern end. The two levels are linked by staircases and ramps which are integrated with the geometry of the architecture, but which are also designed to stimulate and challenge the children's senses and motor skills.

Purpose-built spaces give the children special opportunities: there is a small theater, a motor skills room, and pedagogical kitchens both indoors and out. Another feature is small "loopholes" in the walls, allowing kids to play across the room divisions.

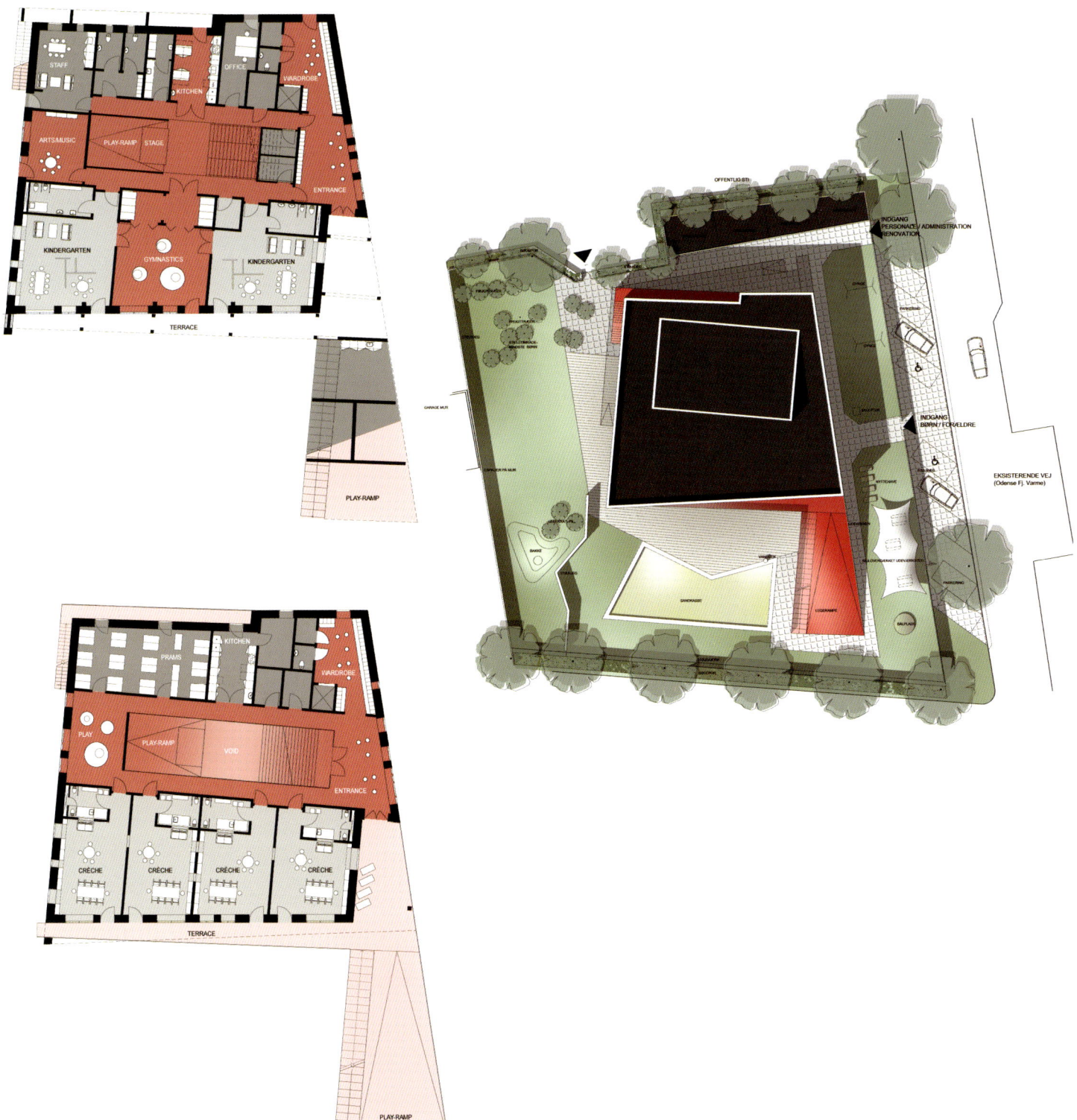

STAFF

OFFICE

KITCHEN

WARDROBE

ARTS/MUSIC   PLAY-RAMP   STAGE

ENTRANCE

KINDERGARTEN   GYMNASTICS   KINDERGARTEN

TERRACE

PLAY-RAMP

PRAMS   KITCHEN

WARDROBE

PLAY   PLAY-RAMP   VOID

ENTRANCE

CRÈCHE   CRÈCHE   CRÈCHE   CRÈCHE

TERRACE

PLAY-RAMP

GARAGE MUR

OFFENTLIG STI

INDGANG
PERSONALE / ADMINISTRATION
RENOVATION

INDGANG
BØRN / FORÆLDRE

EKSISTERENDE VEJ
(Odense Fj. Varme)

SANDKASSE

LEGERAMPE

family box

Location/
Beijing, China
Design/
crossboundaries
architects

Photography/
Chaoying Yang
Area/
5,625 sqm

Family Box is something between an indoor playground and a kindergarten for children up to twelve years old, but it also accommodates their parents' needs. It hosts a variety of activities - from swimming and games to various classes ranging from music, dancing, and crafting to cooking. Furthermore, it has a large playground, a reading area, and a generous café area. Located on the outside corner of a park, the building's placed within a natural environment which enhances the visibility of the building.

The box locations are meant to break the rigid layout of the concrete columns, which are also camouflaged by a series of arches that gives a different rhythm to the environment. Visually, the common areas are treated with low contrast finishes in order to enhance and balance the space and equipment for the children.

The glass façade encloses all of the functions like a skin, following the given building perimeter. It is printed with a pattern which was developed out of simple single-line drawings made by children. The childrens' drawings were modified into a pattern where the graphic motif was reversed: the background is white-translucent and the drawing is transparent. From far away, the objects on the façade are recognizable, indicating the building's function and its relation to children's recreation and fun.

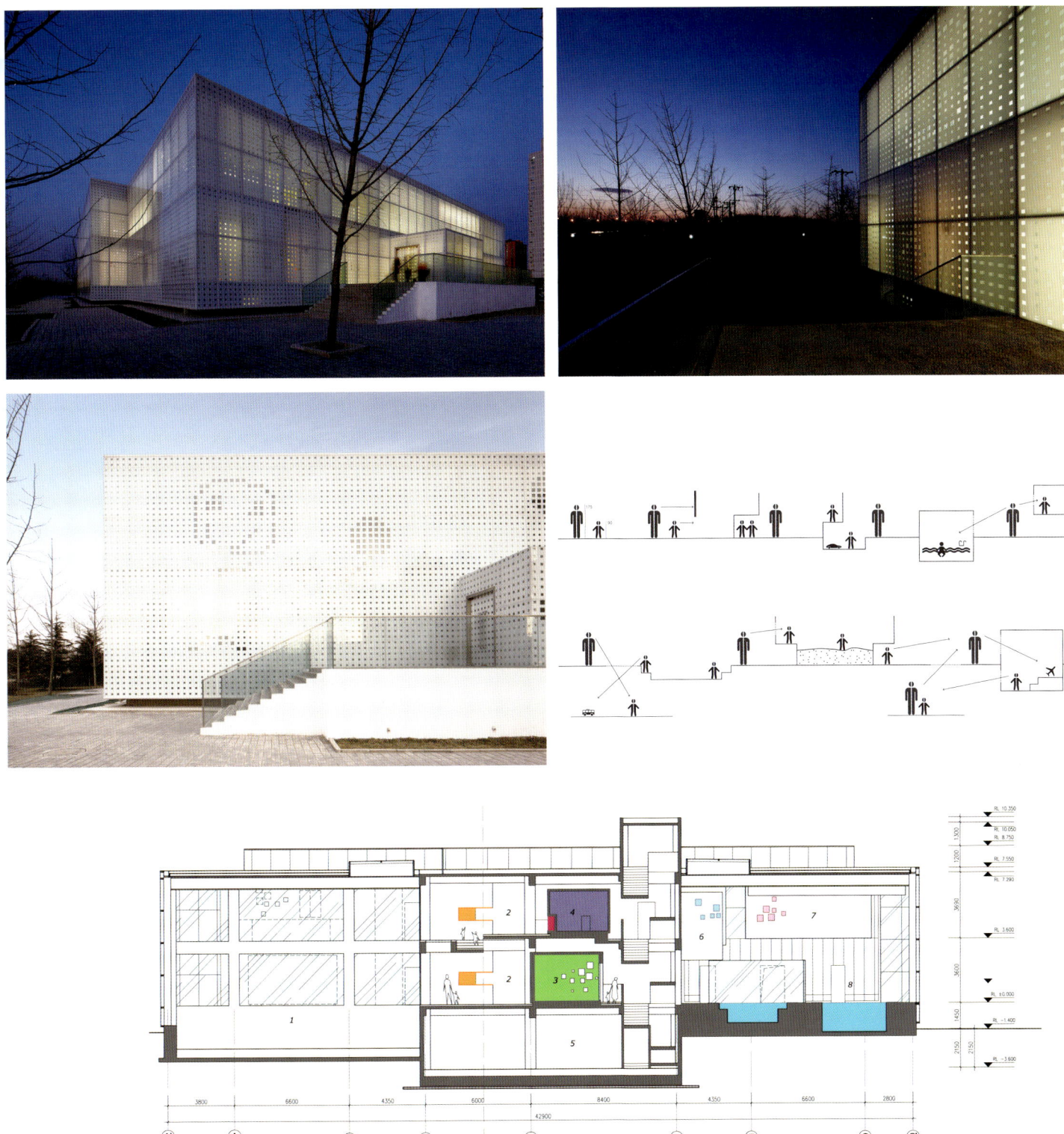

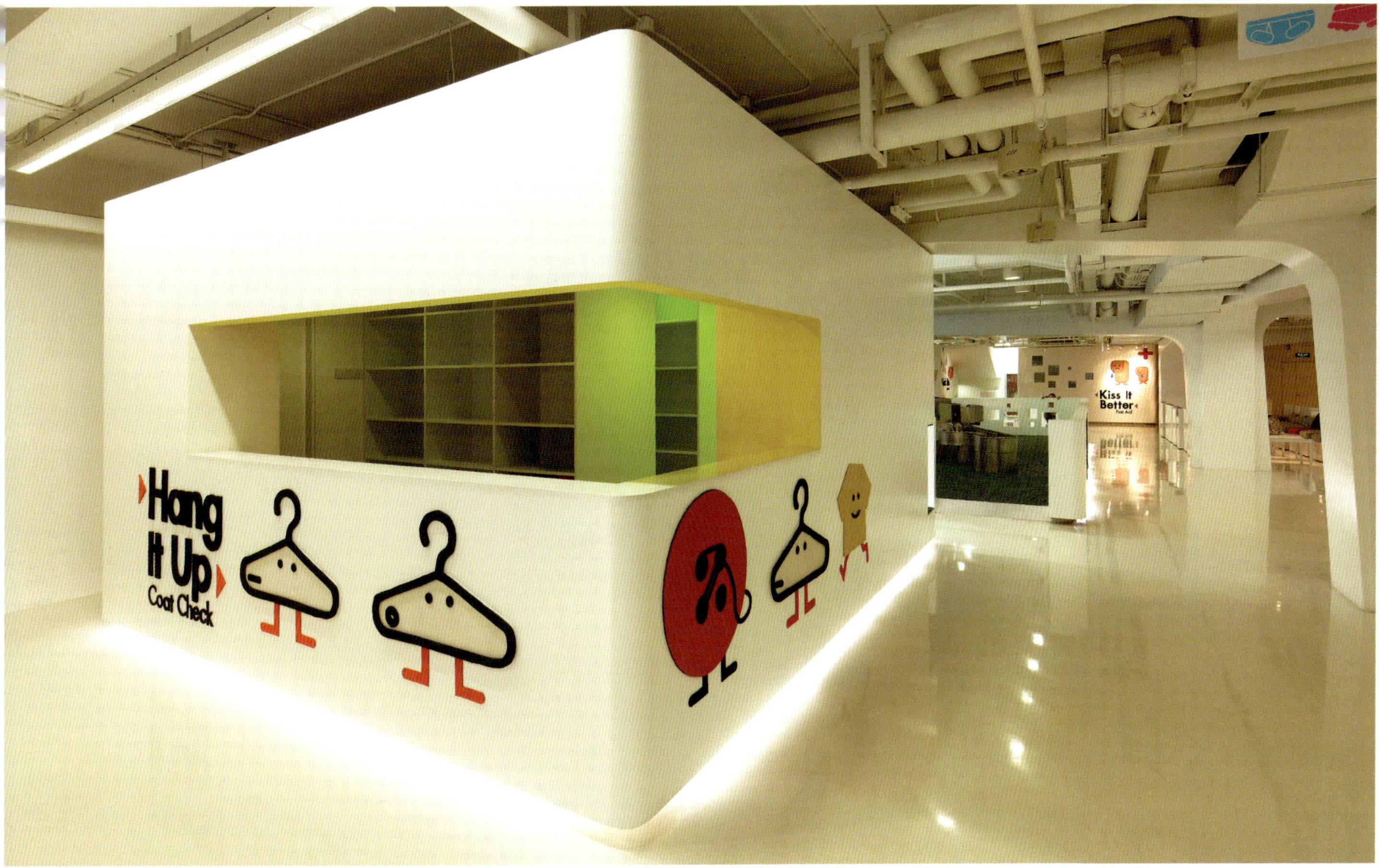
Hang It Up
Coat Check
Kiss It Better

No
Photography

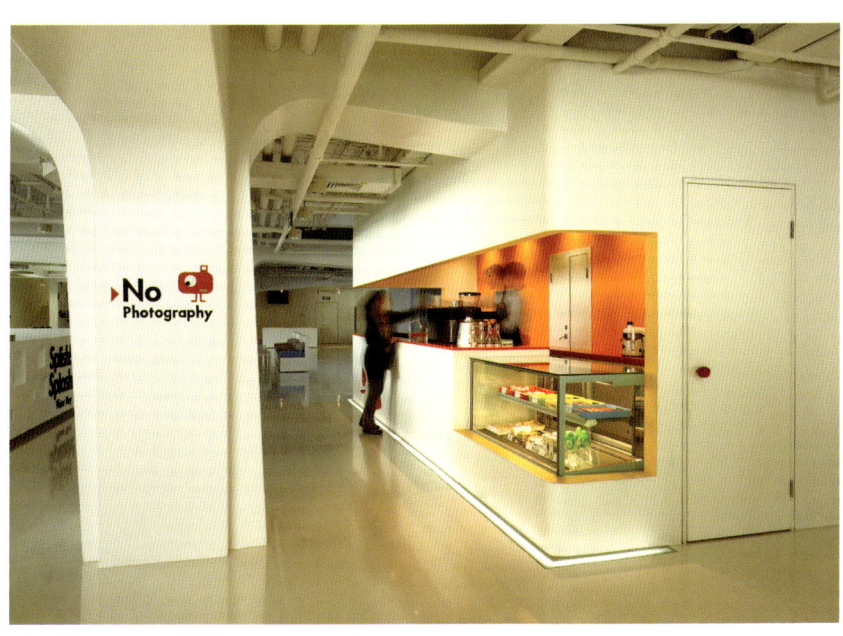

Legend - 图例:

1 Cafeteria - 简餐区
2 Children Play Area - 儿童游戏区
3 Kitchen - 厨房
4 Managers Office - 主管办公室
5 Offices - 办公区
6 Meeting Room - 会议室
7 Finance Office - 财务部
8 Girls Locker Room - 女更衣室
9 Boys Locker Room - 男更衣室
10 Restrooms - 洗手间
11 Storage Room - 储藏室
12 Equipment Room - 设备间

Legend - 图例:

1 Reception - 前台
2 Coat Check - 衣帽间
3 Water Play - 儿童戏水区
4 First Aid - 医务室
5 Boys Locker Room - 男更衣室
6 Girls Locker Room - 女更衣室
7 Baby Pool - 婴儿泳池
8 Main Pool - 游泳池
9 Cafe Bar - 咖啡吧
10 Playframe - 攀登架
11 Little Chefs - 儿童厨房
12 Restrooms - 洗手间
13 Mini Mart - 儿童超市
14 Buggy Parking - 童车存放

272

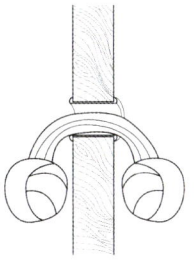

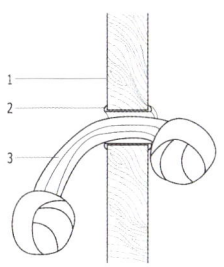

1 door panel, coated white
2 stainless steel ring, 30 mm diameter
3 knotted knob, artificial leather in different colors

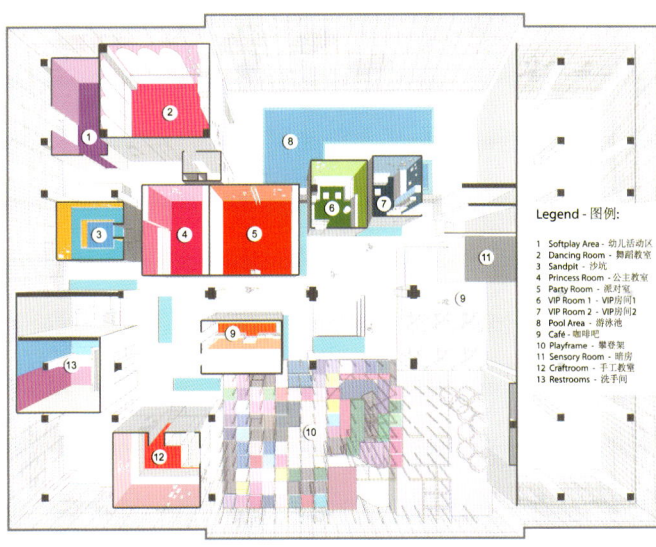

Legend - 图例:

1 Softplay Area - 幼儿活动区
2 Dancing Room - 舞蹈教室
3 Sandpit - 沙坑
4 Princess Room - 公主教室
5 Party Room - 派对室
6 VIP Room 1 - VIP房间1
7 VIP Room 2 - VIP房间2
8 Pool Area - 游泳池
9 Café - 咖啡吧
10 Playframe - 攀登架
11 Sensory Room - 唱房
12 Craftroom - 手工教室
13 Restrooms - 洗手间

lucinahaven - day care centre, taulov

Location/
Taulov, Denmark
Design/
CEBRA

Photography/
CEBRA
Area/
1,200 sqm

Like a flower with its seed grains surrounded by petals, CEBRA has logically arranged the common room of the institution to be a central area with access from shared rooms as well as the entryway. In this way all functions are closely connected to the common room and to each other; at the same time this arrangement reflects an architectural interpretation of the diagram of functions. The arrangement is not only functional, but also symbolic; community is a central point in the spirit and design of the day care center.

As mentioned, the use of hexagons is meant to create recognition. In combination with the use of different colors, a strong identity is created inside each hexagon.

The building design intends to strengthen the identity and community by means of the arrangement of rooms and use of colors in the building. The materials used for the façades and roof are in line with the desire to create variation and diversity in the design. The individual parts of the unified whole are members of the same family but just as unique as each member in a family. In this way, the designers have created a more balanced architectural picture in line with a desire to work in more educational and challenging ways.

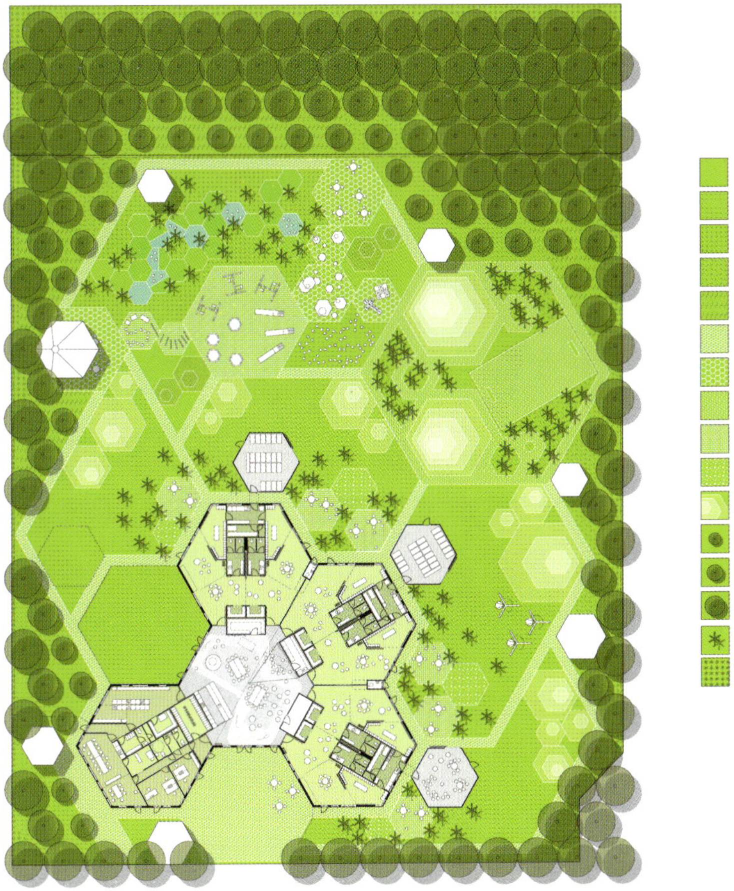

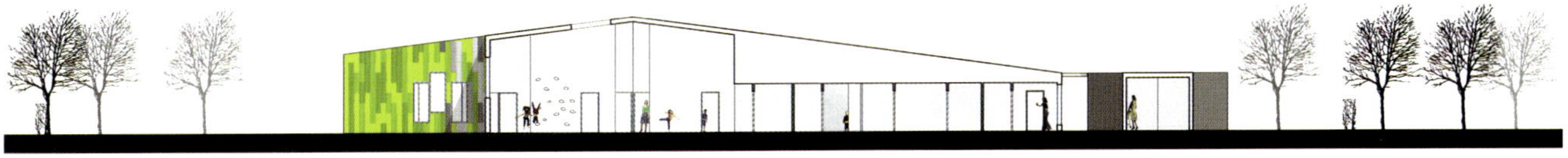

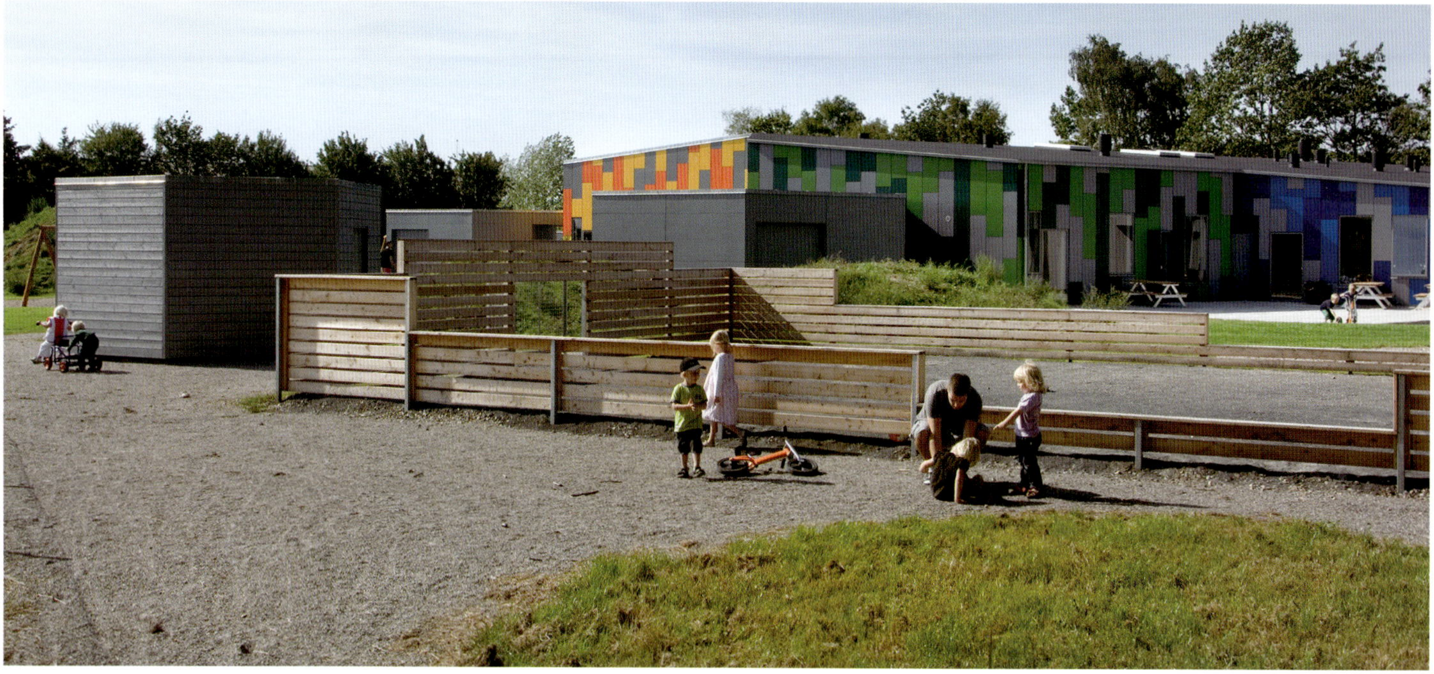

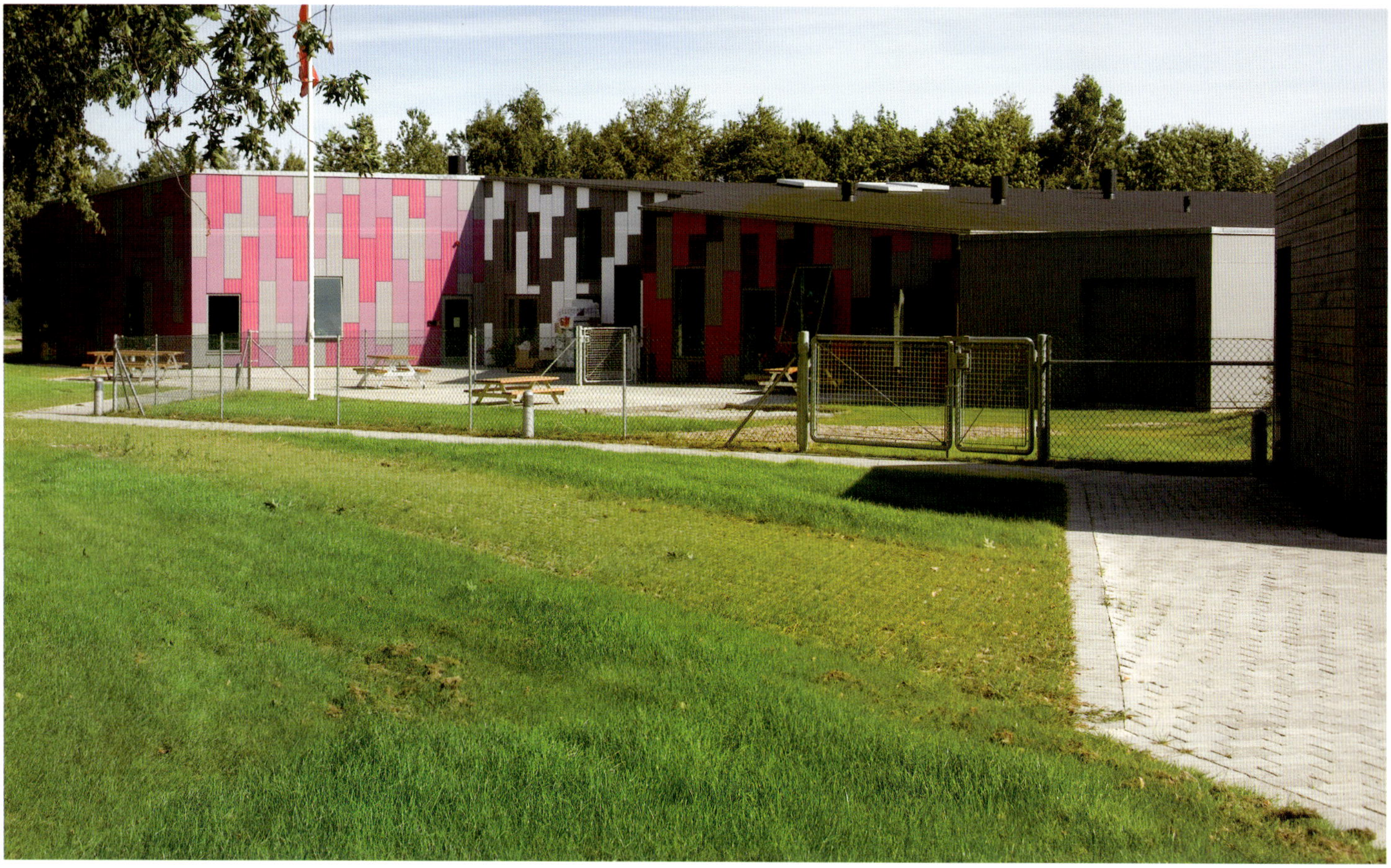

katarina frankopan kindergarten

Location/
Krk, Island Of Krk,
Croatia
Design/
Randić Turato
Architects

Photography/
Robert Leš, Želimir
Gržančić
Area/
2,379 sqm

This new kindergarten on the island of Krk in Croatia is located on the northeastern border of the town within a stretch of tourist apartments and shopping malls. In an uninviting neighborhood, the kindergarten shape is enclosed and introverted, surrounded by soaring stone walls. Inside of the kindergarten, building units are combined with open gardens that are placed next to pedestrian avenues. Due to the rather small area of the kindergarten, the classrooms for the youngest children are located on the first floor of the building. The site is defined by halls, or "kale" - a local name for the small streets characteristic of town historic centers. Within the kindergarten site, these paths interact with the typography and aim both upward and downward. Eastern and western entrances to the kindergarten are used by children, employees, and guests, while service entrances at the northern and southern gates open the kindergarten to a small, sunny playground. In the center of the kindergarten there is a small square, or piazza, which is used for events and celebrations. Besides seven units for older children and four units for youngsters, the school also has an assembly room for sports, recreation, and dance classes.

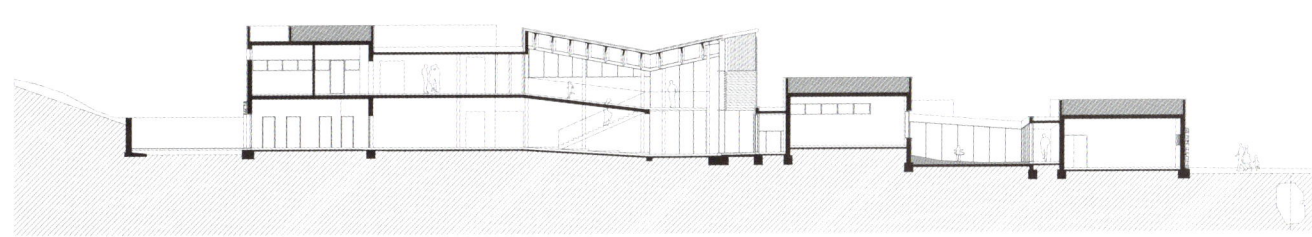

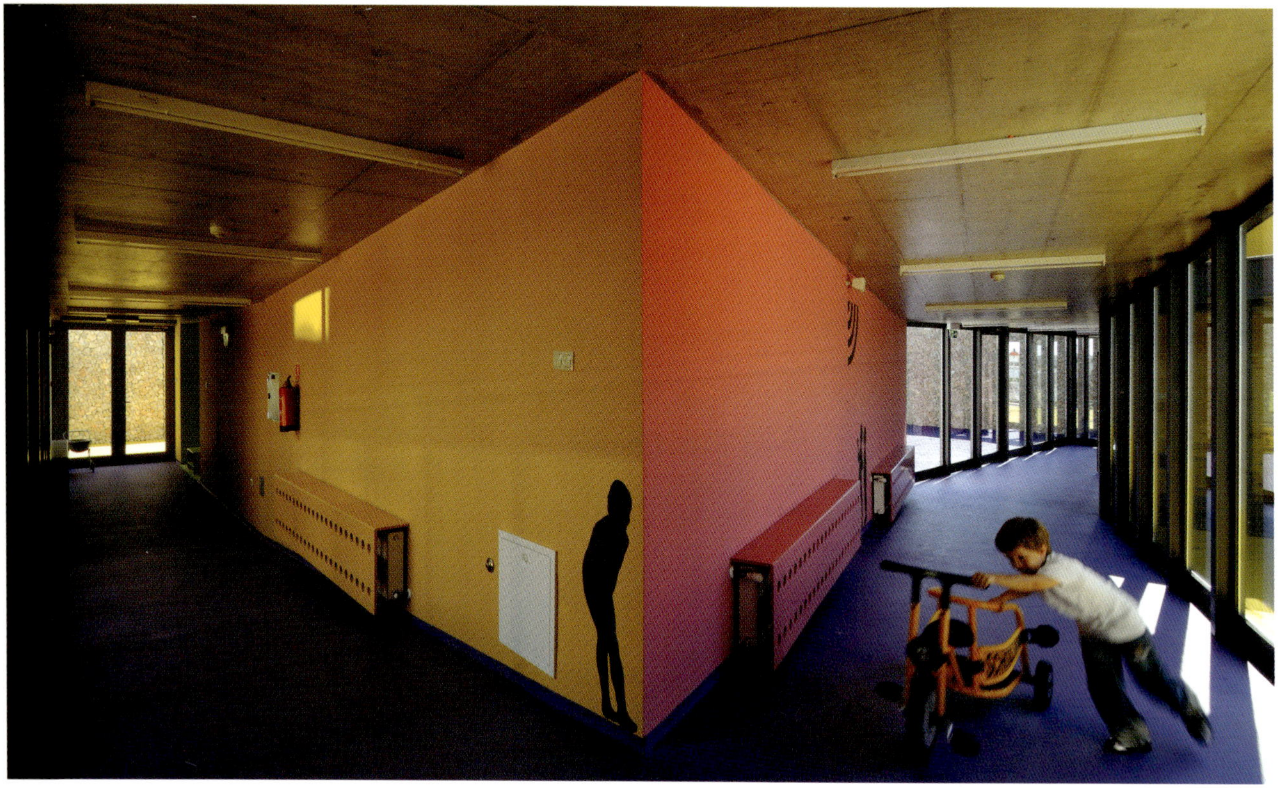

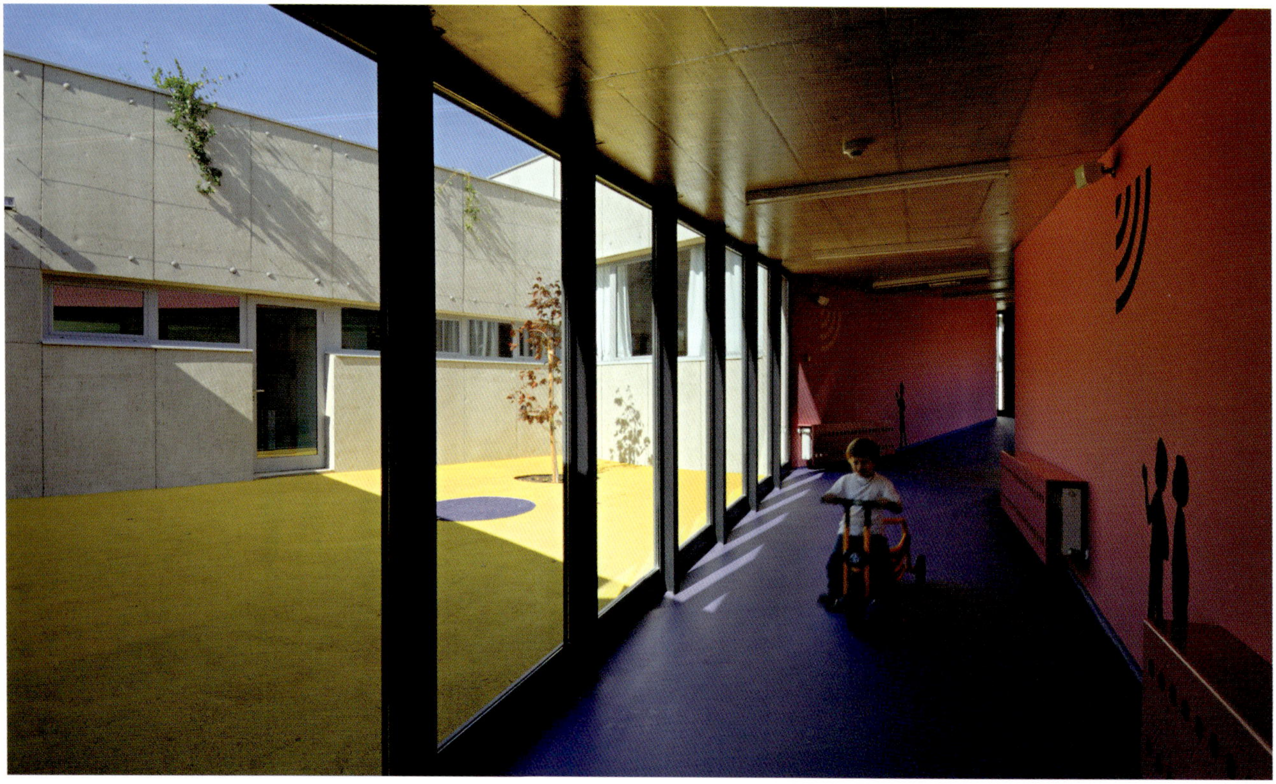

day care centre - bernts have

Location/
Holbæk, Denmark
Design/
Henning Larsen
Architects

Photography/
Courtesy of Henning
Larsen Architects
Area/
1,350 sqm

The day care center has room for 56 children aged 0-3 and 80 children aged 3-6. Situated on the highest point in Bernts Have, the building with its large green roof wedges into the hill while opening up towards the landscape, the sun and a playground to the south.

The simple, minimalistic building is made of glass and wood. It is shaped as a longitudinal section containing the nursery in one wing, with children aged 3-6 in the other wing. A human resources department is housed in the central area and connects the two wings. In the "climate zone," a plant and herb bed was planted for children aged 3-6 and large flowerpots were planted for the nursery.

The climate zone functions as protection from the sun and as a supplement to the preheating and heating of the wings. It is an unheated supplementary area that is very impacted by the changing seasons, making it possible for children to play outside without wearing gloves.

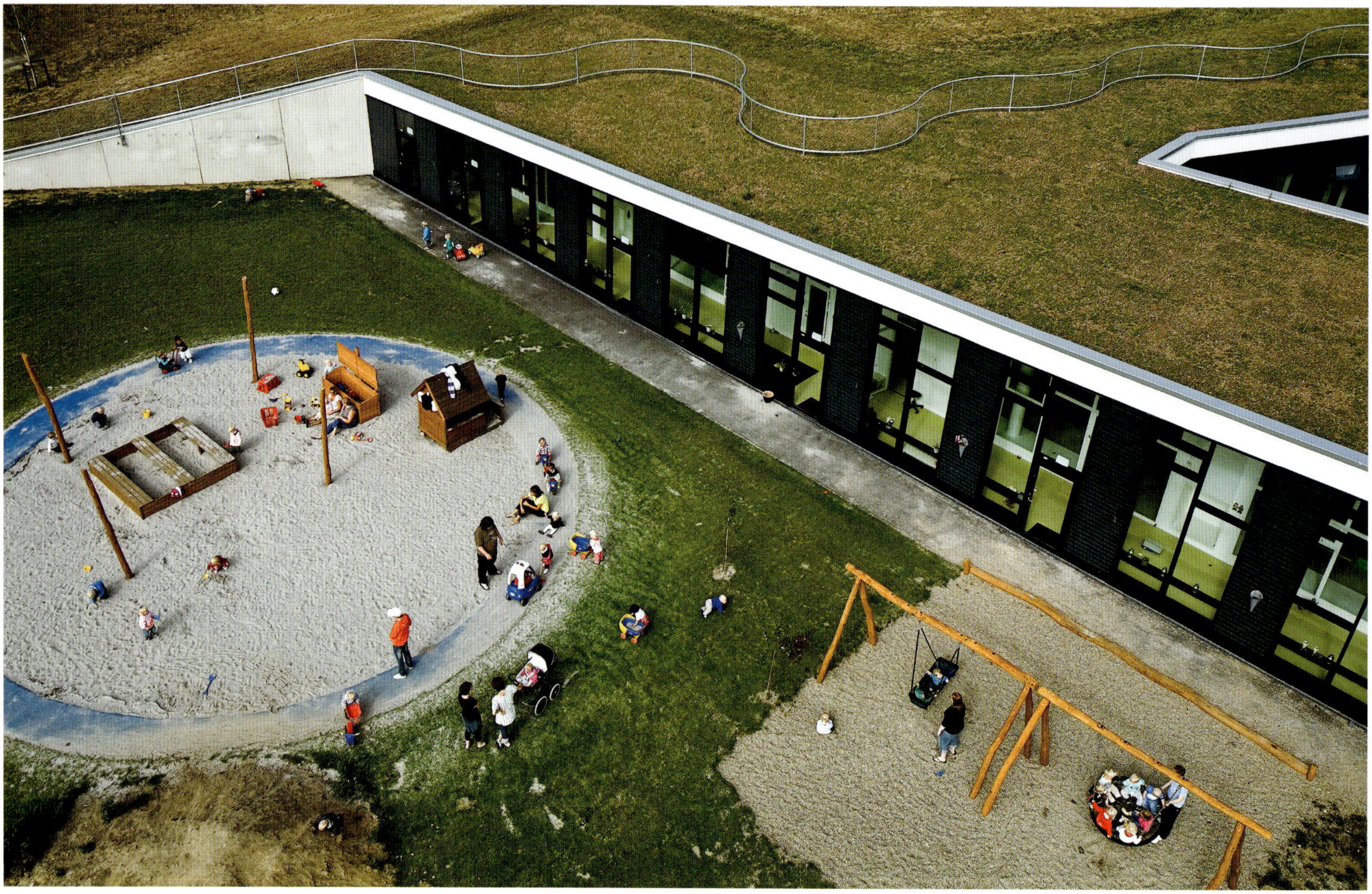

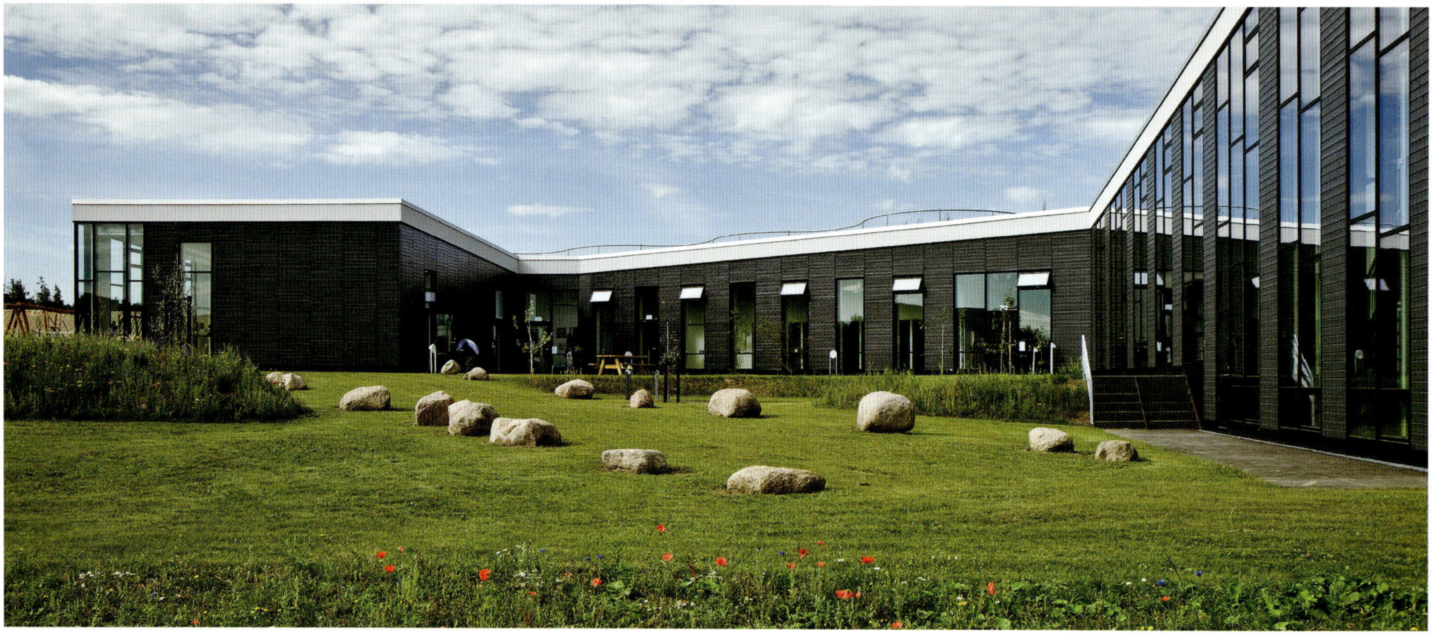

søgaard school

Location/
Gentofte, Denmark
Design/
CEBRA

Photography/
Adam Mørk
Area/
25,148 + 52,584 sqft. new
building and rebuilding

Søgaard School is a school expansion project in the municipality of Gentoftes which CEBRA developed in cooperation with the students and those involved in the school. Søgaard School is a special school for socially challenged children with general learning disabilities. The project is based on the school's value program and the needs expressed during workshops with staff and parents. It has been a goal to reinvent the scattered buildings of the school and integrate them into a coherent structure that enhances the natural opportunities for collaboration across school departments. The architectural intent of the project is to provide elements that are linked with the neighborhood and its scale and characteristics. The new building is therefore divided into sections in the plan as a duplication of the existing building's footprint. The sections are shifted in relation to each other and vary in size. Each section has its own pitched roof - a recognizable form in the surrounding residential neighborhood, and by letting the pitched roofs have the same direction as the existing buildings, a new unified villa is created.

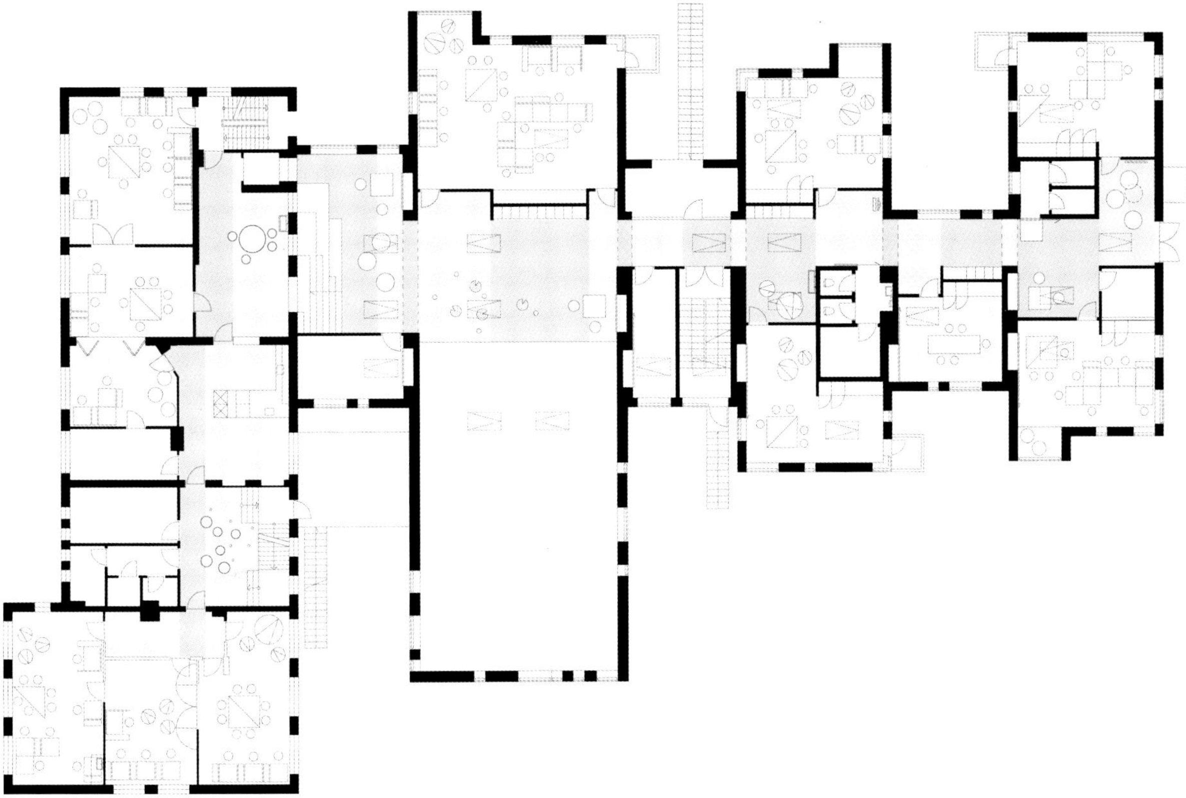

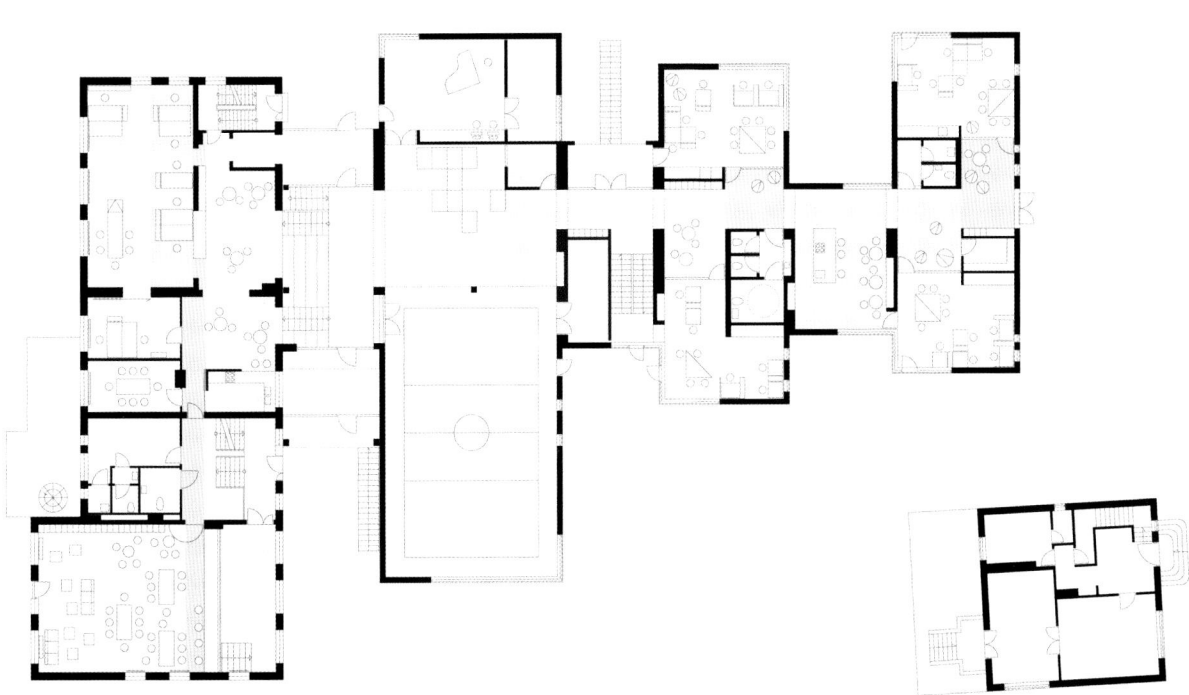

fuji kindergarten

Location/
Tachikawa, Tokyo, Japan
Design/
Tezuka Architects

Photography/
Katsuhisa Kida/
FOTOTECA
Area/
1,094.83 sqm

This kindergarten building is used entirely opened up to the surrounding natural environment for two thirds of the year. This has already been tested, because the building was built in two phases and so half of it has been in use since summer. Therefore, the basic state of this building is with the windows open. The sliding doors directly follow the distorted oval shape. With the ground surface and room interiors at almost the same level, there is no sense of having to take off your shoes, and the distinction between where the outside stops and the inside starts doesn't apply. This kindergarten is an outdoor corridor. Going to each place is like taking off your shoes to visit a house. There are no slippers needed in our school. Even in a residence or a workplace, there are no slippers for the general public. Even in the cold of winter, bare feet won't be cold with the stove-type heating which has been installed throughout the building. This type of heating doesn't have the unnatural heat of floor heating that uses electricity or warm water; instead, it is a microclimate that envelops the entire building.

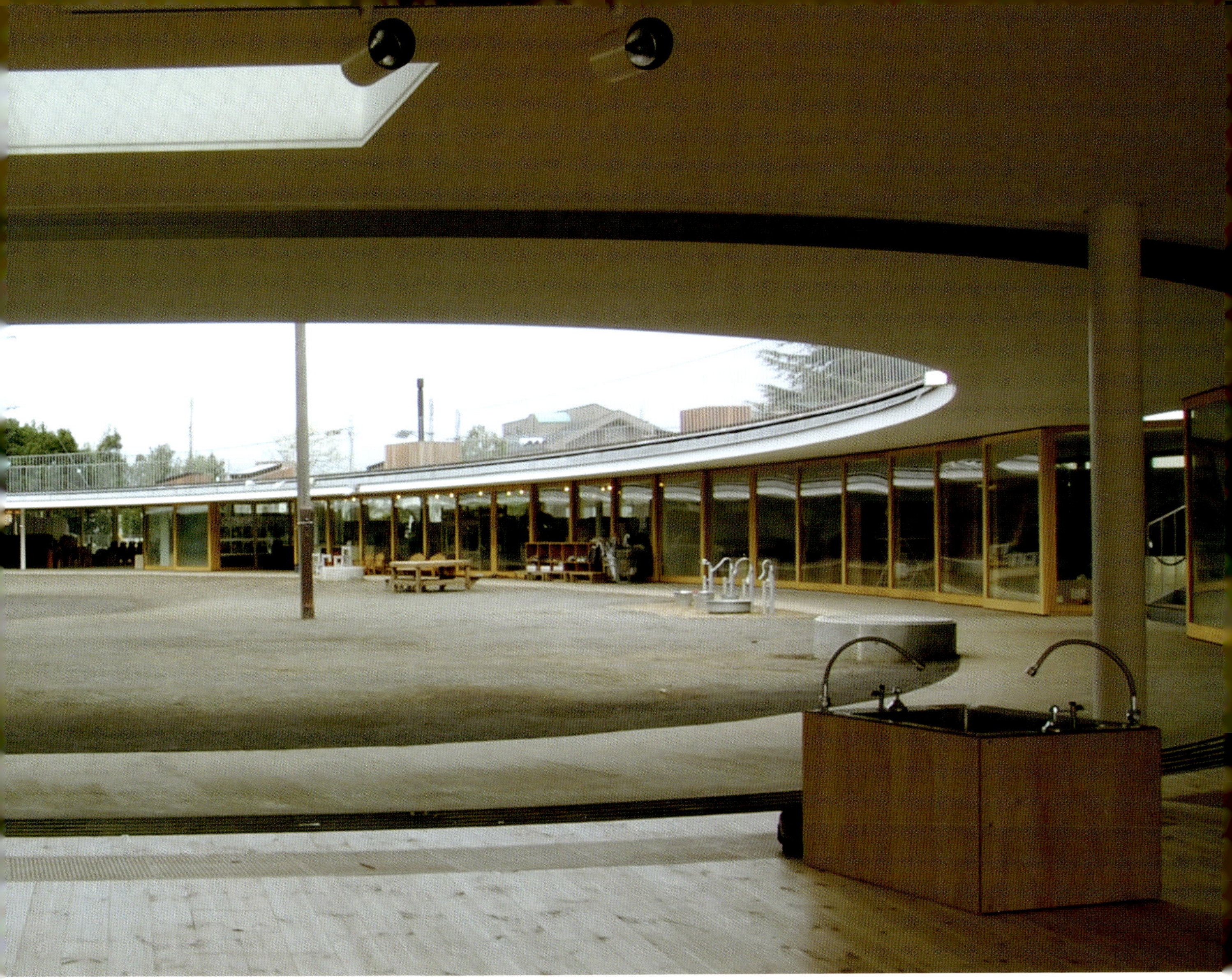

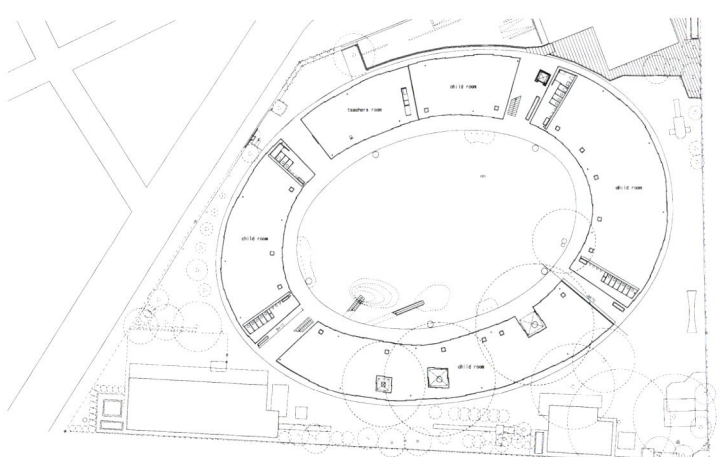

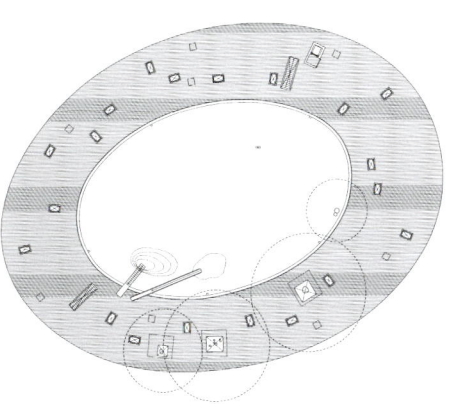

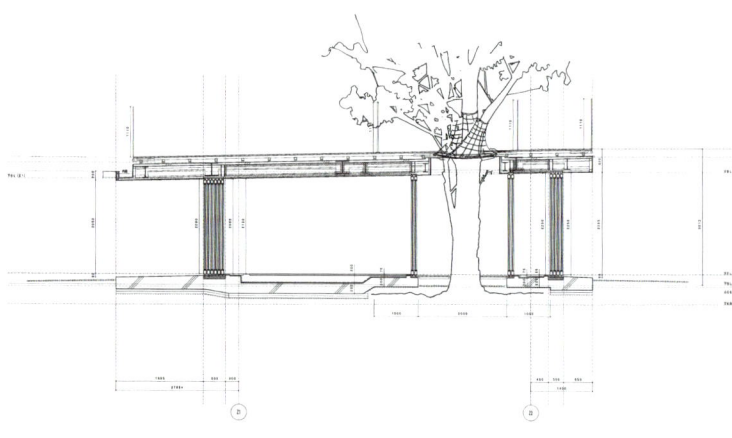

social kindergarden el porvenir

Location/
Bosa, Bogota, Colombia
Design/
Giacarlo Mazzanti

Photography/
Rodrigo Davila, Aereas
Fotos Rudolf, Iwan
Baan
Area/
2,100 sqm

The project was planned as an adaptable system able to respond to diverse situations, like the topographic and urban elements as well as the program goals of DABS.

Based on the construction of an adaptable system, modules are grouped and purposes can be mixed according to the site, solar conditions, topography, and events.

The project seeks to build a model based on the combination of recognizable units: the structure, a rotated-module classroom (the children who enter and exit the school experience), and public use modules (adults). The designers aim to pursue the production of a unique system that can develop a more complex organizational structure that is more adaptive than the sum of the parts.

The interior elements of the structure belong to the children in their classrooms; the design is colorful and youthful with defined sub-spaces for small groups that want privacy. Outside of the building are spaces for public use, such as administration, meetings, etc.

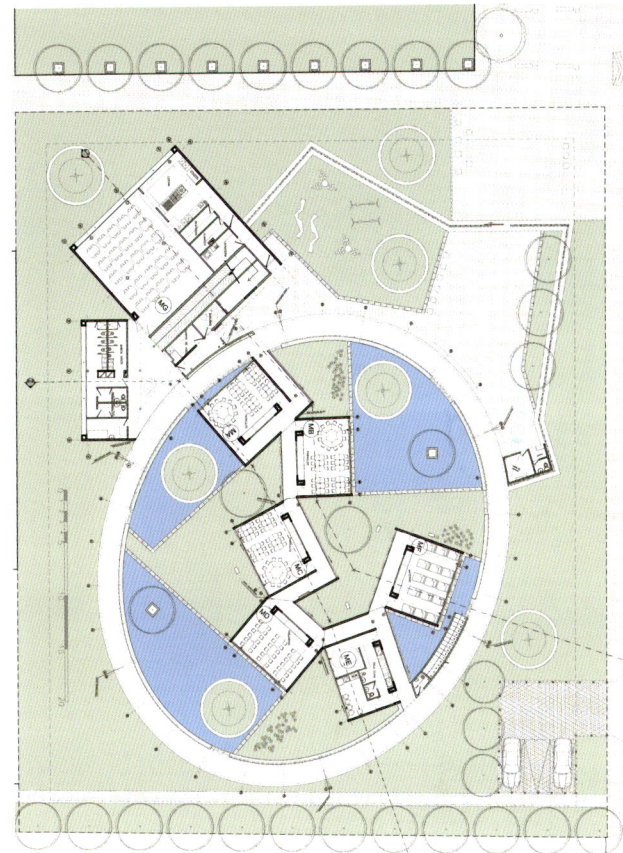

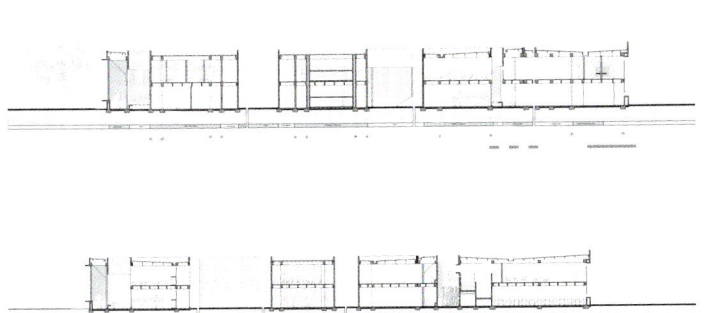

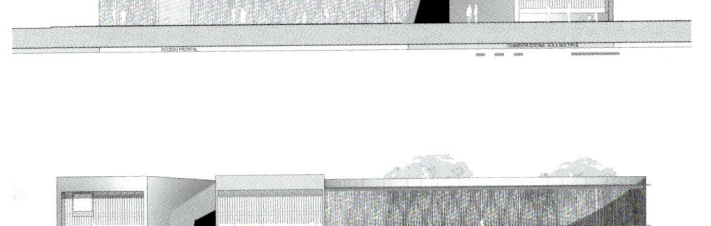

monster's footprint in the citizen square

Location/
Shenzhen, China
Design/
MAD architects

Photography/
MAD office
Area/
120 sqm

MAD architects' design for the Urbanism\Architecture Shenzhen & Hong Kong Bi-city Biennial, the Monster's Footprint debuted in the Citizen Square of Shenzhen. It is a sunken space shade of a giant footprint, paved by pink EPDM material, functioning as the playground for the citizens in the city center.

Shenzhen is a village turned city overnight. Enchanted by the burgeoning power of economic development, the city center is filled with extensive, yet indistinctive, icons. The coarse scale and preposterous symbolism of these icons detaches them from real people's daily experiences and robs them of significance. The Monster's Footprint attempts to change this very surreal reality, and offer a new space of possibility for city dwellers to find their own freedom and joy within Citizen Square.

X=96 X=97 X=98 X=99 X=100 X=101 X=102 X=103 X=104 X=105 X=106 X=107 X=108 X=109 X=110 X=111 X=112 X=113 X=114 X=115 X=116 X=117 X=118 X=119 X=120 X=121 X=122 X=123 X=124
Y=-27
Y=-28
Y=-29
Y=-30
Y=-31
Y=-32
Y=-33
Y=-34
Y=-35
Y=-36
Y=-37
Y=-38
Y=-39
Y=-40
Y=-41
Y=-42
Y=-43
Y=-44
Y=-45
Y=-46
Y=-47
Y=-48

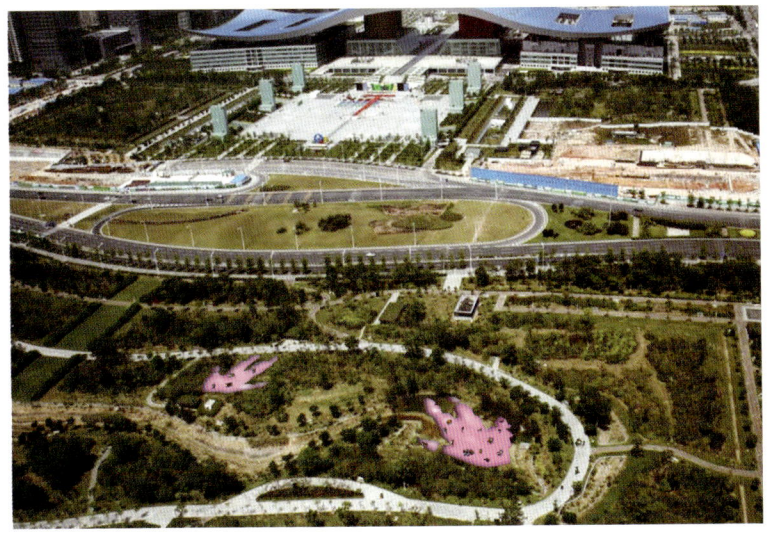

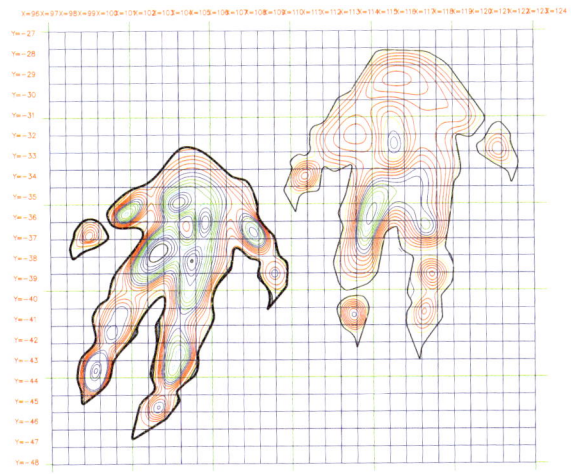

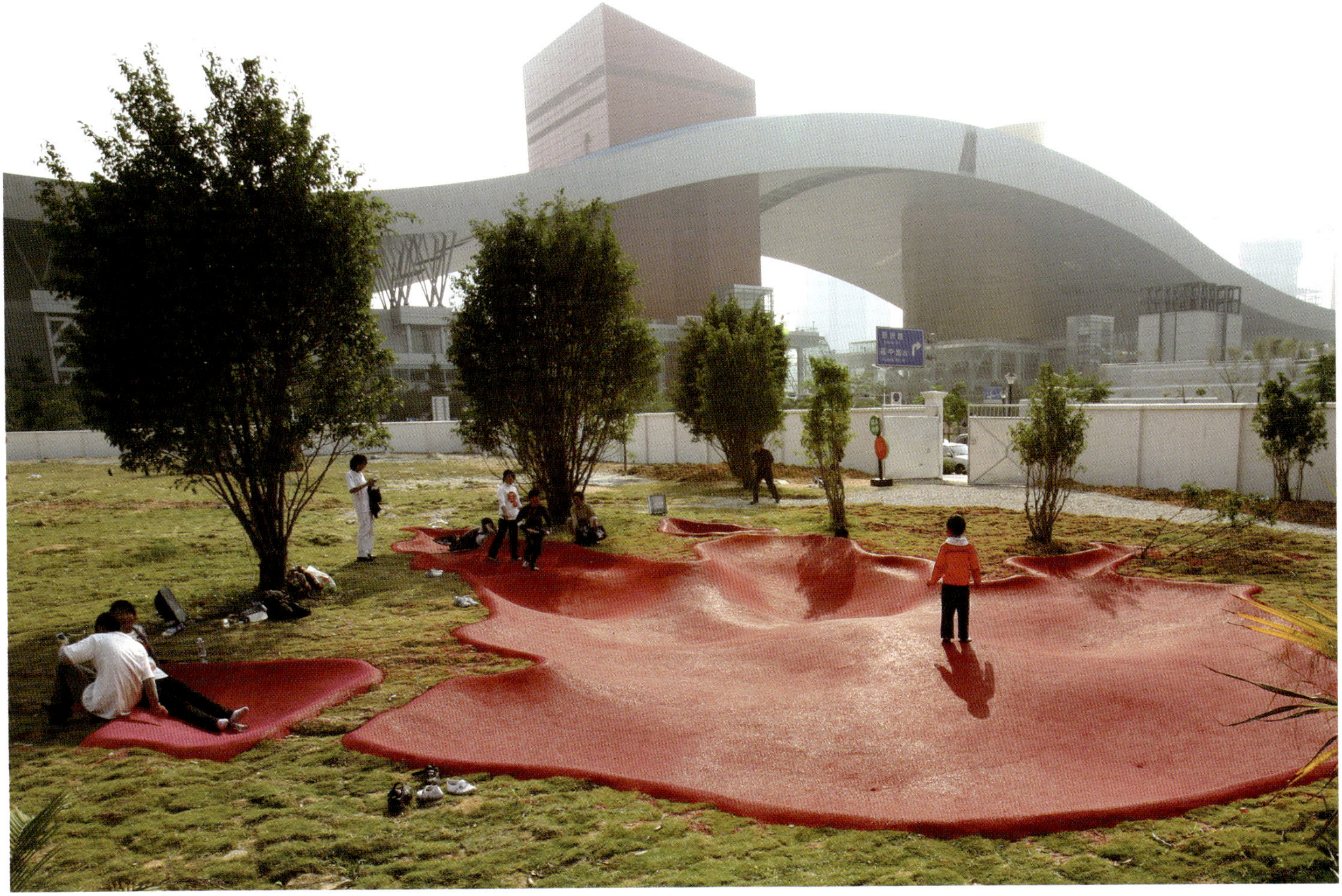

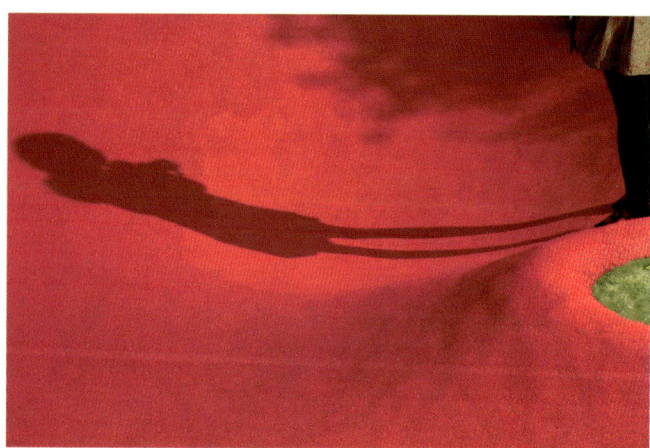

Section A-A

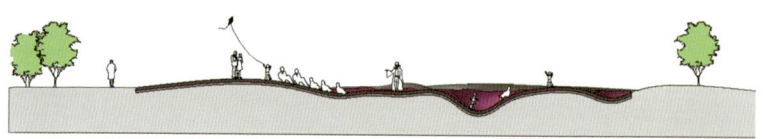

Section B-B

Section B-B

public playground

Location/
Sint-Jobskade,
Rotterdam, the
Netherlands
Design/
Bekkering Adams
architecten

Photography/
DigiDaan
Area/
1,500 sqm

The design for a new space encompassing a school, sports facilities, and a public square is a pilot project resulting from research undertaken in 2007 on the potential of playgrounds for the public domain. The square is located on the Mullerpier in Rotterdam. It is a schoolyard for the primary school nearby, as well a public square. In the vicinity of the square are buildings with different functions, such as a home for elderly people, a business center, a theater, and housing. In the original urban plan, the square was a green oasis in the neighborhood. The reality was an empty plane of asphalt. Because there was no attraction, it was hardly ever used by the neighborhood. Also, schoolchildren found very little variety for play activities.

The new proposal was set up in cooperation with the school, parents, and people from the neighborhood. The plan includes the improved sports square where older children can play more competitive sports, and a smaller square where all children, especially younger children, can play safely in a diverse way.

Around the square is a green hedge, which together with the green rubber underground with a pattern of leaves, relates to the theme of "a secret garden." This was one of the demands for the projects envisioned by the main participants in the project. Today, the playground offers green shelter and many types of play space. The final result of the project encourages children to play in innovative ways, while adults can use the square as an outdoor neighborhood space.

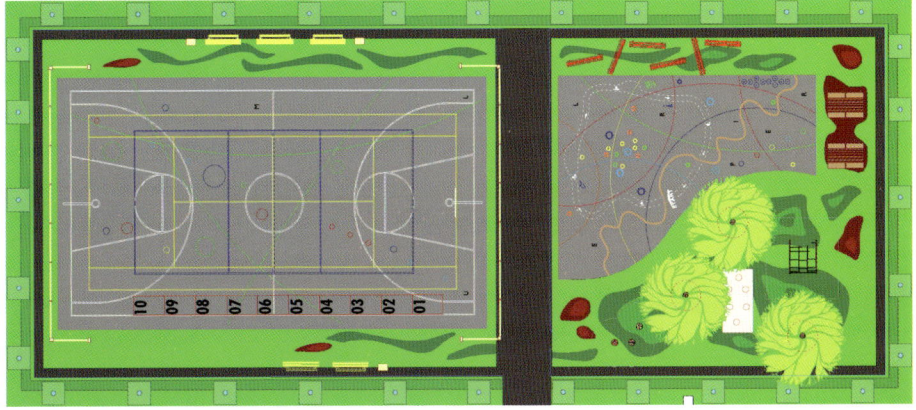

index

70°N arkitektur
Norway
www.70n.no

70°N arkitektur works with all kinds of design issues from small object design, exhibition and set design, and housing projects to area planning and urban design, as well as lecturing and teaching.

70°N arkitektur develops projects, thinking and methods within the whole spectra of architectural practice: buildings, landscape, urbanism, processes/development, theories/ideas, communication/participation and exhibitions. Experimentation and dialogue are fundamental in 70°N arkitektur's practice. Ever since the office was established, architectural competitions have been an important arena for continuous reformulation and development of the office's practice as a reflective, critical and committed approach to architecture and planning, and a vital position in the public debate concerning architecture, urban development and regional planning.

P028-033

AFKS architects
Finland
www.afks.fi

The office was established in 1998 by Jari Frondelius and Jaakko Keppo, after winning the architectural competition of Korso church and parish center. Today there are three partners in the office: Jari Frondelius, Jaakko Keppo and Juha Salmenperä. All together the office employs six professionals.

Our goal is to create projects with rhythm and purpose. We seek architectural vision which originates from the particular features found in every design task and its environment. We attempt to create places that are meaningful, which we believe to be the mission of architecture. We examine the varied scope of building through trial and error to try to find a solution that fulfills the project needs and creates the final form that reaches the emotional level.

P076-081

Alberto Campo Baeza
Spain
www.campobaeza.com

Alberto CAMPO BAEZA was born in Valladolid (1946), first saw the light in CADIZ (Spain) and the Architecture in Madrid (Degree 1971) P.H.D. in 1982. He became Chairman and Professor of Design in Madrid in 1986.

He has built a selected number of very precise buildings and his work has been extensively awarded. A book of his collected writings "LA IDEA CONSTRUIDA" is now in its 7th edition and some monographs on his work have been published. His work has been published in most major architectural magazines in the world and he has been exhibited in many major cities.

P010-015

Alejandro Muñoz Miranda
Spain
www.alejandromunozmiranda.com

Alejandro Muñoz Miranda was recently selected for the exhibition of Young Architects in Spain, organized by the Ministry of Housing and coordinated by Jesús Aparicio Guisado for the Exhibition Hall of Las Arquerías de Nuevos Ministerios in Madrid (2008), the Graduate School of Architecture, Planning and Preservation of Columbia University in New York (2009) and La Casa del Principado de Asturias in Brussels (2010).

The firm's most outstanding recent constructions include the Headquarters of the Granada Business Confederation, the New Syndicate Headquarters in Granada, the Rehabilitation of the Street Gran Vía de Colón, the Project Management of the Boulevard in Avenida de la Constitución in Granada and a house in Barranco del Abogado in Granada.

P112-119

Andrea Tognon Architecture
Italy
www.atognon.com

Andrea Tognon founded his research laboratory for architecture and communication design in 2002 in New York. The office combines practice with research, using a multidisciplinary approach and drawing upon a network of creative, technical and engineering firms for the execution of different aspects of the design and realization processes. Clients include Bottega Veneta, Krizia, Tod's, Lamarthe, and Stiletto NYC...

P244-247

AVA Architects
Portugal
www.ava-architects.com

The atelier began professional activity in 1996, was renamed Carlos Veloso - Arquitecto, Lda. in 1999 and was reorganized in 2007 with the current designation of AVA - Atelier Veloso Architects (AVA – ARCHITECTS).

AVA actively undertakes projects in the areas of architecture, restoration, recovery, urbanism, design, horizontal properties, photography, videography, exhibitions, engineering, consulting, security, and health. The studio has more than fourteen years of experience in a variety of different programs, subjects, and scales.

P178-181

Bekkering Adams architecten
the Netherlands
www.bekkeringadams.nl/

Bekkering Adams architecten is a dynamic and versatile office founded in 1997 in Rotterdam by Juliette Bekkering and re-envisioned with Monica Adams in 2005.

With an enthusiastic team of approximately 8 people the office works on outstanding and innovative projects. The commissions vary from complex building assignments to concept development, from

rivate housing to public buildings, and from urban
o interior design. Over the years a distinct oeuvre
as been established, characterized by remarkable
nd explicit buildings.

Bonnard Woeffray architectes
switzerland

www.arch.ch

C. F. Møller Architects
Denmark

www.cfmoller.com

C. F. Møller Architects is one of Scandinavia's
oldest and largest architectural practices. Our
work involves a wide range of expertise that covers
program analysis, town planning, master planning,
all architectural services including landscape
architecture, as well as the development and design
of building components.

Simplicity, clarity and unpretentiousness are the
ideals that have guided our work since the practice
was established in 1924. These tenets are continually
re-interpreted to suit individual projects but are
always site-specific and based on international
trends and regional characteristics.

C+S Associati
taly

www.cipiuesse.it

The office works internationally in the different
fields of architecture, offering master plans, full
architecture services, and interior design both for the
private and the public sectors.

The office is currently working on about thirty
projects all over the world.

C+S has won many important international
competitions for public and private buildings:
Cinema Festival Palace in Venice, Policlinic Hospital
in Milan, Tenova headquarters in Verese, a housing
complex in Japan, university students' housing in
Murano (Venice) and a law court of Venice which is
currently in the construction phase.

ccd studio
taly

www.ccdstudio.eu

Three engineers animate, organize and coordinate
thoughts and activities of the large workgroup that
forms ccd studio. These engineers graduated in
from the program of Ingegneria edile\architettura
at L'Aquila University. In 2004 they decided to form
an architectural studio. The union aims to develop
current design tools in the architectural field, in
order to provide valid responses to spatial shapes
expressed with contemporary language.

CEBRA
Denmark

www.cebra.info

CEBRA is a Danish architectural firm located in
Aarhus. The office was founded in 2001. Our clients
come from all over Denmark and we are starting
to experience a serious interest in our work from
abroad. We work with just about everything, paying
attention to much more than just the size of the
project. We have been involved in everything from
industrial design to urban planning.

Our ideology is project related. Instead of using the
same mind-set for all of our projects, we treat each
and every project as unique. There is also a common
theme that can be seen in all of our architecture,
a style of our own that unites our many different
projects.

crossboundaries architects
China

www.crossboundaries.net

crossboundaries architects is a young, Berlin and
Beijing based team of international architects aimed
at linking the professional and design experience of
trained architects and consultants.

Our goal is to develop high-quality solutions, derived
from Chinese culture and architectural needs and
based on western know-how and experience.

As the name indicates, crossboundaries architects
maintain an elaborate contemporary definition of
architectural practice with a broad view that looks
beyond the obvious.

dans arhitekti
Slovenia

www.dans.si

dans arhitekti, architectural studio was established in
2004 by Miha Desman, Katarina Pirkmajer Desman,
Eva Fiser Berlot, Rok Bogataj and Vlatka Ljubanovic.
Their work focuses on public buildings; instead of
trying to find spectacular solutions, they try to find
the right design. When assessing the quality of one's
own design, the authors are often only responsible
to themselves and to their ethical judgment.
Architecture by dans arhitekti always respects
the basic human values. It is a good example of
architecture that will outlive its authors and survive
the judgment of time. The architects of dans arhitekti
show respect for the profession which they pursue in
a serious, fair, and honest way.

Die Baupiloten
Germany

www.baupiloten.com

Die Baupiloten create atmospheric architecture and
embolden future users to take part in the creation
of their constructed environment. Their architecture
functions as a social catalyst and promotes spaces of
communication. Spatial atmospheres are employed as
a participatory design strategy.

Die Baupiloten is a group of architects and a design
studio working in cooperation with the Technical
University Berlin. In 2002, Susanne Hofmann AA Dipl.
founded the studio to bridge education, practice and
research. The students are involved in all phases of
the project's design and construction, from the initial
conceptualization and decision making process with
clients to the realization of the (often) tight budget
allowance. The studio guarantees that a wide range
of interdisciplinary skills will be employed in each
project, thereby giving each individual project a
research-oriented component.

Dorte Mandrup Arkitekter ApS
Denmark

www.dortemandrup.dk

The design objective is based on innovation and
continuous investigation into new programs, spatial
relations and building materials and insists on
bringing an original and personal point of view to
any commission.

The office has received both national and
international prizes and is widely published
internationally.

Ecker Architekten
Germany

www.ecker-architekten.de

We reduce a project to its primary components
to discover formal possibilities and a fundamental
language of architecture.

We look for beauty in ordinary things, and strive for
a balance of emotion and reason in architecture.

We respect the art of connection and knowledge of
the building sciences.

We try to make buildings that honor the abilities of
craftsmen and engineers and merit a challenge to
their skills.

When these efforts are successful, the result is a
simple construction, a sensuous use of materials and
a transformation of the familiar into the sublime.

Endo Shuhei Architect Institute
Japan

www.paramodern.com

Endo Shuhei was born in Japan in 1960. He obtained
a master's degree at Kyoto City University of Art in
1986. Two years later, he established Shuhei Endo
Architect Institute. He was Professor at Salzbulg
Summer Academy and is currently a professor at the
Graduate School of Kobe University.

Gaetan Le Penhuel Architectes
France

www.lepenhuel.net

-Gaetan Le Penhuel, Architectes

-Samuel Rose, project manager

-IRATOME, technical engineers

Giacarlo Mazzanti
Colombia

www.giancarlomazzanti.com

GRAFT
Germany

www.graftlab.com

GRAFT, established in 1998 in Los Angeles, California by Lars Krückeberg, Wolfram Putz and Thomas Willemeit, is a 'Label' for Architecture, Urban Planning, Design, Music and the 'pursuit of happiness.' With further offices in Berlin and Beijing, GRAFT has been commissioned to design and manage a wide range of projects in multiple disciplines and locations. Alejandra Lillo became Partner for the office in Los Angeles in 2007, Gregor Hoheisel is Partner for the Asian market.

Grávalos Di Monte Architects
Spain

gravalosdimonte.wordpress.com

Henning Larsen Architects
Denmark

www.henninglarsen.com

Henning Larsen Architects creates vibrant, sustainable projects that reach beyond themselves and become of durable value to the user, the society and the culture they are built into.

At Henning Larsen Architects the professional commitment carries high weight. All employees have skills and experiences that contribute immensely to the projects of which they are a part.

At their office at Vesterbrogade 76, Copenhagen, projects completed all over the world are displayed on the various desk tops, computer screens and bulletin boards.

IA+B arkitektura taldea
Spain

www.iab-arkitek.com

I.AURREKOETXEA ETA BAZKIDEAK SL is an architecture firm which offers its professional services in urban and building design as well as offering consulting services.

IA+B was founded in 1997, and is highly respected

in its field. The team is composed of highly skilled professionals with a wide range of experience in the aforementioned fields.

Our wide range of built projects includes residential complexes, office buildings, sport complexes, schools, hotels, and golf resorts, to name a few, and we have collaborated for various projects with firms such as Arata Isozaki, MVRDV, and David Chipperfield.

Jarmund Vigsnæs AS Architects
Norway

www.jva.no

The practice focuses on projects with potential for outstanding and meaningful architecture, most often closely related to nature and preferably in strong natural settings with a harsh climate. The practice explores modern possibilities with sensual and tactile means, seeking the right character for the place and purpose. Clear and easy to understand strategies create results that are both self-evident and sensational. Larger projects undertaken are often the result of winning competitions, while smaller projects are often received from referrals by satisfied former clients.

Jonathan Clark Architects
UK

www.jonathanclark.co.uk

Jonathan Clark Architects is an award-winning, widely published, enthusiastic and innovative practice providing a high degree of attention and expertise to each individual client.

We specialize in bars/restaurants, retail, educational and contemporary domestic projects, details of which can be found throughout our website.

We aim to look beyond the ordinary to produce architecture and interiors that not only meet our clients' needs and brief but also exceed their expectations.

LAN Architecture
France

www.lan-paris.com

LAN Architecture, a Local Architecture Network, employs twenty professionals (architects, designers, graphic and 3D image designers, communication and development coordinators) and works with specialised external consultants.

In six years of activity, the agency's work has developed a reputation and won competitions both in France and abroad.

The team projects, while respecting contextual, programmatic and site specificities, continue to explore new fields and create new uses with a strong social and urban involvement.

LAN Architecture was founded by Benoit Jallon and Umberto Napolitano in 2002.

LARRAZ ARQUITECTOS
Spain

www.larrazarquitectos.com

LARRAZ ARQUITECTOS is a studio dedicated to architecture, urbanism and interior design founded by Javier Larraz (Pamplona, Spain, 1970, Architect, University of Navarre, Honours Degree in Architecture and National University Degree Prize).

The studio aims to undertake every task with the intensity and exclusivity required to find the balance between form and function, targeting standards such as excellent construction and pursuing specific relevance for each project.

P106-111

MAD architects
China

www.i-mad.com/

MAD is a Beijing-based design office dedicated to innovation in architectural practice, landscape design and urban planning. MAD develops its unique concept of futurism through a persistent investigation of the symbiotic potential of nature and technology. MAD aspires to design in close harmony with nature, offering people the freedom to develop independent urban experiences.

P306-309

MAGÉN ARQUITECTOS
Spain

www.magenarquitectos.com

MAGÉN ARQUITECTOS is an architectural practice founded by Jaime Magén (Zaragoza, 1974) and Francisco J. Magén (Zaragoza, 1980) devoted to architecture, urbanism and interior design.

MAGÉN ARQUITECTOS is interested in architecture as both a technical and cultural process that is deeply focused on unique investigation and development of each project. This method of work allows us to manage different projects, in terms of size, scale and complexity.

The works by MAGÉN ARQUITECTOS have won several awards, such as the Bauwelt Preis 2007. Projects by the studio have also been exhibited several times in Spain, Germany, Italy and France.

P098-105

Mathieu Lehanneur
France

www.mathieulehanneur.fr/

P062-065

Mayslits Kassif Architects
Israel

www.mkarchitects.com

Mayslits Kassif Architects was founded in Tel Aviv by Ganit Mayslits Kassif & Udi Kassif. Since 1994 the practice has been involved in a variety of projects in the fields of urban planning, public buildings, housing, retail, and landscape urbanism.

Since 1997 Mayslits Kassif Architects have won several major public competitions such as: the Remez - Arlozorov Community Campus in Tel Aviv, the regeneration of Ashdod City Center, the regeneration of the Tel Aviv Port and the planning competition for the Natural Gas Stations, held by the National Gas Authority.

P164-167

Mikou Design Studio
France

www.mikoustudio.com

The two partners, Salwa and Selma Mikou, were born in Fes Marocco. After attending school in Paris (Paris Belleville) and Lausanne (EPFL), they received their diplomas in Architecture and Urban design in 2000.

From 2000 to 2005 they worked together at RPBW (Renzo Piano Building Workshop) and AJN (Ateliers Jean Nouvel) in Paris where they were in charge of international projects.

They founded Mikou Design Studio in 2005.

P258-261

MIQUEL MERCE ARCHITECT + MSBESTUDI-TALLER
Spain

www.msbestuditaller.com

MSB estudi-taller d'arquitectura i disseny was established in 2008, after a long and successful experience at RCR arquitectes. They have been collaborating with MIQUEL MERCE ARCHITECT since 2010.

MSB is a path, a story where the essence is creativity, where the work is the projects, the reflections, and the experimentation. The projects are always connected to the world of architecture, interiors, design, and communication. The goal is to develop projects with personality and rigor, evolving concepts and discovering new elements that allow us to go further each time. MSB values pure forms, construction systems, and materials, attempting to reach a natural, tranquil, serene, essential state.

P248-251

Mulders vandenBerk Architecten
the Netherlands

www.muldersvandenberk.nl

Mulders vandenBerk Architecten designs projects of scales everywhere between the moveable form to the metropolis. It is the combination of small scale objects versus big scale visions which makes design interesting. We analyze the ambition behind each project for the greatest possible impact.

We create a clear organization for each design structure and take great care with the final end result and its appearance.

P066-071

nendo
Japan

www.nendo.jp

Giving people a small "!" moment.

There are so many small "!" moments hidden in our everyday lives, but we don't always recognize them. But we believe these small "!" moments are what make our days so interesting and rich - which is why we want to reconstitute the everyday by collecting and reshaping unique moments of inspiration into something that's easy to understand.

We'd like the people who've encountered nendo's designs to feel these small "!" moments intuitively.

That's nendo's job.

P230-235

radionica arhitekture
Croatia

www.radionica-arhitekture.hr

radionica arhitekture was established in 2003 by Goran Rako. During subsequent years the office, located in Zagreb, took part in numerous competitions. In 2004, Goran Rako was a part of 'Days of Oris' with a lecture about his previous work. In the same year, by winning first prize in a competition, project Segrt Hlapic Kindergarten started production. In the following years the team won a competition for Cascade Commercial Center in Zagreb, the Narona Archaeological Museum, the Vladimir Nazor prize, and was part of the Zagreb airport competition. Another important competition was the Memorial Water-tower Park in Vukovar, when Radionica won the first prize again. In 2009, the design firm began work on the Vucedol Archeological Museum project in Vukovar, after winning a competition for the project. The team today consists of: Ana Boljar, Blanka Gutschy, Vedrana Ivanda, Iva Pejic, Goran Rako, Josip Sabolic and Marusja Tus.

P168-171

Randić Turato Architects
Croatia

www.randic-turato.hr

Randić Turato Architects is an architectural office which was established in 1992 by Sasa Randic and Idis Turato. When opened it was defined as the operational platform for architectural activities in a transitional environment of Croatian circumstances. The office has since been transformed into an architectural think-tank, dealing with a wide range of commissions. During the past nineteen years the office has produced a variety of projects that include public, commercial and residential buildings, infrastructure projects, regional physical plans and environmental management projects, and has been awarded with several state and regional awards.

P280-283

RMDM Architects
France

www.rmdm.fr

Truly creative, RMDM Architects agency puts its energy into research for sensible architecture that responds to surrounding events.

Since the agency was founded in 2001 following the receipt of the European VI award, the three associates Eric Dolent, Philippe Maillols and Alexandre de Muizon have been dedicated to an alliance between the unique and the coherent.

The conceptual process leads them to contemporary projects that focus on identity, atmosphere, and practicality, where aims and constraints are mastered.

P172-177

SAKO Architects
Japan

www.sako.co.jp

The design office SAKO Architects was established five years ago and focuses on the highest quality design and construction through a highly skilled 33 person work team. Project locations range from Beijing to Changchun, Shenyang, Tianjin, Weifang, Jinan, Huaian, Suzhou, Shanghai, Hangzhou, Qiandaohu, Jinhua, Mianzhu, Chengdu, Shenzhen, Zhuhai, and also other cities in China. The office has also undertaken projects in Japan, Korea, Spain and Mongolia.

P236-239

Santiago Carroquino Architects
Spain

www.carroquinoarquitectos.com

Santiago Carroquino Architects is an ambitious team of architects located in Zaragoza.

We design with dedication and a conscience, with the primary responsibility of making landscapes into better places through architecture.

We are driven by the diversity and complexity of each new project. The challenge of our work is to find smart, responsible and customized solutions.

Our goal is to develop architecture which derives from common sense. We assume the work of the architect from a sense of responsibility and civic commitment.

To achieve our goals, we have formed a team committed to to excellent communication and close cooperation with the developer, the specialists, the worker guilds, the administrators and the prospective users.

P188-193

sharon taylor designs/Pickwick House
US

sharontaylordesigns.com

Sharon Taylor Designs is an industry-leading creative organization that specializes in interior design and event design. Established in Springfield, Mo. in 2008 Sharon Taylor Designs has been featured in many national publications and industry blogs, including *Better Homes and Gardens*. In 2010, the organization opened The Pickwick House, a design and showcase studio. Sharon Taylor lives in Springfield, Missouri with her partner, Will and her four children.

P240-243

stación-ARquitectura Arquitectos
Mexico

www.stacion-arquitectura.com

We are a young architectural firm based in Monterrey in northern Mexico.

After several years of training and collaboration with international offices of architecture in other countries like Spain, France, Chile and Argentina, our partners have gained great experience in the discipline. Now we develop architecture projects independently. Our members have academic experience as part of the team of professors of the ITESM (Institute of Technology of Monterrey) and other local universities like the CEDIM (Design Center of Monterrey) and the UDEM (University of Monterrey).

P144-149

studio mk27
Brazil

marciokogan.com.br

studio mk27 was founded at the beginning of the 1980s by Marcio Kogan, an architect who graduated from Mackenzie University in 1976, and today the studio is composed of 12 more architects, as well as collaborators located in various parts of the world. The architects of the studio develop the projects from start to finish, and cosign their authorship.

P252-257

Tezuka Architects
Japan

www.tezuka-arch.com

With spatial designs that are skillfully integrated with the outside environment, our designs range from private houses to community buildings. Our most important projects have been the Roof House, in which daily life expands onto the roof, and the Echigo Matsunoyama Museum of Natural Science, which can be buried under 5m of snow. The Fuji Kindergarten takes the form of a 200m-circumference oval-shaped roof space. A total of 320 cubic meters of wood were used in the project.

P294-299

Tham & Videgård Arkitekter

Sweden

www.tvark.se

Tham & Videgård Arkitekter is a progressive and contemporary practice that focuses on architecture and design – from large scale urban planning through to buildings, interiors and objects.

The practice's objective is to create distinct and relevant architecture with the starting point resting within the unique context and specific conditions of the individual project. Taking an active approach, the office is involved throughout the whole process, from developing the early sketch to on-site supervision. Commissions include public, commercial and private clients in Sweden and abroad.

082-085

vaumm arquitectura & urbanismo

Spain

www.vaumm.com

046-051

XVSTUDIO

Spain

www.xvstudio.com

XVSTUDIO is a Barcelona based team that operates in the fields of design, architecture and urbanism.

The multidisciplinary and multicultural team of XVSTUDIO works as a research and ideas LABORATORY that creates projects from the parameters of GEOMETRY, INDUSTRY and SUSTAINABILITY.

058-061

acknowledgements

We would like to thank all the architects and designers for their kind permission to publish their outstanding projects. We are also grateful for the generosity of all the photographers, writers, and publicists associated with each studio, without whom we would not have been able to share these projects with readers.